THE
LIBRARY
of ICE

THE
LIBRARY
of ICE

Readings from a Cold Climate

NANCY
CAMPBELL

SCRIBNER

LONDON NEW YORK TORONTO SYDNEY NEW DELHI

First published in Great Britain by Scribner,
an imprint of Simon & Schuster UK Ltd, 2018
A CBS COMPANY

3 5 7 9 10 8 6 4 2

Simon & Schuster UK Ltd
1st Floor
222 Gray's Inn Road
London WC1X 8HB

Simon & Schuster Australia, Sydney
Simon & Schuster India, New Delhi

www.simonandschuster.co.uk
www.simonandschuster.com.au
www.simonandschuster.co.in

A CIP catalogue record for this book
is available from the British Library

Hardback ISBN: 978-1-4711-6931-1
Trade paperback ISBN: 978-1-4711-6932-8
eBook ISBN: 978-1-4711-6933-5
eAudio ISBN: 978-1-4711-6935-9

Additional copyright information is on page 321.

Typeset in Bembo by M Rules
Printed and bound by CPI Group (UK) Ltd, Croydon, CR0 4YY

for Anna

CONTENTS

On the way a miracle: water become bone.

Riddle 69, from the Exeter Book,
translated by Kevin Crossley-Holland

Introduction

THE BROKEN MIRROR

Upernavik Museum, Greenland

And if the sun had not erased the tracks upon
the ice, they would tell us of polar bears and the
man who had the luck to catch bears.

Obituary of Simon Simonsen of Upernavik,
called 'Simon Bear Hunter'

From Baffin Bay all that can be seen of the island is the museum built on the promontory, its timber frame painted blood red. It's said to be the most northern museum in the world. On some days the building is almost completely buried under snow or obscured by mist. In winter, the whole island is surrounded by a moat of ice.

No ships can navigate such conditions, so my first sight of Upernavik is from the air. The propeller plane stops to refuel often as it flies up the west coast of Greenland. At Uummannaq Airport I descend the folding steps to stretch my legs. The pilot has parked in the middle of the runway and I meander over to the terminal to buy some mints. The sky is a dense indigo, broken only by stars. As we travel on, the weather worsens. By the time we reach 72 degrees north, and begin to make our descent to Upernavik, the storm has intensified and the plane struggles to alight on the short airstrip. But we can't fly back, or onwards to a safer landing.

I can just make out the spot-lit airport sign through the blizzard – each capital letter cut from wood and painted pink. Upernavik means 'springtime place'. The island was named by a nomadic people who once came here by boat when the winter ice broke up, to trade and to fish. Later inhabitants have learnt to adapt, to live here year-round and make use of the ice.

I've been travelling for three days to reach this island – the times, and sometimes the days, of the flights were uncertain, and I felt as powerless as a toy in the bedroom of a child who has abandoned its games and gone to tea. The final stage of the journey takes only a few minutes. As the taxi slaloms from the airport to my new house by the harbour, I pass the lit windows of homes scattered down the hillside. There's an Arctic myth that tells how before the sun came into being, ice could burn. People used ice to fuel their lamps, because no one could go hunting in the dark. Tonight the sea ice is luminescent, and mysterious objects glow by the shoreline in the twilight, their shapes distorted and concealed under snow. It will be weeks until the spring thaw, and sunshine, reveal what they are.

When I received the email inviting me to work in the artist's 'refuge' at the museum, I was offered a choice: summer or winter. 'Contrary to the summertime,' wrote the museum director, 'the darkness of the winter to many southerners seems like a terrible and nasty time lying in wait. But whenever one gets accustomed to the darkness it proves to be a peaceful time that leaves the time for thought that one usually lacks.'

I certainly lacked time for thought. I worked during the day for a book and manuscript dealer in London, and pursued my own projects in the evenings. I liked my job. Authors would bring drafts of their poems and plays to the shop on Seven Dials and I sorted the disordered papers, removing rusting staples and paper clips, and listing the contents. After months of sensitive negotiations, the papers would be sold, either heading in a black cab to the British Library ten minutes away, or being shipped overseas to other august institutions. Drafts were more valuable than fine copies, because they showed the workings of the mind. The words a writer had crossed out, in retrospect, became more valuable than their best lines. I learnt the true value of uncertainty.

Sometimes as I sat among reams of paper and the legal pads with their scribbles, the perforated and punched continuous stationery spilling off my desk onto the floor, I felt as if forests of trees were passing through my hands. I wondered why, in a world that seemed pretty close to ruin, I was spending my days conserving all this paper rather than endangered species. The more archives I catalogued, the more concerned I became about their future readers. Humans had libraries to preserve their fragile records, but the gloomy news headlines put our own survival as a species – and that of the wider world – in doubt. As for my own writing, I was only just beginning to consider what I wanted to say.

One day a photographer brought me a box of transparencies depicting cobwebby window panes, cracked mirrors and shadowy corners. As I held each slide up to the light to see the image in miniature, Claire told me she had taken the photographs at a ruined property in the Irish countryside. Her family's property, which her parents had abandoned after her brother was killed in a motorcycle accident. 'Could you write about this?' she'd asked.

How do you write about that kind of loss? I researched the science behind capturing an image on film: early optics, experiments in darkrooms, how the camera works. I thought about how a photograph can evoke something that's no longer there and studied the rules behind the invisible forces that have such a strong influence on our lives. I read about Einstein, who believed that formulae waited to appear to the right person, like finger-writing on a mirror, revealed when steam hits the surface.

The deadline for Claire's exhibition was tight. I worked through the night for a week. 'Plenty of time to sleep when you're dead,' she said.

I discovered that light was reassuringly predictable: it travelled in a straight line, sometimes over millions of miles, and arrived faithfully on our planet even when the stars it had come from had burnt out. The lives which it illuminated, by contrast, were all too brief. Ice would be a better metaphor for the human condition – part of an endless cycle of change.

'You look exhausted,' Claire said, when we met to talk through what I had written.

'Uh-huh.' That week the shop had also taken delivery of sixty years' worth of diaries from a historian in west London.

'Why don't you get away? If you did a residency, you'd have

the time to make your own work, instead of always dealing with someone else's.'

Claire was right. I would go as far away as possible from this expensive city with its cycle of bank loans and bookselling and brief bursts of free time. I would find out how other artists were recording this temporal world, and immerse myself in archives that nature itself had devised.

I turned my attention from optics to ice. From light to darkness. When I received the offer from Upernavik, I found the idea of the terrible and nasty 24-hour polar night and the midwinter cold appealing. I emailed the museum back: *I will come in January.*

On my last day at work, Bernard rang the bell, and I buzzed him upstairs to the office. He was my favourite of the many writers who passed through the shop, always to sell, never to buy. I was pleased to have a chance to say goodbye. He struggled up the stairwell with a check plastic holdall bulging with correspondence, prescriptions and play scripts, and sank down into a chair. His body was ruined by years of writing and amphetamines. Other authors would deposit their manuscripts and scurry off, but Bernard always stopped to ask how I was – if only to give himself time to recover his breath.

'Fine,' I said, when he asked. 'I'm leaving.'

'Good!' he said cheerily. 'What's next?'

'I'm going to the Arctic,' I said, trying not to sound too pleased with myself.

'That's marvellous. Well done. You need to get away from all this' – he flapped a hand at the vellum-bound editions of poetry, the gilt spines of the classics – 'to find your own voice. Can I have my bag back, please?'

Over the weekend I packed up my cups and candlesticks. Boxed some books, gave away the rest. Handed the key of my Highbury bedsit back to the landlord. Tried to leave a forwarding address with the Post Office: Upernavik Museum, Box 93, 3962 Greenland. But 'Greenland' was not on the Post Office's drop-down menu of nations. I began to wonder if the place I was going really existed, or if I'd imagined it into being.

The morning after my arrival, I walk through the cold museum building, peering into vitrines at the scanty evidence left by earlier visitors. I admire the ornate lettering engraved on a barometer and the entries in a logbook from one of the whaling ships that looted this coast in the eighteenth century. The first European explorers named Upernavik the 'Women's Island'. No one knows why for sure, but people speculate that when the explorers' tall-masted ships passed the island, the men were away on a long hunting trip. Folklore tells of women in such situations, left alone in the settlements, but in these tales the boats that appear on the horizon are not those of whalers. It was believed that when the men left to go hunting, the spirits of the seals they had killed would sail ashore on boats of ice to exact revenge on their wives.

There are no traces of these boats of ice in the museum, but in another room I find evidence of the hunters' craft. A rusting harpoon blade. A mirror lashed onto the end of a pole for watching the movement of sea creatures under the ice. A pair of snow goggles: just a band of whalebone to cover the eyes, with a narrow incision to see through. Hunters wore these on long journeys in the hope that they would be enough to prevent the sun's glare from damaging the retina and causing snow blindness. I stare at them, wondering what it's like to peer through that narrow gap towards a white horizon on the look-out for prey – and predators.

Many of the glass cases are empty. I almost walk past the tiniest object in the museum, the pride of its collection. It's a copy of the Kingittorsuaq Runestone, a piece of soft slate into which a short text was scratched by three Norsemen around eight hundred years ago and left in a cairn on a neighbouring island. Only the men's names survive: Erlingur the son of Sigvað, and the sons of Baarne Þorðar and Enriði Ás; the second half of their message is lost, written in mysterious characters that can't be deciphered, even by rune-reading experts. I wonder what these Viking travellers made of this archipelago. What had they hoped to find here, so much further north than the fjords their countrymen had claimed? Did they ever make it back home? Their truncated story is emblematic of the history of Norse settlers in Greenland, none of whom would survive the fifteenth century, in part because of the cooling climate. During the Little Ice Age this green land was stricken by ice, and the sea trading routes back to Scandinavia and mainland Europe became impassable.

For much of the year there is still ice here, though its extent is changing. The sea ice around Upernavik may cut the island off from shipping, but it forms a bridge to a network of other islands leading back to the interior. (I know this only from poring over maps – even from the cemetery, the highest point I can reach on foot, the mountains looming beyond Upernavik read like one solid mass to me, a basalt barrier. I cannot imagine the waterways that wind between them, or the even larger mountains they conceal, and the ice cap further east.) I wonder about the first nomads, leaving their winter settlements deep within the fjord system, their skin boats laden, arriving at the outer parts of the archipelago as the spring came. They would have quit their igloos hastily while the weather was favourable, taking the cooking pot but leaving a clutter of bones and debris, possibly a few tools – or a shoe, a toy, forgotten in the hurry to round up children and dogs. Years passed, and bitter polar winds blew earth and snow over the midden. Archaeologists now describe the whole region as 'an open-air museum'. In other words, people suspect there are interesting artefacts lying undiscovered everywhere under the ice. No matter that they cannot be seen. They exist, and the museum's empty vitrines await their arrival patiently.

I can smell the filter coffee percolating. I climb a narrow wooden staircase to the office where Grethe, the museum assistant and sole member of staff on the island, is talking to Peter, a hunter who has dropped by to discuss weather conditions. A two-way radio stutters on the windowsill, issuing reports from Grethe's father and brothers who are far out on the ice. It will be difficult to work, I discover, during these mornings at the museum – distracted by a long round of *kaffe* and conversation. Or are the conversations part of my work? Nothing is certain. I arrived full of questions. How long has the museum been here? What had happened to the director who encouraged me to come in winter? When would we hold the children's workshop? In response to each enquiry people smiled at me indulgently, then changed the subject. As the weeks passed, I learnt to stop asking.

*

Each afternoon, Grethe locks up the museum and I stumble the few metres downhill to my cabin. When this building was the island's bakery many people would have used the track. Now, no one but me comes here. As long as there hasn't been a fresh snowfall I can place my boots into the deep footprints I made that morning. On other days, I must force a passage to my door through waist-high drifts of light snow. In the outer chamber, I brush snow from my waterproofs, unzip my goose-down gilet, and force off my damp boots.

I'm not the first outsider to call this place home. The museum has a rolling programme for writers and artists to come and work. Some of my predecessors have left a trace of their tenure, like the German filmmaker who was here last year: I opened the fridge on my first day to find a jar of apple spread (almost full), and there's a packet of herbal tea in the kitchen cupboard. There are books too, in a variety of languages. Someone has left a collection of Hans Christian Andersen's fairy tales. I wonder whether a writer before me brought these, as I'd brought *Treasure Island*, knowing I might want something comforting that reminded me of childhood. Other objects in the house are clearly of local provenance. There's a narrow skull on top of the TV, large enough that I can't identify it as any animal I've seen before. I wonder whether it has any association with the polar bear skin, laid down over the wooden floorboards.

I knew this might be an unusual job. What puzzles me most is a sub-clause in the contract: if you're an artist, you're required to leave the work you make behind. If you're a writer, you're encouraged not to. The museum sets a greater store on images than words. I could paint the sea ice, or film the aurora, and this would be preserved in the museum collections; if I write something, no one wants to read it. Should I be relieved or offended that I'm required to take any words I write about Upernavik away with me?

The proviso offers me a rare opportunity to relax – I could do the little required of me, hunker down in this cosy house and dine with the neighbours. But the problem intrigues me. It is so different to the symbolic power that books have in my own culture. There must be some words I can write for the islanders.

I think of everything I do leave behind, every day. My carbon trail from all those flights to get here, for a start. The empty packets of little marzipan biscuits from the store, and the beer bottles that are building up in my kitchen. And worse, there are no sewage pipes on this rocky island, so every few days I have to extract the heavy-duty plastic bag from the toilet bucket, tie it carefully, carry it sloshing outside to wait in the snow for the waste disposal boy. It's impossible to live and leave nothing behind, and my work ought to reflect that conundrum.

The one thing I want to leave behind as a trace of my tenure – words – isn't wanted. Before I can challenge that rule, however, I will have to write something. I crumple up the sheet of paper I have been doodling icebergs on and start a new one.

No door in Upernavik has a lock. On a small island it would not do to imply that your neighbour is a thief. And since no one wants to be thought to be doing something secretive, people are free to come and go to each other's houses at any time. But not me, Grethe warns. 'You have to wait until the first time you're invited, only then it's okay.' After a pause she adds, 'You should come to us for dinner tonight. We have some seal.'

Sitting at my desk overlooking the harbour, a cup of black coffee beside me, in the twilight I spot flashlights bobbing away from the island across the shore-fast ice. Shadowy figures step carefully, pausing often. Nevertheless, their progress away from the island is steady; each time I look up, the lamps have grown more distant. Over dinner that evening, I ask Grethe's husband what the men were doing. He explains they were on their way to drill through the ice and fish for halibut, testing the ice with their chisels before putting any weight upon it. They have to be adept at interpreting patterns and sounds in the ice, which tell them where to step to avoid falling into the freezing water. Each man's understanding of the ice is essential to his survival. Grethe interrupts him. 'My cousin drowned last month,' she says matter-of-factly. 'He just disappeared under the ice.' Now I understand why she keeps an ear to her radio.

The ice, always mutable, is now dangerously unpredictable. During one of his many visits to the museum, Peter tells me that for the last few winters there has scarcely been sufficient ice for him to leave the island on his sled. Other times there's too much snow: he must take along a shovel to clear the way to his fishing nets. No wonder he has so much time for coffee! He is pessimistic about the future. His beloved dogs are restless. Without their regular sled journeys over the sea ice, they are getting no exercise. Hunters cannot afford to feed animals that do not work, and he knows men who have been forced to shoot their dogs.

In an attempt to comprehend the changing way of life
and presence of death on Upernavik, I turn to the bookshelves in the museum. There's not much available. Most of
the books are pictorial or practical: photograph albums and
manuals on how to build a kayak or carve a paddle. I browse
through a Greenlandic–English dictionary from the 1920s,
not looking for any words in particular but rather letting
chance definitions catch my eye. I discover that *ilissivik*
means 'bookshelf' while *ilisissuppaa* means merely 'a shelf or
cupboard'. A subtle difference. They are clearly related to
the verb *illisivit*, listed further up the page, meaning 'to put
it away'. And for those with too many shelves and bookcases,
the dictionary informs me that *ilisiveeruppaa* is the verb for
'having put something in a safe place but being unable to
find it again'. I begin to see why this culture feels ambivalent
about the printed word.

In an old newspaper I find an obituary of Simon Simonsen,
a famous hunter from Upernavik, whose sons followed his
profession. A tribute to his skills concludes: 'And if the sun
had not erased the tracks upon the ice, they would tell us of
polar bears and the man who had the luck to catch bears.' It
dawns on me that tracks on the ice are considered a better
way of telling hunting stories than any words. Even their disappearance is part of the story – an indication of time passing,
as the hunter and hunted move on. When the last of the ice
has melted, I realize, the records of the past will be the least
of our concerns.

As January rolls into February the skies begin to grow
lighter. Behind the high mountains the sun is returning. A
few miles to the north, glaciers churn their way through the

basalt cliffs and thunder into the icefjord. With each new day these icebergs drift slightly further south and crumble a little more into the water. These scarcely perceptible changes are just enough to suggest, disquietingly, that icebergs might be living things with minds of their own. In silhouette, the varied forms – domes and pinnacles, and a few great tabular bergs – look like a line of writing. I feel I might understand what it said, if I looked long enough.

Grethe is pleased I am taking an interest in the environment beyond the museum. It's what she has been secretly hoping for, I know. She finds my obsession with objects, with books, with *typing*, curious and a little unhealthy. Every day I walk down to the shore and make a short film at the same spot. I hold my breath as I record the ice, trying to hold the camera still for as long as possible in my clumsy gloves. The ice here is uncanny, having been broken down by tides and storms, and reformed by cold, like Japanese porcelain repaired by a *kintsugi* master with a seam of silver lacquer. The view through the lens is always different. Sometimes water trickles over channels in the melting ice, which gently rises and falls with the incoming tide. On other days a thick rind of ice covers the sea, or a blizzard obscures everything. The shore-fast ice creeps across the bay, extending the shoreline by a mile and more, only to vanish on a stormy night. Making the film is a means to encourage my own close looking – but it's hard to see the boundaries of an object when I don't have words for what I'm seeing. Where does one ice formation end and another begin?

As the brief daylight fades, I return indoors. I relish the

terms I find in an online oceanographic dictionary: *frazil ice* describes fine spicules and plates of ice suspended in water; *nilas*, the thin elastic crust that bends with waves and swell, and grows in a pattern of interlocking fingers; and easiest of all to spot, *pancake ice*, those irregular circular shapes with raised rims where one 'pancake' has struck against another.

When I'd been filming for a couple of weeks, it was time for a new vantage point. I dared myself to take a few steps out onto the shore-fast ice, like the fishermen I'd watched. I stepped gingerly, all too aware of the ocean just inches under my feet. I hoped that by standing upon the ice I'd achieve some kinship with the islanders. As I tiptoed back again, Grethe came down to the shore to meet me, and I wondered if she was going to reprimand me for my risky behaviour. But she was laughing. A little hurt, I asked her why.

'Because you have been walking on the ice all this time,' she said, pointing to the snow we stood upon, which I had assumed covered a rocky shore.

Ice does not always look like ice. I think of the origin myth, of the time when ice could burn. In those days, people had powerful words that when spoken could transport the speaker – home and all – to places where they could settle and find food. The saying of the words brought the place into existence. I wondered what words might have the power to carry people to a place of safety today?

Grethe taught me to say, '*Illilli!*' when I passed her a cup of coffee, 'There you go!' She told me proudly that now I could be identified as coming from Upernavik: 'If you were from Ilulissat, you'd say *illillu*.'

It was flattering to think I was becoming part of the community, but I was all too often reminded of my difference.

'You work too hard,' Grethe said one day. 'You should be careful or you will never get a husband.'

It wasn't the future husband I was concerned about so much as my existing friendships. Grethe kept a close eye on how often I plugged the ethernet cable into my laptop. Connectivity in Greenland is expensive, sporadic and slow. I treasured the letters that made it to me in a mail sack in the front seat of the plane, and even occasional parcels: the box of spices which my friend Ruth bagged up and labelled – turmeric, ginger, coriander – bringing scents of London to my rudimentary kitchen cupboard. The hand-printed poster that Roni, a former colleague, sent from Manhattan, which featured a quote from Gertrude Stein's 'Valentine for Sherwood Anderson': 'If they tear a hunter through, if they tear through a hunter, if they tear through a hunt and a hunter ...' I ran my fingers over the unmistakable deep bite of metal type on the luxuriant paper.

One night, after a quick supper of fish fingers, I take the book of Danish fairy tales down from the shelf and curl up on the sofa to read the story of the Snow Queen again. Like many fairy tales, it's disturbing: it deals with an abducted child, whose eyes and heart have been pierced by shards of glass from a goblin's broken mirror. I empathize with Kay, imprisoned by his regal kidnapper in a great northern castle formed from over a hundred halls of drifting snow, enduring her ice-cold kisses and trying to make sense of his situation by writing new words in the sharp, flat pieces of ice she has given him to play with. The Snow Queen tells Kay that when he can form the word 'eternity', he will be his own master; she will give him the whole world – and a new pair of skates. Kay drags the ice around, composes many figures, forms different words, but he can't manage to make the word 'eternity', however hard he tries.

When I first read this story years ago, I longed to travel with Kay on his dizzying sledge-ride to Spitsbergen, and I fell in love with the wayward robber girl – a minor character, but not to me. Andersen's words have a different meaning for me now. I read on, stretching my feet out on the polar bear rug. 'I must hasten away to warmer countries,' says the Snow Queen. 'I will go and look into the black craters of the tops of the burning mountains, Etna and Vesuvius. I shall make them look white, which will be good for them, and for the lemons and the grapes.' Away she flies, leaving Kay alone in her castle. And there his friend Gerda finds him, still looking at his pieces of ice, thinking so deeply, and sitting so still, that anyone might suppose he was frozen. It is Gerda's tears that wash the piece of enchanted glass from his eye, and set them both free.

The sun appeared for the first time on Valentine's Day. A golden line split the mist above the snowy peaks, rested there for a moment, and then slipped away. I expected it to rise a grudging inch each day, but the days lengthened with bewildering speed. By March the darkness was just a memory, and I grew as complacent about sunlight as I had been about snow. I found I could go outside without wearing two pairs of gloves. The ice surrounding Upernavik began to fragment, and down by the shore the creaking of floes was replaced by the more harmonious sound of water trickling over stones. I was ready to fly south too, eager for luxuries like lemons and grapes again.

'Why don't you change your flight?' Grethe asked. 'You could stay another month, come with me on the motorboat to the settlements.'

I was tempted – but I knew that if I stayed another week I'd never leave. Besides, the book that was beginning to take shape in my mind as a gift for the museum required more than the laptop I was equipped with. I would need a printing press, and gouache paint, and perhaps a particular 'velvet' paper made by a mill on the River Axe in Somerset. I knew where I could find the press, and hospitality while I set the type. I boarded the plane as planned, leaving Upernavik to enjoy its springtime. The warm weather was coming, and archaeologists would arrive in the archipelago hoping to discover new objects to place in the museum while I was making mine. The tiny plane accelerated down the runway, and the pilot lifted its nose towards the sun. As the plane banked, the island seemed to tilt away from me. I looked over the ice floes tessellated upon the ocean like Kay's puzzle. I wasn't going to try spelling out eternity. There was not enough time left for that. The ice was beginning to disappear – and before it vanished I wanted to learn what words it would teach me.

I

SCIENTISTS

CALLING TIME

Bodleian Library, Oxford
Halley VI Research Station, Antarctica

But we need the books that affect us like a
disaster, that grieve us deeply, like the death of
someone we loved more than ourselves, like
being banished into forests far from everyone,
like a suicide.

Franz Kafka, letter to Oskar Pollak

I

A few months after returning from the Arctic, I sit at a
wooden bay in the Upper Reading Room. Beyond the
leaded glass windows the afternoon sky is indistinct. The
forecast was bad this morning: rain is on the way. The clouds
hanging over the spires of All Souls' are such a static shade
of white that the Gothic building looks like a cardboard

cut-out stuck on a sheet of paper. The weather vane, a cast-iron arrow decorated with the initials of the compass points, doesn't move.

My view is interrupted by decorative rosettes set within the window panes. They show human figures in sacred and secular pursuits: praying, tending animals, drawing water. Sundials used to be made this way, glass roundels hung against a window, painted with lines through which the light fell. You looked out of the window to tell the time.

The old glass distorts the view, as though it is raining already, as though the glass is running with water. Some students zip up their laptop cases and leave for lunch.

While spring returns I have been revisiting Upernavik in my mind: refining my sketches of icebergs, mixing inks to evoke the colour of the skies. I can't forget the museum's proviso and try to tell the story of ice using as few words as possible. The studio I have borrowed is still under construction, with walls on only three sides and a tarpaulin for a roof, but the printing press and drawers of metal type are already in place. I crank the cylinder forwards and backwards to print each page while builders drill into the walls beside me. Their radio plays classic love songs and breaking traffic reports. Not the usual conditions for fine press work, but within a few weeks I have managed to complete the book I will send back to Upernavik for the museum's collection.

Rather than bringing my investigations to a close, this new publication just marks their beginning. My curiosity is growing. Living in the Arctic suggested new ways of thinking about language and landscape and time, but I want to ground these ideas. An appreciation of science would deepen my understanding of the ice formations I saw around Upernavik, and how they are changing. As I browse the entries in the library catalogue, I admire the informative records: each one is a book in miniature, composed by an anonymous author. A long list of fields: Title; Author; Publisher; Publication date; Format; Language; Identifier; Subjects; Aleph system number; Miscellaneous notes; Call number. A code for every book that has ever been printed in England, whether it is likely to find a reader or not. A register to bring order to this vast collection of information, buried in vaults beneath the ancient building.

I order *The White Planet* from the stacks. On the book jacket is a photograph of a stark icescape. The credit on the back flap tells me it is Fox Glacier on New Zealand's South Island, the other side of the globe from Upernavik. The frozen sea looks violent, and somehow invites violence. I think of Kafka, who said that a book must unleash something painful, a terrible knowledge, it must 'shake us awake'.

The book has been translated almost seamlessly from the original French. There are only a few places where the word choice makes me furrow my brow. I need to read quickly – I got to the library late this morning after a hairdresser's appointment. I usually book in for a trim every six weeks or so, as soon as my short cut begins to grow out. While I was in Greenland, my style ran to seed. I am reassured now by the dull ritual: the hairdresser's scissors orbiting my skull, snipping away the excess. More and more grey hairs these days, she points out, hoping I will book for a colour.

I shake my head, feeling how light it is. Tiny clippings fall onto the page as I read, and lie in the gutter of the book until I blow them away.

'But we need the books . . .' I begin to type the words that I will quote at the opening of this chapter. They precede Kafka's more famous statement, 'A book must be the axe for the frozen sea inside us.' I type that too, and then I pause. Am I alone in liking the idea of possession by a frozen sea, more than that of the axe that would release the water? I doubt it: surely that is why the metaphor has become so famous. I let the cursor run back and delete it. I'm sure Kafka – who requested that his diaries and letters be burnt unread after his death – would understand.

The White Planet mentions ice cores, and I want to see an image. Online, I find a short documentary film that I watch with the sound off so as not to disturb the remaining researchers. I read the subtitles.

Dr Nerilie Abram is talking about her work with the British Antarctic Survey, analysing ice cores in order to understand past climates and predict those of the future. She has about two minutes to explain the complex science behind her research to a lay viewer.

The opening shot shows Dr Abram holding a circle of ice cut from a core. For a moment she is completely still; she looks like a painted saint in an icon, or a Roman emperor with an *orbis terrarum*, the symbol of one who holds the Earth – and all earthly power – in their hands. Until she blinks. She's wearing a bright red waterproof; it's the same colour as the expedition tents huddled on the Antarctic ice cap, which are already covered with a thin layer of snow. The colour of her jacket bleeds through the thin cross-section of ice, which is laced with tiny air bubbles. Disposed to find patterns, my eyes join up the bubbles. Now the ice appears to contain a hedgerow flower – cow parsley perhaps, or Queen Anne's lace. Dr Abram holds the disc with as much anticipation as a child might hold a snow globe, but no amount of shaking will disrupt this snow scene.

When I was a child I longed to possess a paperweight I'd once seen, a dome of glass in which a dandelion clock was trapped. I used to pick dandelion clocks in the garden and blow away the seeds with their fine hairs. I never really believed that the number of puffs was a way to tell the time. Weren't they more likely to indicate the power of my breath, like the tube the doctor made me blow into to test my lung capacity? Maybe the dandelion clocks would tell me the time I had left? But this dandelion was perfect and preserved under glass for ever. It would not grow, or wither, or let its seeds fall. It would place me outside of time.

Dandelions, cow parsley, Queen Anne's lace: such plants are unknown in the Antarctic where this ice was found. The camera zooms in. Without Dr Abram's fingers in the frame to set the scale, the disc could be as small as a communion wafer or large as a planet.

An aerial view of the Antarctic appears on the screen. That familiar irregular circle. Its neat circumference is interrupted by a scrawny peninsula jutting out into the ocean, looking for all the world as if it had been sketched by Dr Seuss. The continent's circular appearance is down to the ice shelves that form three-quarters of the coastline, covering the many bays and inlets. Some of these shelves have begun to disintegrate; from the air you can see places where the ocean's dark eclipse curves in towards the ice cap.

Antarctic ice shelves disperse in many ways. Bergs calve from the ice front, ice melts into the ocean beneath the shelf and drifting winds erode the surface. But the snow that falls on the central ice cap does not melt away. Each winter's snow-flakes are buried beneath further snowfalls. Over millennia, these layers compress and form *firn*, a grainy substance that contains pockets of atmospheric gases and even solid matter: infinitesimal specks of dust, ash and radioactive particles. Deep in the ice, the firn is pressed thinner. In the tiny spaces between the snowflakes, evidence remains of the environ-mental conditions at the moment they fell.

On research stations across the Antarctic ice cap – Halley VI, Dome F, Lake Vida, Vostok – scientists have begun to send drills down thousands of metres to extract cylinders of this ancient ice. Dr Abram reads a tracking device; she judges the click-click of depth readings and makes pencil notes. Her hands are gloved (red again) to protect them from the sub-zero temperatures. The great drill is winched lower. A core of ice is extracted and placed in a trough where it will be marked at intervals, and then cut along the marks with a rotary saw. Once a section has been sliced and stored in cold chambers dug out beneath the ice cap, another one will be drilled.

And another, and another. The 1.5-metre cylinders continue to be raised to the surface, until at last the drill touches the base of the ice sheet – or it breaks. There is no way to retrieve delinquent drill parts, stuck deep in the ice.

The work is gruelling and may take several polar summers. The South Pole: the name suggests a long cylinder embedded at the end of the Earth, as if scientists could extract the essence of the Pole itself. Once, explorers rammed their flagpoles into the ice as proof of conquest; now science leaves behind only a cylindrical absence, tempered by chemical traces.

These giant icicles are witnesses to global climate and its history. Within them is evidence of past temperature, the gas composition of the lower atmosphere, solar variability, ocean volume, volcanic eruptions, rainfall, the extent of deserts and forest fires. Under the magnifying glass the cross-sections of the core glow like magic lantern slides. Summer and winter snowfall have an entirely different appearance: the coarse-grained summer hoar is covered with a fine-grained layer, densely packed by the winter winds. This pairing is known by scientists as the 'depth hoar/wind slab couplet'. It is a surprisingly poetic term, which calls to mind the neat closing lines of a sonnet. The couplet forms an annual marker that – like the growth rings of trees – can be counted to date the core. One of the longest cores extracted to date, at Vostok, reached back 420,000 years. Its ice had lasted through four previous glacial cycles – surviving every time ice has formed on the planet's surface, and then melted away.

Human beings, lodged on Earth's thin crust, must drill deep or soar high to understand their environment. Knowledge comes from far beneath our feet, from distant outer space. The Antarctic ice stretches back to an era before the Cold War, before the competition between nations to reach the Poles, and the era of exploration that preceded it. By mining a single spot beneath the ice, scientists travel in time to a place beyond human memory, before any of the books here in the Bodleian Library were written. The polar ice is the first archive, a compressed narrative of all time in a language humans have just begun to learn. Only a few people are fluent: we rely on scientists to read the alphabet of elements and isotopes for us. I imagine Dr Abram recording her research, compiling graphs, the lines of which ascend and descend like ice formations. Drip, drip. The slow accumulation of data, the meticulous accretion of science.

II

'For the Lord spake unto Job: Hast thou entered into the treasures of the snow? Out of whose womb came the ice?'

Surely no contemporary scientist would quote the Bible in their work? My interest in the patterns in the firn has brought me to an early study of snowflakes. Its author, Johannes Kepler, describes himself as a man 'who has nothing and receives nothing'. The seventeenth-century mathematician and astronomer was concerned with harmony in nature and made significant advances in the field of optics, inventing – among other things – an improved version of the refracting telescope, which bears his name.

Kepler did not only investigate the vast reaches of the solar system. He also examined tiny forms close to hand, using his understanding of the stars to look at snow, which 'falls from the heavens and looks like the stars'. His treatise on the spaces between snowflakes suggested a new theory of the tessellation of spheres, but it remained conjecture, and in time it acquired the dubious honour of being the oldest problem in geometry. In 1900 David Hilbert included it in his famous list of twenty-three unsolved mathematical problems. Eventually, over four hundred years after the publication of Kepler's work, as I write these words, the BBC news announces that Thomas Hales's 'Flyspeck' project has presented formal proof of Kepler's conjecture.

Kepler's research all began quite light-heartedly. *De Nive Sexangula* had its origins in a winter walk through Prague. 'For as I write again it has begun to snow, and more thickly than a moment ago. I have been busy examining the little flakes. The water vapour thickened through the cold to snow, and single small snowflakes fell on my coat, all were six-cornered with feathered spokes . . .' Kepler considers their symmetry. Why were they all six-cornered, he wondered? I can't read any further, as the next page is uncut. Then I notice that every other page in the book is uncut – in other words I'm the first person to read this copy. There are library guidelines for situations like this. I go to the librarian's desk to explain, and he gives me a silver paperknife. I'm astonished that I am allowed agency in this act – when I first joined the library, I had to sign a form to say I would never 'kindle a flame' in the building – but I take the knife back to my desk. I feel like a thief as I slip the knife into the fold and slice along the top edge of the page with two swift strokes. In doing so, I reveal a spread of information that previously I could only squint at. It is a privilege to be the first person to have access to these pages – but I don't start reading them yet. The destructive action is addictive. I slit the next signature, and the next, all the way through the book. The paper sighs: I can almost feel the text escaping.

Now there's a light fluff at the top of each page where my knife has passed. Kepler's text – jaunty and self-effacing by turns – considers not only snowflakes but also the hexagonal cells of a honeycomb, the shape of pomegranate seeds, the arrangement of peas in a pod, three- and six-petalled flowers, regular Platonic solids, semi-regular Archimedean solids, the tiling of planes and the filling of spaces. Kepler contemplates the best way to stack cannonballs in order to occupy the smallest area.

Cannonballs for snowflakes: an unexpected conflation. Another conundrum faced by Kepler – one that I *can* understand – is how to anchor something as ephemeral as a snowflake in language, in order to explain his study of it. In the end, the snow comes to symbolize the very insecurity of his life. He hopes to be able to bring the snowflake that has fallen on his jacket to his patron and the treatise's dedicatee, Imperial Councillor Baron Johannes Matthäus Wackher von Wackhenfels, but the moment he notices it, it melts away. Ironically it is his own existence – the warmth of his body – that destroys it. 'Now quickly bring the present to my benefactor, as long as it exists and hasn't through body warmth disappeared into nothingness.' But it *has* disappeared into nothingness. The written word of his treatise must suffice to describe it.

At a climate conference in London a few weeks ago I paired up, during the one-minute speed-meeting session, with an amiable, bearded scientist, who told me that he'd held a piece of the Vostok ice core in the palm of his hand. Chris used up his whole minute describing the experience. 'The thing is, it *fizzed*,' he said. 'It was melting with the warmth of my palm, and the air was under such pressure that it exploded out of its ice pockets. It fizzed,' he repeated, 'then it melted, and I just wiped it on my shirt.' He passes his hand across the checked cotton covering his chest, an expression of mild bewilderment on his face as he relives his Keplerian encounter with a 20,000-year-old piece of ice.

I download a paper on the Vostok core from a science journal, hoping it will help me understand the work of cryologists. It joins other PDFs, chapters from PhD theses on modelling ice flow and UNESCO conservation reports, cascading across my screen, long slivers of text on a radiant white background.

I open the file with a single click and scroll through the text, which is crammed into two columns between a list of multiple authors and the dense footnotes. Science has so many authors! The tone is less personal than Kepler's: these days, scientists must appeal to their sponsors not through friendship or the use of wit but by other means. This study describes eras of time that defy conventional numbering and must be represented by numerals crouching above the line like little deities. One language cannot convey the ice's properties: symbols – Greek letters, geometric shapes – stand in for words. Charts saw-tooth across the page, recording variations over time, a silent sonograph between the regular, linear text.

Something causes me to look up from my computer. It has

begun to rain. After a minute my screen, through inactivity, grows dim. Time telescopes. I'm summoned back from the Ice Age to my own era, the Anthropocene. Instead of struggling to comprehend millennia, I watch as the rhythm of raindrops on the glass quickens.

Somewhere in Antarctica, the snow that may never melt is falling, preserving isotopic evidence of my daily actions. Years from now, a scientist not yet born may read this story in the ice.

III

Sunlight filters into the University Museum through the glass-vaulted ceiling, the struts of which were designed to mirror the animal skeletons below. I haven't come to see bones on my lunch break, but a rather special skin. I hurry to the back of the building where an almost-hidden archway gives access to the collection next door – the Pitt Rivers Museum. I descend to the gallery where objects from the Arctic are exhibited. I came here before I went to Greenland, hoping to learn something about the place I was travelling to. I've returned to look at an object that I haven't been able to get out of my thoughts: the skin of a seal on which an outline of the Bering Strait has been painted. Did the irregular shape of the skin suggest a map to the artist? The coastlines of America and Russia almost follow its edge, an inch or less away in some places, in others slightly more – just enough to fit in a vignette of figures firing arrows at a bear, or a herder leading his reindeer.

It's winter, and the sea is covered in ice. We know this

because a man is standing in the centre of the yellowed skin, harpooning a seal at its breathing hole. The anchor line of a ship extends for several inches to the shoreline, a precaution often taken when wintering in a harbour where the ice might shift. Two dog teams pulling sleds approach the three-masted vessel. None of these activities would take place unless the seas were frozen. The sealskin is not only a map of winter hunting grounds: it also depicts the story of Europeans coming to the region in the 1850s and 1860s, making this a historical, as well as a geographic, chart.

Chronologies and cartographies were once very similar in Europe too. While the map-makers of the sixteenth century were making strides in their depiction of the globe, historians still faced the challenge of how to give form to time. They knew that the way they presented chronology would influence the perception of time itself. One solution was a chart in which individual events, reigns and crusades were listed in separate boxes. These remind me of the pages in my diary which show miles between train stations, hours between airports. Or even the periodic table. Out in the world, the chemical elements don't stay in discrete boxes like distances do: they combine and mutate – and time doesn't always do what you expect either.

To express the peculiar passage of time, some chronographers began to produce charts of world history that looked like maps of the globe, with different areas for different eras. This fashion culminated in Friedrich Strass's *Der Strom der Zeiten* (1804) which shows history as a 'Stream of Time'. It is an extraordinary production, which even follows a folding model like a map. At the top of the document, storm clouds gather and streams flow out from them. In fact, this landscape is nothing but water, with scarcely even a sandbank between the colourful tributaries, waterfalls and lakes – representing dynasties and nations – that crowd the paper, more like thirsty pot-bound plant roots than streams. The chart's English translator William Bell wrote:

> However natural it may be to assist the perceptive faculty, in its assumption of abstract time, by the idea of a line . . . it is astonishing that . . . the idea of a Stream should not have presented itself to any one . . . The expressions of gliding, and rolling on; or of the rapid current, applied to time, are equally familiar to us with those of long and short.

How small a step it is from a river of time to an ice core. Long before the bore-hole technology used to collect ice cores was invented (ironically to facilitate drilling for oil), the use of a line was mooted by scholars to order world history. One of the first uses of a linear narrative to depict the passage of time was a magnificent, untitled, 336-page work published in 1493, only a few decades after the invention of metal type in Europe. The book, known to English readers as the *Nuremberg Chronicle*, divides history into eight ages. Its author Hartmann Schedel began with the First Age of the World, which lasted from the Creation to the Deluge. 'We wish to write briefly of these first days and the beginnings,' he wrote, 'as much as befits things that lie so far in the past.' Schedel may have been inclined to brevity from an awareness that any accurate dating of those 'first days' was impossible: holy books in ancient Hebrew and Greek differed on the interval between the Creation and the Flood by six hundred years. Schedel was on surer ground with more recent, and better documented, events. His Sixth Age culminated in a careful account of the election of Maximilian as Holy Roman Emperor in 1486. Between 1486 and the end of the world, Schedel left three blank pages for readers to fill with any significant events that might occur between publication and the Apocalypse.

Christopher Columbus's first sight of Jamaica in 1494, John Cabot's voyage to Newfoundland in 1497, Vasco da Gama landing in India in 1498: these were still to come. When I think of all the events that have unfolded between then and now, the three pages in the *Chronicle* seem a laughable allowance. Not even the most talented scribe could fit into them a comprehensive narrative of the last five hundred years – and if humans are lucky, there may be more decades ahead. (If only Schedel had been able to harness the seemingly limitless dimensions of the internet.) While he did not know the immediate future, the events of the Apocalypse itself were reassuringly preordained by biblical accounts. The Eighth Age would end in the Last Judgement. Schedel wrote:

> On the first day the sea will rise 40 cubits above the highest mountain, replacing it like a wall. On the second day it will recede to a level where it may barely be seen. On the third day the monsters of the sea will appear on the waters, and their cries and howls will reach to the heavens. On the fourth day the sea will be aflame.

A historian is no longer obliged to predict the future.

Alongside postcards of shrunken heads and puffer fish, the museum gift shop sells 'History by the Metre', a novelty folding ruler that lists the major events of the last 2,000 years. (It does not include the relatively late adoption of the metre as a standard unit of length following the French Revolution in 1789.) I unfold it from the middle, finding the invention of printing with moveable type in Europe in 1448, followed on the next flange by the publication of Kepler's laws of planetary motion in 1609. Eras pass swiftly when each centimetre represents a decade and each year is only a millimetre in length. Yet even a ruler this long can't encompass eternity: it stops at the millennium, the last notable event being the fall of the Berlin Wall in 1989. It is a handy crib for school history exams. The graphic representation of time as a line we travel – whether straight or crooked – rather than a space we inhabit is a convention arrived at through centuries of experiments, so commonplace that it even makes it onto a novelty ruler. But as Kepler discovered, the straight and sure line is not the first form in nature. Our planet has always moved in an ellipsis around the sun.

IV

The ruler may be a toy, but it reminds me that time is short – I should press on with my research. I walk past the Radcliffe Camera, a former science library which now houses literature and history. I hop off the pavement onto the wet cobbles to avoid passing between two tourists, one of whom is holding up a phone to snap the other in front of the neo-classical dome. Across the High Street, behind the crenellated wall of University College, there is another cupola. It's built on the site of the rooms rented by Robert Boyle, one of the founders of modern chemistry. His lodgings in Cross Hall are long gone, as are fellow members of the mysterious 'invisible college' which Boyle mentions obliquely in his letters. Born into a wealthy family in Lismore on Ireland's east coast, Boyle moved to Oxford in the mid-seventeenth century to be close to a group of like-minded natural philosophers who sought to acquire knowledge through experimental investigation. This was an era in which chemistry and alchemy each held the promise of the other: knowledge might lead to riches, but riches could be defined as knowledge. The transmutation of lead into gold, the creation of an elixir of life, were no longer the only business of the laboratory. Boyle remained in Oxford for over a decade, until 1668. I imagine him walking up Catte Street, the paved alleyway which I take daily. The medieval street would have seemed old even then by comparison with the sandstone quadrangle of the Bodleian Library, built just fifty years before. The book trade was centred in this part of town: binders, printers, copyists, were all within Boyle's reach.

However, it was in London, at the Sign of the Ship in St Paul's Churchyard, that Boyle's *New Experiments and Observations Touching Cold* was first printed. I consult an edition from 1665. It's a small volume, but chubby. The leather hinges are so worn with use that the front and back boards have come away from the spine and are now held in place by a ribbon tied around the book; the faded tail-band hangs by one silken thread. I place the book carefully on a foam rest. All the edges are gilt, protecting the pages from dust; an ancient hand has scrawled the accession number 8°B.16.art.BS over the shining fore-edge in black ink.

Poor Robert Boyle. This was one of his first published books, and it seems he was unprepared for the tribulations of seeing his research to press. There's an introductory note from the publisher: 'The Noble Author being at *Oxford*, when the Book was printed at *London*, he hopes the Reader will not impute to him the Errors of the Press, which yet he is perswaded will not be many'. This might seem to be the usual publisher's caveat, but the story becomes more complicated. He warns the reader to expect a blank section or two, and explains:

> the Authors Papers being near two years since given to be transcribed to one, whose skill in writing was much greater, than (as it afterwards appear'd) his knowledge of what was, or was not good sense, or true English; this person suddenly going for *Africk* before the Transcript had been examin'd, and not taking care to leave all the first copy, the Author found, (beside several Blanks, that he filled up out of his Memory, or by repeating the Experiments, they belonged to) one or two where he was not able to repair the Copyists omissions.

The 'very many Passages so miserably handled' almost caused Boyle to write a new book.

This incident was not the only cause for delay. The publisher warns the reader that while some 'passages are so penned, as to suppose the book to be published early in the Winter', this was misleading. While much of the book was sent to the press, Boyle held a section back. He was hoping for an opportunity to perfect an experiment that seemed essential to his subject – but he was hindered by the weather. The trouble with doing research on cold in an era before artificial refrigeration was that work was entirely dependent on the climate. 'I was fan to Wait for, and make use of a Fit of Frosty weather (which has very long been a rarity),' he wrote, 'as solicitously as Pilots [of ships] watch for, and improve a Wind.' However, the winter frosts came late in the season, and furthermore 'the Coldness did within a while arrive at that degree, that by its operation upon the moisten'd paper, it long put a stop to the Proceedings of the Press'. (The handmade paper would be dampened to soften it, the better to compensate for uneven thickness, and increase the bite of the type and adherence of the ink. But once the moisture in the paper started freezing, printing would be impossible.) Perversely, the experiments and their publication required opposing conditions. Yet Boyle was determined to keep to his intended deadline and, at the end of 1664, 'in the first or second week of the Frost', he presented some copies of the incomplete version of *History of Cold* to the Royal Society, 'though the Book were not then quite printed off'. Of twenty-one sections, the printer had completed around nineteen, and Boyle protested that he had the manuscript of the twentieth in his hands, ready to supply it whenever the weather should permit printing.

'Cold is so barren a subject,' Boyle opens his book unpromisingly, 'and affords so few Experiments, that are either very delightful for their surprizing prettiness, or very considerable for their immediate use.' Not useful or pretty then, but perhaps worth pursuing for its own sake? In a manner that is familiar in academic discourse today, he protests the importance of investigating 'the Phænomena of Cold', and condemns the scarce attention it has received from previous scholars – 'they commonly take leave of the subject, as if it deserved no further handling, then could be afforded it in a few Lines'. I find his irritable tone, across the space of three hundred years, quite charming.

Next, Boyle excuses his lack of consistent experimental method and forestalls criticism of the unequal nature of the sections in his book by pointing out that since the material covered in each of them differs so much, some must be long and others may be short. He does not want to expand the shorter ones 'by untruths or impertinences'. He defends his prolix passages: he wants to record in detail 'the Manner of the Trials', either so that readers can repeat them, or at least be satisfied they are true – for often they could not be done 'but by the help of Glasses Skilfully Shap'd, and Hermetically seal'd and other Instruments and Operation, that require more tools, and more of manual dexterity, then every ingenious Man is Master of'. He also excuses his way of working, for, 'sometimes I wanted conveniently shap'd Glasses, sometimes the Implements necessary to seal them up with, sometimes such ingredients as I needed to work on, oftentimes frosty Weather ... and not seldom Ice and Snow for artificial congealations; sometimes Weather-glasses, especially seal'd ones.' The unfortunate scientist broke two weather-glasses in quick succession, which foiled a number of his experiments.

Boyle was confident enough to admit to the imperfections

of his work on *Cold*, and indeed confess that, had he the chance to write the book over again, he would not. 'I have other work enough, and that of a quite other Nature upon my hands; the Truth is, that I am plainly tired with writing on this subject, having never handled any part of Natural Philosophy, that was so Troublesome, and full of Hardships, as this has proved'.

Science can still be troublesome. This morning, the *Guardian* reported that a freezer malfunction at the University of Alberta in Edmonton has melted part of the world's largest collection of ice cores from the Canadian Arctic. An ice core from the Penny Ice Cap on Baffin Island lost about a third of its mass, equivalent to about 22,000 years of history, and a core drilled from Mount Logan, Canada's tallest mountain, saw 16,000 years melt away. The dozen cores – 1,400 metres of ice – had only recently been acquired by the university, and had been moved just a few days previously into its brand-new, custom-built, million-dollar facility. Then one of the freezers activated a high-heat alarm.

'The way in which the freezer failed meant that it started to pump heat into the freezer,' explains glaciologist Martin Sharp. 'So it wasn't just a question of it gradually warming up ... It was actually quite rapidly raised to a temperature of 40°C. It was more like a changing room in a swimming pool than a freezer.

'I've had better days, let's say that.'

Robert Boyle intended his frankness to encourage other scientists by proving that good work can be done without advanced instruments and 'where the measuring of things by *Ounces* and *Inches* will serve the turn, without determining them to *Lines* and to *Grains*.' Amateur research was of value, laying down 'hints' that other, more accurate trials might investigate later. Boyle was in the vanguard of Enlightenment scientists, his laboratory, a place where nature could be manipulated. He believed that 'the History of Nature would make too slow a Progress, if it were presum'd, that none but Geometers and Mechanitians should imploy themselves about writing any part of that History.' As someone who is neither a Geometer or a Mechanitian, I warm to his argument.

We may take the everyday transformation of water into ice for granted, Boyle writes, but in some parts of the world where the climate is warmer men have been looked on as liars for suggesting such a thing is possible. 'And certainly, if custom did not take away the strangeness of it, it would to us also appear very wonderful, that so great a change of Texture should be so easily and inartificially produced.' Boyle made no assumptions in his investigations into the formation of ice and its behaviour. (After all, it had recently been suggested by Robert Hooke that ice was caused by wind.) He investigates bodies capable of freezing others; bodies that are disposed, or indisposed, to be frozen; the tendency of cold upwards or downwards; he wonders: does the degree of cold vary the compactness of the ice? (He makes enquiries of 'an intelligent person, who lived some years in Russia', who informs him that the ice in Russia is much harder than that in England.)

Reading Boyle is a lesson in perseverance and close observation and imagination: the scientist as poet. He experiments on various shapes and sizes of ice. He prepares cylinders of ice (the forerunners of ice cores) by freezing water within a metal tube. He uses flat sheets of ice of uniform thickness with the sides cut parallel and cakes of ice a quarter- to an eighth-of-an-inch thick. He adds salt to the surfaces, likewise *Aqua fortis* (nitric acid) and *Oil of Vitriol* (sulfuric acid), and notes their relative effects. He judges how much weight ice can bear, and puzzles that while ice is so strong that it cannot be broken with levers or even by a man standing upon it, yet a shard of glass 'will readily scratch it deep enough' and even 'common Knives would cut it, and that with great ease'. He puzzles that when he scatters salt on a sheet of ice laid out on a table, this action both melts the ice and also causes it to freeze again to the wood beneath. He even listens to the ice: 'I once caused divers [*sic*] pieces of thick ice to be brought out of a cool place into a somewhat warm room, and listening, observed a noise to come from them, as if it had been produced by store of little cracks made in them.'

Water is not the only liquid Boyle tries to freeze: during snowy weather, he experiments with 'Urine, Beer, Ale, Milk, Vinegre, and French and Rhenish Wine', finding the wine the slowest of all to become solid. He even sees what effect cold air has on 'a strong solution of *Gum Arabick,* and another of white Sugar, of Alume, Vitriol, SaltPetre, and Sea salt, a strong solution of Verdegrease in fair water (which was thereby deeply coloured).'

While Boyle protests that most of his experiments are entirely new, and not the work of others, in one respect he had to rely on hearsay. He was not able to travel to the far north to see for himself the ice formations reported in books of exploration. These 'great Islands of Ice' are so big as to be almost unbelievable, he says, but he never suggests his readers should not believe in them. Section XV, 'Experiments and Observations Touching Ice', contains some 'Collections out of Travellers, and Navigators, into those Colder Regions, that afford much considerabler, or at least much stranger Observations concerning ice, than are to be met with in so temperate a Climate as ours.' Boyle excuses his practice of quoting other authors, saying it is better than missing out the material altogether – especially as many of these books, being long out of print, would have been hard to procure even in England's centres of learning. Besides, he adds, if the reader is lucky enough to find such a volume, to get to the useful matter they must labour through 'melancholly Acounts of storms and distresses, and Ice, and Bears, and Foxes'.

I smile. My own journals are not free of such accounts.

Boyle considers what he has read of icebergs. Although these 'great Islands of Ice' are found floating in the sea, he does not think they are composed of frozen sea water, suspecting rightly that they have travelled from inland, created perhaps 'upon the shattering of ice in Bays and straits, partly by the heat of the Sun, and partly by the Tides, may be afterwards by the winds and currents driven all up and down the seas, to parts very distant from the shore.' His belief is supported by the tales of travellers, who melted the ice, finding it to be fresh water and good to drink. He notes comparisons of the height of icebergs to the leads of Westminster Abbey, to the tops of the masthead on ships, to steeples, and finds that they may offer mixed terrain: 'flat in some places like vast Champions, and high in others like frightful hills.' He believes that ice increases by the snow falling upon it (as scientists working on firn would prove). He wonders whether 'such Hills of Ice' are entire and solid or rather 'vast piles or lumps, and masses of Ice, casually and rudely heap'd up and cemented by the excessive Cold, freezing them together by the intervention of the water that washes them, which piles of many pieces of Ice are not made without great Cavities intercepted, and fill'd only with Air, between the more solid Cakes or Lumps'. He considers whether the azure colour observed in ice in Nova Zembla and other regions is inherent or permanent, 'or else one of those that are styl'd Emphatical'.

I wonder what libraries Boyle had access to in making his selection from these narratives. The Bodleian was new in those days, and far from the encyclopaedic collection it is today. His sources range from a scholarly Latin work by the Swedish cleric Olaus Magnus, subtitled 'a little book that more closely explains the map of the northern cold', to the sensational tales of the Dutch explorer Gerrit de Veer – both writers who in their own way have greatly influenced the way we see the Arctic, and whose names I will encounter repeatedly in my reading.

While I'm curious how Boyle achieved such wide-ranging research, long before the internet, I'm even more intrigued how he compiled his notes without the convenience of a digital desktop. Almost as soon as I print out an article it gets crumpled in my bag; when I pack up to move on, these accumulated papers have to be left behind. Files are only really safe when they are saved as diminutive icons on my screen. During the era in which Boyle was testing the boundaries of chemistry, other aspects of knowledge were up for debate:

even how best to study. For a long time scholars had sub-scribed to the idea that taking notes was lazy, that memory was diminished by writing things down. When a friend of the Greek philosopher Antisthenes complained of losing his notes, Antisthenes replied, with little sympathy: 'You should have inscribed them on your mind instead of on paper.' Thinkers with great memories were still celebrated in Boyle's day. John Aubrey, in his *Brief Lives*, describes how John Birkenhead, the founder of Oxford's short-lived Royalist newspaper *Mercurius Aulicus*, 'had the art of locall memory; and his topiques were the chambers, &c, in All Soules colledge (about 100), so that for 100 errands, &c, he would easily remember.' A building is a good mnemonic, especially when the building you live and work in is as labyrinthine as an Oxford college. But wouldn't the chambers fill up? What if Birkenhead had more than a hundred things to remember? Some humanist scholars believed that the very act of writing notes helped engrave ideas on the memory and that, in addition, the existence of the note, by acting as a prompt for later, would free up space in the mind – which however well trained, was finite.

Boyle had a good memory and poor eyesight. He did not need to take notes, but he chose to, even though in later life he required the services of an amanuensis. In an age when an orderly system represented coherent thought, Boyle seems to have been perversely, even proudly, unsystematic. While humanists advised scholars to keep a tidy commonplace book, Boyle jotted down ideas and quotations on loose sheets of paper. Sometimes these thoughts might be given order by being haphazardly bound together, or even, like those of his contemporary Francis Bacon, organized in methodical sets of one hundred, or 'centuries'. Some of the experiments on cold, he later told a friend, went 'in a kind of Note-book, wherein I had thrown them for my own private use.' His tone is careless, as was his note-keeping. After Boyle's death, John Evelyn told a mutual acquaintance William Wotton that Boyle's bedchamber was crowded with 'Boxes, Glasses, Potts, Chymicall & Mathematical Instruments; Bookes & Bundles of Papers.' After later making his own inspection, Wotton concurred that 'His Papers were truly, what he calls many Bundles of them himself a Chaos, rude & indigested many times God knows.'

V

My own thoughts are a chaos of facts gathered from five centuries of science. Ice is the solid state of water, I read. When water freezes to ice it increases in volume. Ice is an inorganic solid. Ice absorbs light at the red end of the spectrum. Ice is found in nature. Ice does not violate the third law of thermodynamics. The density of ice is $0.9167g/cm^3$ at $0°C$. Its chemical formula is H_2O.

I learn that the structure of the water molecule is one of the simplest in existence: it is formed of two hydrogen atoms bonded to a single oxygen atom, in a shape that resembles the letter 'v'. Simple or not, its behaviour bewilders me.

I leave the library, crossing the Old Schools Quadrangle. The finials and crenellations of the roof are silhouetted against the last of the daylight. A glow spills onto the flagstones from the high windows. Within the reading rooms librarians are still at work, placing volumes on readers' shelves and classifying new publications. I know there are secret chambers under the library that have grown out beneath the city to hold ever more books.

I have been staring at diagrams of ice too long – even the library is crystallizing.

Once you know the structure of a small part of a symmetrical crystal, I discover, you can predict its structure into infinity. Scientists have drawn up three-dimensional renderings of ice crystals, which show lattices with coloured spheres at each intersection. The spheres remind me of the decorative stone bosses that stud the soaring perpendicular vaults on the library ceiling – except that these spheres represent particles that, while even more durable than stone, cannot be seen by the naked eye. I marvel at physicists' ability to depict the hydrogen and oxygen atoms that so few people have witnessed – although they affect us – and plot the bonds between them. They make infinitesimal bodies big enough to see and bring incomprehensible forces within our grasp. I find it hard to even conceive what the lab equipment looks like, let alone the objects under examination: a thermometer sensitive enough to measure the heat within a chemical reaction, an electron microscope which can magnify objects by a level of 10 million. Would Boyle and Kepler have envied such advanced apparatus, dependent as they were on fragile glass instruments?

Glass is closely related structurally to an 'amorphous' form of water that can be made by very fast cooling of water: physicists define both as 'disordered condensed matter'. I imagine a scientist putting a sample of this form of ice into a glass flask, containing potential disorder within yet more potential disorder, creating a kaleidoscope of potential chaos. I am surprised by how frequently I encounter the term 'disorder' in my reading. I realize that physicists use it more precisely than I do, not to convey chaos and confusion but rather an absence of symmetry in a system of many particles.

Most of the ice on Earth and in the surrounding atmosphere is underpinned by the six-cornered symmetrical crystal structure that Kepler observed. It is named ice Ih – 'h' for the hexagonal pattern, and 'I' to indicate that it is only the first of many possible phases of ice. Under high pressure and at low enough temperatures the structure of ice Ih breaks down. The hydrogen bonds rearrange themselves, and a new rhombohedral lattice is formed. This phase, known as ice II, does not occur naturally on Earth – even the weight of the Antarctic ice cap exerts only one-quarter of the pressure necessary to create it. Ice II may exist in the outer solar system, perhaps in the cores of icy moons, such as Jupiter's Ganymede. And science indicates that there may be other phases of ice in space, each characterized by a different crystalline structure: the tetragonal lattice of ice III, and rhombohedral ice IV. When Ice Ih is cooled to -213°C it transforms into ice XI, and the hydrogens in the hydrogen bonds, which are arranged at random in ice Ih, finally achieve order.

Since the 1980s a group of researchers at University College London have been seeking new phases of ice, testing the behaviour of the bonds of the water molecule at the very highest pressures and lowest temperatures. In 1996 they discovered ice XII, which can be created in a number of ways, including by careful heating of one of the amorphous ices which lacks a crystalline structure. Twenty years on, the scientists have identified the crystal structures of ice XIII and XIV, and discerned the diffraction pattern of ice XVI. One of the team, John Finney, has described this work as being like that of the artist, making new 'sculpted ice structures'. 'A good forger can reproduce the pattern,' Finney writes, 'but the painter creates something new and original that has never existed before. Anywhere. Perhaps it was similar for ice XII. Perhaps it was the first time that water molecules had been persuaded to link together in this particular way to form this structure? We could easily argue that the same pressure, temperature and cooling rate conditions that we used to "create" ice XII would be unlikely to be found anywhere else in the universe. In which case, perhaps we could look at the first making of ice XII as an original act of creation. How many other forms might ice take?'

While Finney and his fellow scientists work to create the conditions of outer space in the laboratory, and predict the phases of ice on distant moons, the view back from space to Earth is helping scientists understand changes in the composition of ice on our own planet. Space travel has changed the way humans think about the world, from the moment in 1969 when astronauts first walked on the moon and audiences back on Earth were enchanted by images of the planet taken from space – and more aware of its fragility.

All through the 1970s, Nimbus satellites travelled the Earth in near polar orbits. These spacecraft were intended to document rainfall and collect atmospheric data to help everyday weather forecasting, but the later missions would reveal something far more momentous. When Nimbus 7 launched in 1978, its sensor technology allowed scientists to map sea ice concentrations across the globe, distinguishing newly formed ice from older ice. As observations accumulated, another pattern started to emerge: a hole which appeared in the ozone layer over Antarctica each winter.

The environment was already a matter of concern: the first connections between CO_2 emissions and climate change were made in the 1930s. In 1957 Revelle found that CO_2 produced by humans would not be readily absorbed by the oceans; Keeling measured CO_2 in the atmosphere and detected its rise in 1960. In the 1970s models of glacier flow revealed an instability in the Antarctic ice sheet, and ocean geologists found huge deposits of methane-bearing ices in the world's seabeds. Increasing numbers of scientists chose research topics relevant to climate change. It was little surprise when these discoveries were followed by the announcement that 1981 had been the warmest year since records began.

NASA launched an Ice, Cloud and Land Elevation Satellite (ICESat) in 2003 to measure the polar ice sheets; it de-orbited in 2010 after a seven-year mission. ICESat-2 was launched in 2018 to pursue research in a very different public 'climate'. Now researchers have found the collapse of the West Antarctic ice sheet to be irreversible and confirm that it will lead to a rise in sea level over future centuries. The topic of climate change is no longer restricted to specialist conferences and research programmes, but is reported by the mass media. In July 2017, when a 1.1-trillion-tonne iceberg calved from the Larsen C ice shelf, it made headline news around the world. Some channels dwelt on the fact that the Antarctic ice shelf was now at the lowest extent ever recorded. Others celebrated the awe-inspiring dimensions of one of the ten biggest icebergs ever seen.

How to calculate the magnitude of an iceberg? Boyle, who worked so hard to create modest pieces of ice in his laboratory, notes with some admiration the 'stupendiousest piece of single ice ... which our Famous English Seaman Mr. *W. Baffin* (whose name is to be met with in many modern Maps and Globes) mentions himself to have met with upon the coast of *Greenland*.' Or rather 'ſtupendiouſeſt', since the word looks even more impressive with the long *s* of the seventeenth-century font, its tip curling like an incomplete *f* above the character's x-axis. Baffin calculated the size of this most stupendous object as 'one hundred and forty fathoms, or one thousand six hundred and eighty foot from the top to the bottom.' Baffin and Boyle both knew that to calculate the size of these ice islands one has to consider the ice that lies hidden below the waterline.

This problem of 'the proportion betwixt the extant and immers'd parts of floating ice' hinged on understanding the way ice behaves in water. Some men, Boyle writes, report 'that there is but one seventh part of Ice above water ... This proportion I know doth hold in much Ice, but whether it do so in all, I know not.' After some calculations, he comes to believe that the part of the berg underwater ought to be eight or nine times as deep as that seen above the water.

Today's glaciologists place the figure even higher, at around 91% – although the exact amount will depend on the character of the ice. Such percentages suggest that the iceberg can be easily divided into upper and lower parts, whereas it is no respecter of the waterline – it soon enough slips sideways, turning as it melts. In this it echoes the evolution of the percentage sign itself. The zeros, which in Boyle's day were written above and below a horizontal fraction line, now balance precariously either side of a diagonal solidus.

VI

I have no desire to go to Antarctica, but I'm curious. The artist-explorer Emma Stibbon RA has just returned from a residency on board the Antarctic research vessel HMS *Protector*, and we meet in a café on Turl Street to compare notes. As HMS *Protector* sailed down the Antarctic Peninsula towards Rothera Research Station, Emma observed the ice formations – and the navy personnel who were studying them. 'Everyone had their work to do,' Emma tells me. 'There were specialists in meteorology and hydrography and navigation, as well as the ice experts.' In contrast to the remote recording technologies used by navy personnel to capture data, Emma made her records from chalk and water and pigment. She believes that this human, tactile response is as important as ever in understanding the world.

Emma tells me that the coastline of Antarctica is so inaccessible that it has not been surveyed for nearly two centuries. Ships are still navigating with charts made by sailors on whaling ships, who would have dropped a sounding line down to take a depth reading and used a sextant for positioning. 'Obviously,' she continues, 'that leaves room for error. So the new data gathered by HMS *Protector* is really going to contribute to modern mapping. The ship is fitted with sonar that emits beams of sound energy off the seabed. The ship tracks the mapping area (a bit like mowing a lawn) and this produces lines of sonar data that is then sent to the Chart Room on board. Here, the data is expertly cleaned by the surveyors to remove any excess noise – and then digitally converted into positions and depth.' This detailed, high-resolution data is transferred to the Admiralty UK Hydrographic Office in Taunton, where it will be used to make new navigational charts.

The users of the maps will be the temporary inhabitants of the Antarctic, most of whom arrive at research stations to analyse the environment. They will tell you that a trip to Antarctica is like a journey back in time as well as over many miles: Europe experienced similar conditions during the Ice Ages, when glacial sheets covered the planet as far south as London and Oxford. Emma questioned how to record this ancient landscape. 'Working in my sketchbook in such cold temperatures meant I had to draw quickly. I tend to use wet media such as Indian ink or watercolour and this would some-times freeze on the brush. Drawing on board a ship means the landscape is continuously slowly sliding by and that requires a swift response.'

Emma's drawings of ice are shape-shifters, making the viewer wonder not only how the image is made, but also how such strange visions can exist at all. Are they glaciers or ghosts? Back in her studio she would deliberate about which media to use, 'I sometimes work with gesso, graphite and silverpoint which gives a silvery effect.' Her Antarctic works record all three states of water – solid and liquid and gas – and the permeable line between them, a reminder that it is the only substance to exist naturally in all these forms on Earth.

Once a museum conservator of works of art on paper, Emma has a sense of the longevity of materials. She uses processes with an awareness of archival permanence. 'When I consider the amount of time I invest in making art it gives me some consolation to think that it will be around for a while yet.' But then, she adds – 'we have to think in wider circles of time, beyond those our minds can comprehend. What can last for ever?'

Our conversation is interrupted by a hailstorm. Emma wipes the condensation off the window and we watch the transformation of the street. Bikes come to a halt and tourists scurry into the bookshop for shelter; students rush towards the porter's lodge, burying their faces in books and scarves. When hailstones strike they hurt like hell, but they are nonetheless glorious in their dynamism. There is something comical in the way the pellets fall and then immediately bounce back upwards, their downward trajectory less certain than it seems.

Hail's ambiguity has puzzled humans since ancient times. People once believed it only fell during the day. The author of the nineteenth-century classic *Meteorology* admitted that – even in his enlightened era – no one could agree on its cause. 'How are we to understand that during the fine season, and the hottest days, considerable masses of ice fall?' wrote Ludwig Kämtz. 'Why certain countries are ravaged by hail almost every year, while adjacent localities are almost entirely spared?' Another mystery was that hailstorms took place over a very limited area: 'At a few myriametres from the place where the hail has fallen, not even wind has been felt.'

Kämtz was impressed by record-breaking data: he reports that on 29 April 1697 hailstones fell in Flintshire weighing around 130 grams; and the following week a Mr Taylor of Staffordshire found hailstones 3 centimetres in circumference; a hailstorm ravaged the banks of the Nile on 13 August 1832; and at Utrecht in 1736, Mr Mussenbroeck observed a heavy hailstorm, of which all the hailstones were the size of pigeons' eggs and even those of hens. But these are as nothing: on 5 October 1831, hailstones the size of a fist fell in Constantinople.

Hailstones fall in brief stints. It's as if the sky can't maintain the dramatic detonation of ice for more than a few minutes. A short hailstorm is like those uncomfortable condensed forms in poetry, the limerick or the triolet, which often have a sting in the tail. The short form requires wit, and wit sometimes tips over into malice. If snow were falling now, it would be a soft accretion, the flakes lying in sheltered nooks of the old buildings. It's hard not to get lyrical about snow, which falls so gently that it seems to slow down time; hail speeds time up like strobe lighting does a pantomime. Snow commands a respectful silence, whereas hail elicits a noisy reaction as car alarms are activated by the pellets.

Yet snowflakes and hailstones begin alike as drops of water in the clouds, where they freeze into ice crystals. The snowflake has a simple journey; an ice crystal floats down through a cloud, and further crystals adhere to its extremities. Hailstones originate in vast cumulonimbus clouds, above the altitude at which planes fly. The hail has further to fall, and may be thrown back into the cloud by updraft. As it passes through alternating layers of warm and cool air above the ground it melts, and then refreezes, accumulating ever more layers of ice. Ice buried deep in the ice cap can be preserved for centuries, but ice falling through the atmosphere can change state by the second.

The torrent stops as suddenly as it began, but the pellets remain. Some have collected in the statues over the archway opposite: the Virgin Mary standing on the globe, wearing a red cloak over her more traditional blue, and St Mildred, riding a flock of geese like a wing-walker. When Emma and I step outside, our feet crunch upon the tiny, opaque balls of ice.

II

EXPLORERS

PAPER TRAIL

Rijksmuseum, Amsterdam
Scott Polar Research Institute, Cambridge
National Library, Greenland

We had seen God in his splendours, heard the
text that nature renders. We had reached the
naked soul of man.

Ernest Shackleton, *South*

We left no footprints, even.

Ursula Le Guin, 'Sur'

I

Around every corner in Amsterdam, the Arctic is there to
meet me. It's January. The new feature film *Nova Zembla* has
just hit the cinemas, and the poster is pasted onto bollards

57

down dreary stretches of Damrak and all along the Amstel. The handsome face of an explorer framed by fur cap and grizzled beard, the frozen rigging of his ship behind him: these don't look much out of place in this city of waterways. The film is a historical drama about Willem Barents's voyage, which set out for the north from Amsterdam four centuries ago. I'm intrigued, but can't afford the cinema admission.

Almost a year has passed since my return from Upernavik. I long to go back to the Arctic; I have a pressing feeling of unfinished business. Meanwhile, money is scarce, too scarce to settle anywhere. When Eva asked me to keep an eye on her harpsichord, I spent fifteen pounds on a ticket for the overnight bus from London Victoria to Amsterdam. Groggy with lack of sleep and fresh air, and the monotony of motorways between Calais and Rotterdam, I arrive in the De Baarsjes district, where Eva lives on a street that was the setting for a Dutch police procedural drama in the 1980s. Now recovered from TV fame, it is quiet and relatively crime-free. Nevertheless, Eva is pleased to have me in the flat with her treasure. Before catching her flight to Tallinn, she shows me the meter which I'll use to check the temperature and humidity of the room morning and evening. Dusting the harpsichord is optional. 'And give the cat some pollock every day,' she adds.

These duties leave me several hours during the day to wander the city. My mind is still so occupied by thoughts of the Arctic that I'm not surprised to see a polar bear standing on its hind legs sniffing the air in Erasmus Park as the afternoon light starts to fade. I'm impressed by its size and its poise; edging closer I discover it's a statue in white marble by

Simona Vergani, installed during recent renovations. I cross Mercatorplatz, which honours the creator of the first map of the world, and stroll along the sluggish Admiralengracht. The streets in this neighbourhood are named for navigators of much tougher waters. Among Marco Polostraat and James Cookstraat, I find tributes to the iconic polar explorers: John Franklinstraat, Shackletonstraat, Baffinstraat and Hudsonhof. Their names look strange on the blue enamel street signs fixed to the apartment buildings. I'm used to encountering them on the maps of the waters they charted: Baffin Bay, Hudson Bay. They are equally out of place there, of course – those regions were home to others, and not theirs to name. Indigenous Arctic dwellers would never think of naming a place after a person, but rather after its own attributes. As the Greenlandic politician and poet Aqqaluk Lynge wrote:

> They explored and explored
> and every island or fjord
> river or mountain was named
> to honour this or that or themselves

Like those earlier explorers, over time I become more adventurous. One afternoon I pass the Rijksmuseum. It's closed for refurbishment, and most of the building is concealed behind netting and scaffolding, but part of one wing is open. I enter through a side door, and in a dimly lit gallery I find a collection of objects that travelled to the Arctic in the sixteenth century. This was ambitious baggage, even by the standards of the time: a carriage clock, muskets with ornate silverwork and, most unexpected of all, a cache of engravings.

The prints depict mythological and religious subjects, like Spranger's *Paradise*, and famous historical scenes including Goltzius's *Roman Heroes* and the patriotic *Defenders of Haarlem*. In those days connoisseurs kept their prints in albums or folders, not framed like paintings. These images were once bundled up and carried as cargo by Willem Barents on his final trip.

Barents was searching for a sea route to China which must, he reasoned, exist north of Siberia. He believed that the midsummer sun would melt any ice in the region. He was wrong. The expedition passed Bear Island and, at 80 degrees north, met the pack ice, sailing along its edge. They reached Nova Zembla, a long pennant of land that stretches up from the coast of Russia towards the North Pole, on 17 July 1596 and pushed on round its northern tip, which he named 'IJskaap' or Ice Cape, before turning into the Kara Sea. Ice began to surround the ship. Anxious to avoid becoming trapped as the weather grew colder, he started to retreat, but *Mercury*'s progress was confounded by icebergs and floes. Barents could go no further. By 28 August *Mercury* was frozen in. Its timbers began to creak – and then to crack – under the strain.

Gerrit de Veer, the ship's carpenter, survived the ordeal to write a memoir. An etching in the first edition depicts the dramatic wreck in the 'IJshaven' or Ice Harbour: the unlucky ship, listing sideways, its rigging slack, the poop deck raised up on a great spar of ice, and the anchor hanging forlorn and useless from the bow. Barents and his sixteen crew were forced to spend the winter on the bare peninsula, gaining the dubious honour of being the first Europeans to winter so far north. They built a small log cabin using driftwood that had floated from Siberia and, when there was no more driftwood, lumber from their ship. Even working swiftly against the worsening weather, care was put into the construction of 'Het Behouden Huys' (the Saved House). The engravings in de Veer's memoir show a well-proportioned single-storey building with an impressive chimney rising from the roof. It looks cosy, but I wouldn't have wanted to live there. The shelter was not merely a means to keep out the cold, but also the polar bears that prowled the area, lured by the prospect of food.

For some months the crew were able to survive on their salt beef, smoked bacon, dried fish, ship's biscuit and beans. A shortage of beer was declared on 8 November (the beer had frozen inside its barrels, bursting them, and then it leaked away) and the explorers began to drink melted snow. The rationing of bread began the same day, and that of wine on 12 November. Not long after, the workings of the clock froze, and from then on time had to be calculated using the ship's instruments and an hourglass. The wonders of Western Europe that Barents had intended to sell in China were put to unexpected uses that winter. One by one the fine prints were taken from their wrappings and used to fuel the fire.

After ten hard months, the crew left the Saved House to attempt the seas again. They piled supplies into two small boats, Mercury no longer being seaworthy; many things had to be left behind. Barents was to die on the homeward voyage, midway across the sea that now bears his name. Over the centuries, ice overtook the contents of the Saved House, transforming the prints that had escaped burning into frozen papier-mâché blocks. But the house was not forgotten: in

NANCY CAMPBELL

Mercator's map of the northern lands from 1620 't'Behouden huys' is written from the tip of Nova Zembla across the Kara Sea. The northern coastlines had been charted, but few explorers had landed on the frozen nations coloured green, yellow and pink that stretch between them, on which barely any towns or settlements are marked. This temporary dwelling was an exception. The size of the text gives this tiny encampment the same significance as the whole of the Orkney Isles.

The ruins of the Saved House were discovered by a Norwegian seal hunter in the nineteenth century. Some of the surviving artefacts were sold back to the Dutch government; others were plundered by pilgrims over the years. The prints were transported to Amsterdam, where conservators at the Rijksmuseum slowly separated the frozen layers of paper. Only fragments of the original sheets survived, but these were identified and ordered again and backed with a strong Japanese paper, which shows through in many places. These operations saved the prints – and perhaps even improved them to modern eyes like mine, conditioned to find fragments more romantic than complete narratives.

I peer at the prints, oblivious to the gallery behind me reflected in the glass. I look closer, and the lines etched by the artist dissolve under my gaze. The original sheets of paper pull apart like ice floes and the blank spaces in between seem to possess the raw promise of new ice on the surface of the ocean. Tree branches have been ripped from their trunks. The limbs of soldiers are plates of armour, disembodied. Landmasses become islands. My eye seeks coherence from these fragments, reads the absences as a history of the shifting bodies of water

62

and ice in the Arctic, which promised advancement to explorers, but often clinched them in stasis.

II

I returned to England when my harpsichord duties were done, taking a berth on the overnight ferry from IJmuiden to Newcastle-upon-Tyne. I spent my last few euros in the bar, and stood on deck in drizzle watching the port disappear. The propellers boomed below me, churning the water to a bright foam that soon dispersed on the dark sea. When I woke in my bunk later, and drew back the swaying accordion blind to reveal the lights of a coastal town, I had no sense of how far we'd come. The ferry was far out from land, so far in fact, that I could see two lighthouses at once through the oval window, repeating their different sequences of signals, as if endlessly interrupting each other in conversation.

The North Sea was calm and ice-free, but I was looking for a Saved House, somewhere I could hunker down and continue my writing about Upernavik. The Arctic ice had become an obsession that would not release me. I'd scoured opportunities for writers who wanted to live and work in the north, and sent off a couple of applications. While I waited for the responses I had to live as frugally as I could, which meant moving between house-sits. Sometimes I sofa-surfed for a few nights, or spent the night on a train concourse, or holed up in an airport or bus station toilet cubicle, leaning against the door, ignoring the lock when it was rattled by the cleaner early in the morning. I wasn't writing much, or not as much as I wanted. Too much time was spent packing and unpacking. I began to feel a disproportionate affection for familiar points of departure, such as Golders Green bus station and King's Cross in London, which punctuated my weeks more consistently than the locations that came between them. The sporadic nature of my work and my lost hours seemed less of a concern when I read in the newspaper of a notebook which had been closed in 1912, and wasn't opened again until a century later.

Every summer, melting snow carves new channels in the *scoria*, the cinders that cover Ross Island, a small volcanic outcrop embedded in the ice sheet that surrounds Antarctica. Robert Falcon Scott's 1910–13 *Terra Nova* expedition, which aimed to be the first to reach the South Pole, set up base camp on its barren shores. The hut they built still stands today. Once it seemed such expedition sites and the artefacts they held would be preserved for ever by cold temperatures. Now the work of preservation is delegated to conservators who specialize in Antarctic heritage. Lizzie Meek was making a circuit of the hut in the summer of 2012 when she noticed a clump of paper in one of the melt-water streams. When she investigated, she found a notebook, half-buried under the black rocks. Lizzie carefully pulled the sodden bundle free and took it to the field laboratory. As the paper dried she was able to discern pencil marks on some of the pages. Pencils were the writing implement of choice on polar expeditions as ink tended to freeze. But even pencils were not infallible. While writing, Scott reported, 'not only would one's fingers freeze very rapidly, but one's breath would form an icy film on the paper through which it was difficult to make the pencil-mark'. Nevertheless, in this instance the pencil had been sufficient.

Lizzie was just able to make out a series of numbers, followed by a few words: 'ice flowers', 'panorama', 'spoilt', 'missing', 'accidentally exposed'.

The text on the title page was still clear: *The Wellcome Photographic Exposure Record and Diary for 1910*. It was a popular choice of notebook for photographers. The preliminary pages contain reference sections on 'Modern Photographic Methods' and information on permits the British photographer might need when working in foreign countries (the polar regions are not included). There is helpful information on everything from fixatives and gold toning to night photography. Conversions between British imperial measures and the metric system. Like my own run-of-the-mill, week-to-view diary, it lists the hours between time zones and British public holidays: a mass of helpful information that is rarely glanced at during the course of a year.

Back in New Zealand, Lizzie's conservation team separated the pages from their gatherings and repaired the worn areas with tiny pieces of paper, then sewed them together again. The canvas case binding opens onto endpapers decorated with an elegant pattern of a unicorn, which repeats over and over. The metal stud has rusted, leaving a great circular stain in the centre of each page. The paper is only slightly yellowed but its edges have eroded. Lizzie found a name on the flyleaf and realized that she was looking at the exposure notes and subject matter of the glass plates created on Cape Adare by a member of Scott's Northern Party, George Murray Levick. 'We seldom find objects that have such a strong personal connection to individual explorers,' Lizzie says. 'This has Levick's signature, it has his handwritten notes. Did it fall off a sledge, did it fall out of his pocket? We don't know the answer to that, but I bet that he missed it.'

Levick's journal did not make it back to England, but he and his fellow members of the Northern Party did. In this, the men who were chosen to explore Cape Adare were more fortunate than those selected for the trek to the South Pole. Robert Falcon Scott and a party of four others successfully reached the Pole on 17 January 1912, only to find they had been beaten by Roald Amundsen's Norwegian team thirty-four days earlier. Scott and his fellow explorers died on their return journey. Their fate touched many hearts, and donations to a relief fund were generous enough to establish a library in Cambridge, which would hold the results of past and future polar research. After an email exchange with Lizzie Meek, I decide to pay a visit to the Scott Polar Research Institute, which recently celebrated its centenary, to look at Levick's photographs.

I arrive early, and find Graham the caretaker blowing the tiny yellow leaves of the acacia tree from the steps. 'Hoovering the cornflakes,' he says, wryly. I step over the deciduous breakfast and pass through the glass doors. This museum feels like home to any traveller. People disappear for months or years, and then they come back, their skin raw from the elements, sometimes direct from the airport lugging a ruck-sack. Conversations are picked up again after a six-month absence. A year or two later, a book or a thesis may be added to the collections. The polar regions aren't considered exotic here – most people's minds are on ice, anyway. This is only my second visit, and my research is not sanctioned by any laudable institution or grant, but I'm welcomed warmly. Within moments of spotting me in the building, a researcher disappears to photocopy a report on Operation Iceworm (the secret system of tunnels for nuclear missiles planned by the US military under Greenland's ice cap). He thinks it will be of interest to me. It is.

In the reading room above the museum, the librarian gives me a pair of white gloves, and a tub containing at least twenty lead pencils. Pens can't be used here – not, thankfully, because of freezing conditions. She brings out several files containing Levick's photographs. I have learnt to interpret Levick's old-school script by scrutinizing the digitized version of his diary. I swivel between the yellowed pages on my screen and the pristine images, arranged in clear archival pockets.

Levick was a surgeon and zoologist, as well as photographer to the *Terra Nova* expedition. Another member of the party dispatched to Cape Adare, the geologist Raymond Priestley, sniffed at the area – it had been occupied by previous explorers. The Northern Party's ship had steamed on towards Robertson Bay, examining the coast for an alternative landing place, a region where Scott's men could make their own mark. They found nothing but towering cliffs and walls of ice. A section of the Dugdale Glacier seemed to offer a chance of landing, but this was rejected; the explorers were later grateful for that decision when the area of ice they had considered camping on sailed past them. Instead, they turned back, and settled for the cape's safer, 'second-hand' surroundings.

A series of nine photographs presents a panorama of the Admiralty Range from the Northern Party's base at Cape Adare. I imagine Levick setting up each scene, standing on the ridge and steadying his tripod on the uneven surface of the ice, moving the camera gradually sideways for each of the nine shots, careful not to miss a peak of the monotonous range. (Taking photographs was considered the best way to record the geography of the Antarctic so that cartographers back home could draw up maps.) Then he would move in closer to the crags, making studies of the steep outlet glaciers that run between them. In most of these photographs, a member of the party stands in front of the glacier to set the scale, one arm raised as if pointing out a difficult to spot geographical feature – although no one could miss the wall of ice, which fills the frame. The figures look tiny compared to the striations of the ice. Despite their small size, they alter the mood of the composition: this is now an inhabited landscape. These monochrome images can't do justice to the ice formations which Levick describes in his notebook as 'ice crystals', 'ice floes' and even an 'ice tapestry'.

Next, a few images of the hut at Cape Adare. Levick's home for the year is barely visible: it's buried in snow up to the windowpanes, as was the baker's house on Upernavik. I know how welcome the sense of the snow's enclosure would be, even though it would also remind the explorers how far from home they were. The walls of the hut were just two thin layers of pine boards, stuffed with hessian and shredded seaweed, but they offered shelter and safety for Levick, and storage for his few books and clothes. Inside the hut, Levick took photographs of his five fellow explorers engaging in gentlemanly pursuits. There's even a self-portrait – he is seated on his camp bed, hands in his pockets, reading and smoking his pipe. Chemicals for developing film are lined up in jars on the shelf above him. Another shot captures him shaving by candlelight, with his mirror propped up on a pile of jackets. The camera flash must have cast a sudden light on the grimy interior, momentarily diminishing the candle's weak flame.

Such moments of relaxation are rare. Living on the ice requires industry. Many photographs show the men actively shovelling snow or posing for a moment, holding their ice axes. As well as studying the physical environment, the explorers were keen to understand the animals that lived on the ice, the traits that enabled their survival – and which in turn might help mankind to survive. In one photograph, Levick stands over a dead seal. It has been laid out upon a sledge inside the hut, its limp flippers looking eerily like hands. He appears to be paying his respects. A knife lies beside him on the table. In another, Levick is outdoors: he skins and guts a seal, knife in one hand, blood stains on the other. Victor Campbell, the group's leader, looks on, nonchalantly balancing a cocked rifle under one arm. A later photograph shows Levick sporting long sealskin gloves.

Seals were not the only creatures with whom the explorers shared the ice. Turning back to the panorama shots of the Admiralty Range, the distant mountains smoky with blown snow, I notice some black spots scattered in the foreground. They look like specks of dust on the lens, but when I look more closely, I can make out the pointed tips of the penguins' wings.

It seems appropriate that, of all the expedition paraphernalia, it should have been Levick's notebook that lay so long under the ice, as his writings were dogged by self-censorship and silence. At Cape Adare he spent an entire breeding season with the penguin colony. The behaviour he observed there was unexpected. He confided in his notebook that 'hooligan' males engaged in 'depraved' sexual acts, mating with dead females, abusing chicks, and even trying to breed with other males. His affection for the creatures soon turned to horror. Later, he pasted over his original notes with a transliteration into Greek letters to spare others in the party from discovering the distressing truth about their companions on the ice shelf. On his return to England, fellow zoologists urged him not to include this material in his monograph on penguins. He followed their advice. However, the Natural History Museum has kept a file on Levick, in which there is an offprint, circulated in an edition limited to a hundred copies for close colleagues. The reader is forewarned by a message in bold type on the first page: 'THE SEXUAL HABITS OF THE ADELIE PENGUIN, NOT FOR PUBLICATION'. Later scientists would confirm Levick's observations (which seem less surprising today) and did not make any moral judgements on the penguins' behaviour.

I feel sorry for Levick, his faith shaken by the penguins, and with worse to come. In January 1912, after nearly a year at Cape Adare, the Northern Party were collected by the *Terra Nova* and taken 200 miles south, where they explored another region by sledge and Priestley collected geological samples. They returned to the main depot as arranged five weeks later, and waited there for the ship to reappear. Meanwhile they charted their immediate location: an outcrop of granite and gneiss, almost completely bare of snow, bounded by glaciers on the west and on the east sloping down to the waters of the bay. They named it 'Inexpressible Island'. For some weeks they continued to watch for the ship, at last so eager for the sight of it that it began to make its way into their dreams, but, as Priestley wrote: 'The waters of the bay were lashed to fury by the wind, and all we could see to seaward was one constant procession of white-caps sweeping across the bay.' Although the stranded party saw only open water, beyond it was thick pack ice, through which the ship was unable to pass.

I find Priestley's journal on the shelves, and I am so horrified by the men's predicament that I end up staying in Cambridge an extra day to read it. When I return to the library the next morning, Graham is working his way round the shelves, dusting and straightening. He tells me that when he gets to the end he starts all over again. Books require upkeep, they don't survive on their own: you learn this when you work with them.

I was beginning to make a home of the Scott Polar Research Institute, just as the explorers I was reading about lost theirs.

The Northern Party found themselves facing the winter alone on Inexpressible Island with only summer supplies. Lacking even materials to build a shelter, the men dug a cave from a deep snowdrift, lining its floor with sealskins and its walls with snow blocks, and creating a door out of biscuit boxes. It was just big enough to hold the six of them lying side by side. Priestley wrote in his diary of a journey back to the ice cave, having visited a depot nearer the coast: they struggled 'across half a mile of clear blue ice, swept by the unbroken wind, which met us almost straight in the face. We could never stand up, so had to scramble the whole distance on "all fours", lying flat on our bellies in the gusts. By the time we had reached the other side we had had enough. Our faces had been rather badly bitten, and I have a very strong recollection of the men's countenances, which were a leaden blue, streaked with white patches of frostbite.' To add to the indignity, the party's sleeping bags had been left behind, and they had to share two men to a bag that night. (A return trip to the depot was made to rescue the sleeping bags.)

Some hardships become bearable in retrospect. Levick, who accompanied Priestley on that depot mission, wrote later: 'It is a pleasing picture to look back upon now, and if I close my eyes I can see again the little cave cut out in snow and ice with the tent flapping in the doorway, barely secured by ice-axe and shovel arranged crosswise against the side of the shaft.'

With scarcely any food remaining, their knowledge of wildlife was more necessary than ever. They bagged as many penguins and seals as possible before total darkness descended, cached them in the snow and settled in for a gruelling winter. Priestley was quartermaster in charge of the meagre stores. He describes the routine:

> Every few days there were bones to be fetched from the dried seal carcasses, seaweed from the beach, penguins from the depot near the icefoot, and seal meat and blubber from the caches where we had stored the dead seals. Heavy loads had to be carried either over the huge boulders ... or else along the smooth, glistening surface of the icefoot, on which it was necessary to walk with stiff legs, feeling every step with the sole of the foot, and avoiding unevennesses as much as possible.

Once the meat was back in the cave and unfrozen, it was made into watery 'hoosh' or gruel. As time went by various flavourings were introduced to vary the taste of the hoosh: dried seaweed from the beach, seaweed from the cave floor, ginger and citric-acid tabloids and even a mustard plaster from Levick's medicine box. Seal brains were the only ingredient all agreed were a good addition, but these were hardest to come by. The meat in the hoosh supplemented their strict rations of more familiar food: less than one biscuit a day, a mug of weak cocoa five nights a week, a mug of tea once a week, a little chocolate and sugar, and twenty-five raisins each month and on birthdays.

As well as providing the substance for their shelter, ice was an important ingredient in their diet. It could be melted down for drinking water, and Priestley notes its use in the hoosh, especially when soaked in seal's blood: 'Our one great discovery in the eatable line, was . . . when a seal was butchered, the hot blood melted down into the ice, and the pool thus formed froze solid a few hours later. Then one of us would go down with a pick and shovel and a sack, dig up this mixture of blood and ice, and carry it to the drift. Part of it was then boiled up with the hoosh, and this made a gravy in which it was possible to stand a spoon upright.'

The daily routine centred around food, with time allowed for torpor; the men who were off-duty lay in their sleeping bags until about eleven o'clock each morning, digesting their first dose of hoosh. After occasional forays into the blizzards, the cave seemed almost snug. Even the worst storms were only apparent from the 'sibilant hiss of the drift on the roof, or the murmur of an unusually strong gust'. Such sounds were sufficient to increase the men's feeling of security by reminding them that however bad their lot was, without the walls of ice enclosing them, their chances of survival would have been very much worse.

After the evening meal was over, the day's appointed mess-men finished their chores, while the others wrote their diaries or reread old letters from home. Once the mess-men had also turned in, Levick would read a chapter from *David Copperfield*. This welcome escapism lasted the group for around sixty nights. I imagine their reaction to Dickens's description of Tommy Traddles in the final chapter, who also lives in a house with 'no room to spare', so crowded out by a happy family that he 'keeps his papers in his dressing-room and his boots with his papers'. Other reading matter followed Dickens: several novels by Max Pemberton, *The Decameron*, and two copies of the *Review of Reviews*, which were read from cover to cover, the advertisements relished as much as the articles.

As a special treat on Sundays, Priestley read aloud from his Cape Adare diary, and the men contrasted their life the previous year with existence in the snow cave. Then Campbell would pull out a pocket edition of the New Testament, and everyone sang what hymns they could remember as bravely as they could. Fortified by music, the men would often protest that they were happier in the ice cave than they had ever been at Cape Adare, but their accommodation had obvious drawbacks. The polar winter was interminably dark, and the cave did not even offer a window onto that darkness. The only source for artificial light was melted blubber, and the soft yellow glow it dispensed was hard won. Priestley describes an ingenious method of making lamps by combining strands of lamp-wick, a safety pin, and a small Oxo tin filled with melted blubber oil:

> The little reading-lamps gave light sufficient to read by if the book was held fairly close to them, but they were of very little use for illuminating the hut generally. Two of them were usually available for the use of the mess-man and cook, and of these one had to be kept handy for the cook to light his spills so that he could examine the hoosh from time to time. The mess-man, therefore, had the use of one lamp, which gave about half as much light as a match. This was just sufficient to throw a small circle of light on the joint he was quarrying, and no more.

No doubt the smell of lamps tempered the other odours of the space. Cave life was a constant battle between cold and heat, between keeping the stove going and avoiding a thaw. As the weeks passed the sooty walls grew as striated as a glacier, gleaming where the melting ice washed away the dirt.

'The term "smoke" did not seem adequate to express the oily brown fumes which rose from the blubber-stoves,' wrote Priestley. Luckily Browning offered a word from his West Country dialect: 'smitch'. Everything was besmitched. As the months passed, their eyes developed 'smitch-blindness' and since it became too painful to read, they would doze instead. 'I myself could never have believed that I could have been happy without something to read,' Priestley wrote. 'Yet ... many times when I could have been reading *Hints to Travellers* or the *Review of Reviews* and I preferred to lie and let my thoughts wander at their own sweet will.' And so they acclimatized. It was a surprise to Priestley, and probably a relief to Campbell, that the party settled down to their new existence in a docile manner.

I began to wonder about the psychological effect of this lifestyle. Would it be worse to be trapped in the ice unable to return home than to long for the ice but be unable to return to it? The members of the Northern Party formed a strong bond with each other and with the polar landscape, learning its characteristics and how to survive in it – a knowledge they were unable to use in their subsequent lives. Priestley seems almost nostalgic for the ice cave in *Antarctic Adventure*, his account of that winter. Perhaps the determined camaraderie of the snow cave seemed simple, compared to the war the explorers faced on their return to Europe. Even so, it was a miracle that Campbell maintained discipline in such a demoralizing situation. To do so, he divided the cramped cave into two virtual messes: one for himself, Priestley and Levick, as 'officers', another for those of lowlier rank. It was a naval custom that men in one mess were not to pay any attention to conversations held in the other. Towards the end of the winter, as the officers prepared for the long sledge journey south to Cape Evans to join the rest of the expedition, this polite fantasy of privacy was not enough. Since everything could be heard throughout the cave, a silent dialogue was carried out by notebook. In Campbell's 'cave-diary' – alongside his lists of diminishing stores and other calculations – several pages were used to confer with Levick on sensitive matters without the other men's knowledge. He used the diary to discuss issues of discipline, and express concerns about Browning's health. His words scrawl haphazardly down the page: he was either too cold to care about lineation or just struggling to see: 'How about giving Browning a spoonful of brandy?'

Levick's response is more precise: 'I think he'll be alright now he's got rid of the stuff ... If he is not quiet in an hour or so I'll give him some.'

The diary's 'silent conversations' have been painstakingly deciphered and dated by Don Webster. His research reveals Levick as a reassuring presence, who shakes off Campbell's fears for Browning: 'this morning was a little panic and nothing more.'

Later in the winter, other men began to struggle. Campbell wrote to Levick: 'I meant to tell you P. [Priestley] got rather exhausted out today so I suggested his coming in: he tells me he feel [sic] very run down after this last attack.'

Levick replies: 'I had a yarn with him when he came in: I told him a tonic he was taking would set him up. I hope it will.'

It did, and all survived. Levick took a triumphant, over-exposed photograph of the six men as they emerged from the cave after seven months. Their sooty garments are silhouetted against the ice, only the sheen in the sun suggesting the filth they have endured: 'dirty and dishevelled' as the Freeze Frame cataloguer at Scott Polar Research Institute tactfully puts it. The clothes, encrusted with blubber, would have stood up by themselves. The photographer has to position the camera a good way off to fit six men in the frame: as if in celebration of their escape to freedom the upper half of the image is full of sky.

The debilitated party took five weeks to sledge to Cape Evans, where they discovered that Scott and his men had met the fate they so narrowly avoided. (Their leader's last act had been to write in his diary.) Back at the subdued base camp, Campbell set about rewriting his diary, and Priestley borrowed Apsley Cherry-Garrard's typewriter to type up his own account of the ordeal. Meanwhile, Levick developed the photographs taken at Cape Adare. Despite the long period between exposure and development, and the conditions they had endured that winter, the images were perfect. The ice of Inexpressible Island had kept both the films and plates frozen, so that no chemical reaction could take place.

III

These days there's an annual BBC midwinter radio broadcast to Antarctica, and the relatives of staff overwintering on research stations come into the studio to record short personal messages. Their embarrassed tones are beamed instantly to the other side of the world, and everyone in between can listen if they tune in. Levick and his companions had no such comfort, but they read letters from home until they fell apart, and toasted absent friends. What was it like for the Northern Party, with no possibility of sending a message even to the *Terra Nova*, nor receiving reassurance that it would return for them? Most polar explorers have had to carry their messages themselves, whether delivering an SOS to the nearest settlement or tucking last letters home safely inside their journals to await delivery later. Hard as it was for explorers to travel across the ice, sledging over crevasses, standing upright in a blizzard, making out the horizon through frost-caked eyelashes, it was equally difficult for messages to travel.

The Scott Polar Research Institute is the only library I've ever been to where people are not told off for whistling. Or shouting. 'Hugh!' a plummy voice calls from one bay of books to another, 'Hugh, do you think it's worth me talking to that admiral about the briefing?' I take down a volume of the letters of John Irving, third officer aboard the ship HMS *Terror*, which was being repaired in Woolwich, and head for a more peaceful alcove.

'My dearest Katie,' Lieutenant Irving wrote to his sister-in-law on 18 April 1845. 'Our *Terror* in her last voyage with Captain Back was so crushed by ice that she could not have been kept afloat another day, when she got in to Loch Swilly. Two years is a long time without any tidings, and perhaps we may be three years at least. Do not give us up, if you hear *nothing*.' This was not exaggeration for effect: the voyage was bound to be long. *Terror* was about to depart on Sir John Franklin's ill-fated expedition to find the final section of the Northwest Passage, an ice-free marine trade route around North America. Katie would have read Franklin's bestselling account of his first Arctic journey, *Narrative of a Journey to the Shores of the Polar Sea*. Just before sailing a month later, on 16 May, Irving wrote again: 'We take two years' provisions, and a transport accompanies us with a third year for each ship; so if you do not hear of us for three years, you need not think we are starved.'

There's no chance of me starving here. There are punctual breaks for coffee and cake at ten-thirty in the morning and at four in the afternoon. Time is calculated according to the naval watch and sounded on the great brass bell from Scott's *Terra Nova*, which sits in state in the stairwell. The honour of sounding the watch is delegated to me this morning: two short bells, then a long one. All work stops. The echoes die away, and there's a rattling of crockery as the tea trolley is wheeled in and parked beside the spiral staircase. When, I wonder, biting into a brownie, did Irving get his time to write? Did he sit with pen and paper in the mess room after his watch, listening to the hull of the ship straining against the sea and thinking of home as icebergs sailed past on the horizon?

Back to my desk. Four locations are given in Irving's letters as he journeyed north. Woolwich and, further down the Thames, Greenhithe, were followed by Stromness in Orkney, and later the Whalefish Islands, Greenland, where the last packet of letters was entrusted to the harbourmaster. Woolwich – Greenhithe – Stromness – Greenland: these names recur in explorers' letters as the only predictable post-marks in the voyage into oblivion. The ship was the constant, not the lands through which they passed.

Irving's letters were often written in haste, but they are characterized by postscripts that relive difficult leave-takings. He tries to communicate his extraordinary travel experiences in a long, last letter to Katie. Firstly, he draws a sketch of his ship in the Greenland harbour. Although it is high summer – 'probably 10th July 1845' – 'there is plenty of ice floating about and scraping our sides, and we have sometimes a little snow.' He finds the Whalefish Islands (perhaps modern-day Disko Bay) barren and rocky, and notes 'the openings betwixt some of the islands are choked up with ice'. During his journey he has observed many icebergs, which, he informs Katie, 'are huge piles of ice and snow floating about. Some are 200 feet high. These are formed by avalanches from the

Greenland mountains, which are very high and precipitous, and one sheet of snow to the water's edge'. Anticipating his lack of opportunity to send a letter, he tells Katie to read 'the Polar voyages of Parry, Ross, and Back ... as they describe exactly what will be our difficulties; and you will, I daresay, like to know a little what I may be about for so long.' He also encloses 'a little Polar chart', saying, 'I have put the track of the Expedition in red, and proposed route dotted red.' His lines look hesitant, surrounded by the expanse of white paper. I think of the Bellman's speech in Lewis Carroll's *The Hunting of the Snark*, published in 1876, two decades after Irving set out:

> 'What's the good of Mercator's North Poles and Equators,
> Tropics, Zones, and Meridian Lines?'
> So the Bellman would cry: and the crew would reply
> 'They are merely conventional signs!
>
> 'Other maps are such shapes, with their islands and capes!
> But we've got our brave Captain to thank:
> (So the crew would protest) 'that he's bought us the best—
> A perfect and absolute blank!'

'As you observe,' writes Irving from the Whalefish Islands, 'there must now be a long blank in our correspondence.' They will set sail tomorrow, 'in the first place, for Barrow's strait, and after, as best we can.'

Irving worries that former expeditions were stopped 'by a Barrier of ice so thick and solid that the summer, which is only ten weeks long, passed away without dissolving it.' But he trusts they will be able to find a passage through the ice using charts and their experience – besides, they have a fine library on board, 'the best books of all kinds, consisting of 1200 volumes, and shall be able to pass the time very well . . .' Even the ice offers the promise of activity to Irving: before the ship is completely frozen in the crew will be busy 'sawing the ice and working the ships on, whenever a single mile can be gained', and parties may be sent off the ship to explore from time to time. Irving was the ship's astronomer, in charge of winding and comparing the chronometers, those 'little clocks' which were accurate enough to calculate longitude (the ship's distance west or east of Greenwich). So these activities will keep him occupied, he says. He sounds certain, but I wonder if his words convinced Katie.

After dropping off the last letters, the expedition ships *Erebus* and *Terror* were seen on 26 July by a European whaling vessel, making their way north. Then, all their correspondents could do was wait.

Katie had two years to work through the reading list Irving gave her, by which time, concerned at having heard nothing further of Franklin's expedition, Lady Jane Franklin, Members of Parliament and the British press urged the Admiralty to send a search party. The disappearance of Franklin became a Victorian sensation and, in the ensuing decades, over thirty expeditions joined in the search. Meanwhile, in the Arctic, Franklin's desperate crew had left messages in cairns for whoever might find them. No longer personal correspondence to dearest Katie, these documents address unknown, imagined readers. They demonstrate the authors' firm faith, not only

that someone would read the words, but also that future readers believed in the texts' existence sufficiently to travel across
the icy tundra to find them.

The regions the British Admiralty had commanded
Franklin to chart were haunted by expanses of ice that
seemed to defy the seasons. A map by the cartographer R.T.
Gould (now in the National Maritime Museum, Greenwich)
delineates the last known movements of the expedition. This
map depicts an area marked not by geographical features but
punctuated by ominous 'x's: the caches of letters, pemmican
and bones found by search parties. These clues to Franklin's
disappearance, linked by a red dotted line, eventually peter
out in a question mark surrounded by blank paper. (The
similarities to the Polar chart which Irving sketched for Katie
are poignant.)

Over time, Franklin's expedition acquired the attributes
of the environment in which it perished, becoming, like the
Northwest Passage, a mystery to be solved to win money and
glory. But the humans were harder to find than any geographic entity – indeed the final sections of the Passage were
pieced together by those looking for the lost explorers. In
this muddle of harsh elements, speculative maps and missed
connections, the search parties tried to conscript the environment as a mail delivery system. One search expedition trapped
eight wild arctic foxes and buckled iron collars engraved with
messages around their necks, before releasing them into the
tundra, hoping they would be hunted down by Franklin's men
and the messages read. Only one fox was ever seen again, and
there was no sign that it ever encountered Franklin during
its travels. The collar, now downstairs in the Polar Museum,

reads: 'HBMS ENTERPRISE WQ [WINTER QUARTERS] LAT 71.35 N LONG 117.39 W XX XII [20 December] 1851'.

Unlike foxes, carrier – or homing – pigeons have been used as messengers since classical times. The pigeons supporting polar expeditions provided their keepers with companion-ship and entertainment before being despatched, and were given special status, despite a poor record of success. On 8 April 1851, Erasmus Ommanney advised Sir John Ross, 'Pray take care of the Pigeons, may they be "Messengers of glad tidings."' The pigeons were released into the sky in baskets attached to balloons, each with a portion of split peas to sustain them. Ross told the secretary of the Hudson's Bay Company that he had great faith in the birds, hoping that if released into a fair wind they would be carried into the path of whaling ships, where they would alight for a free passage to England. Unfortunately, the few birds which survived the long flight only did so by virtue of having shaken the heavy papers they had been entrusted with out of their tail feathers.

In 1852 Edward Belcher took command of the search expedition aboard HMS *Resolute*. His ship carried a novel airborne message delivery system which did not require birds. On 16 August 1852, *Resolute* was in relatively unknown waters near Dealy Island when it was struck by an enormous ice floe, which leaned it to port, so that it struck a second floe. After over a week trapped between the floes, with the nights lengthening, the thermometer starting to drop, and with ice as far as the eye could see, the crew decided to test the system. Officer Emile de Bray noted in his journal that the weather had been squally, but the wind fell towards evening. 'At 7 o'clock we released our first balloon, which carries with it about a thousand little squares of paper spaced along an iron wire with a slow match.' The balloon was a couple of metres wide, and filled with gas – presumably hydrogen. Printed on each piece of paper was *Resolute*'s precise position. De Bray continues: 'As the balloon was released, the match was lit so that the pieces of paper would fall at well-spaced distances; distributed at various points in the arctic landscape they may fall into the hands of some travellers and thus give Franklin or his companions news of us.' The first balloon rose high, and headed north-north-west. As they watched it disappear, the crew knew they must soon ship the rudder and make preparations to winter in the same ice pack which they believed had destroyed Franklin's ships.

Resolute was never released from the ice. It was still beset in the spring of 1854, and by May the crew had decided to abandon ship. They were luckier than Franklin's men. They were rescued. The government printed a formal announcement in *The London Gazette* that the ship was still Her Majesty's property, but there was no attempt at salvage. *Resolute* found her own way out from the pack ice. The following year, an American whaler spotted her adrift off Baffin Island, over a thousand miles from where she had been abandoned. Captain Buddington boarded and found everything stowed away according to the rules for desertion – spars hauled up to one side and bound, and boats piled together. The hatches were closed and the hold was silent.

The ship was returned to England, where Queen Victoria ordained that its timber should be used for commemorative objects, including a magnificent desk. The original design of the desk called for carvings of the Arctic and Antarctic circles

at each corner, but it seems these were never added. In 1880
the unadorned 'Resolute Desk' was presented to President
Rutherford B. Hayes; in 1961 First Lady Jackie Kennedy
transferred it to the Oval Office. There it remains, and is still
the desk at which the president sits to write letters and sign
bills into law.

Qivittut or 'mountain wanderers' are heartbroken individuals
who leave society and become wild and solitary in the mountains, never to be seen again. They are often said to acquire
supernatural powers, or adopt the language of the creatures
they eat, such as ravens and grouse. In Greenland, wildness
is an emotional state, often symbolic of rejection by a community; it is defined by loneliness as much as geographical
isolation. There are many tales of *qivittut*. One tale from the
south of Greenland, tells of Alinnaata, who would have been
a near contemporary of Franklin. She ran away from a cruel
husband, who would not let her eat. 'It was impossible to find
her'. After a long and fruitless search her community had to
give up looking for her. No one was able to claim the find-
er's fee, which had been offered by local missionaries – even
though the sum was increased several times. This was a person
who wished to leave no traces for others to follow. Later, some
hunters were kayaking in a remote fjord when they noticed
that the water was no longer clear and the breeze sounded like
'a swarm of bees'. On the shore they found items of female
clothing, turned inside out, and then discovered Alinnaata's
naked body: 'At first sight she looked just like an animal'. Her
arms were bent at unnatural angles, and her head was craned
back over one shoulder.

They lifted Alinnaata's distorted body on a piece of sealskin and took it for burial:

> When they came to the burial place, they laid the paper with a text from the holy scriptures that the missionaries had given them, on her, over her poor clothes. When they had buried her, they covered her completely with stones. The missionaries had forbidden them to sing hymns, so no hymns were sung for her. They just heaped stones on her grave.

Alinnaata's mourners may have been silent, but the grave was not. After the burial, sounds were heard from the grave whenever there was a change of weather: sounds like the calling of great black-backed gulls.

Although the fate of her husband was unknown, Lady Franklin continued to write to him for eight years after his departure. Some families of the crew shared her persistence. John and Phoebe Diggle decided to send a New Year's message to their son John, the ship's cook on board HMS *Terror*. It is dated 4 January 1848, almost three years after his departure: 'Dear Son, I wright these few lines to in [*sic*] hopes to find you and all your shipmates in both ships well as it leaves us thank God for it but we fears we shall never see you again . . .' The letter was carried to the Arctic by one of the expedition search party ships and returned with a brusque stamp over the copperplate address: 'RETURNED TO SENDER THERE HAVING BEEN NO MEANS OF FORWARDING IT.'

Meanwhile, Franklin's party had also written messages

which there was no means of forwarding. In May 1859, towards the end of their two-year mission, the search party led by Francis McClintock found a boat moored by the shore of King William Island in the archipelago north of Hudson Bay. In the boat, they discovered a copy of *Christian Melodies: Home and its Scenes*, a tiny book of verses that fits in the palm of the hand. An inscription on the flyleaf indicated that it belonged to Lieutenant Graham Gore, HMS *Erebus*. McClintock searched the island, finding a cairn which contained a small, sealed tin. The rust-stained document inside was the standard Admiralty accident form, printed with delivery instructions in six languages: 'WHOEVER finds this paper is requested to forward it to the Secretary of the Admiralty, London, with a note of the time and the place it was found.' On the form were two messages written a year apart which offered conflicting messages from different members of Franklin's party. The first appears optimistic, but there are already signs of trouble. The writer, Gore, gives their bearings and notes: 'H.M. Ships *Erebus* and *Terror* Wintered in the Ice in 1846–7'. But he gets the date wrong: this should read 1845–46. The error has been ascribed to memory loss, indicative of the lead poisoning which was to kill many of the party.

One year later, the remaining crew had left the icebound ships and returned to the cairn to update the form, before setting off overland into the tundra. Their message was ominous: 'HM's Ships *Terror* and *Erebus* were deserted on 22nd April, 5 leagues N.N.W. of this, having been beset since 12th September 1846. The Officers and crews, consisting of 105 souls, under the command of F.R.M. Crozier, landed here ...' The manuscript rambles on, but fails to provide any information that would have been of use to a rescue party. The only clue as to where the men were headed is an afterthought, the incomplete and almost illegible sentence: 'And start tomorrow, 26th, for Back's Fish River'. Cramped copperplate fills the margin, imprisoning the original text; a calligraphic metaphor for the claustrophobic ship frozen in pack ice for two winters. The signatures run around the edge of the page at a contrary angle to the intended Admiralty layout: to read them the document has to be turned upside-down. There could have been little pride for the deserting officer who placed his signature on the official Admiralty stationery. The erratic arrangement of text made necessary by the limited paper stock recalls the circuitous lines on charts of lost expedition routes, which show forward progress hampered by the unpredictable drift of ice. In the Arctic, even official correspondence was governed by environmental rather than social laws.

We don't have Irving's account of those long last weeks. But stories from survivors of other icebound ships reiterate the discipline and camaraderie, the attempt to pursue a rational, familiar existence amid apparently boundless ice and faced by an uncertain future. Regular readings from the Bible and hymn-singing satisfied some, while games of football and rations of spirits on festive occasions gave others something to anticipate. William McKinley, who was iced-in with the *Karluk* in the Beaufort Sea above Alaska during the same years that the Northern Party were exploring the southern hemisphere, recalls the pleasure of discussing horticulture with Bartlett, the ship's skipper, on a rare visit to his private cabin. The Glaswegian writes, 'I noticed on his table a copy

of Dean Hole's *A Book About Roses*, with its glorious chro-
molithographs of the softly shaded petals. As I picked it up he
asked, "Do you grow roses?"' The two men sat for a while,
in freezing temperatures and 24-hour darkness, miles from
the nearest garden, talking about roses. And the ice offered
its own soft colours, a less comforting but more transcendent
beauty. I hope that before Irving and his companions abandoned ship they had a chance to observe such scenes as this
one, described by McKinley:

> One night when there was a full moon I went for a walk
> on the ice and stopped about a hundred yards from the
> ship. The larger hummocks of ice stood out in all their
> weird shapes and sizes, casting fantastic shadows in the
> moonlight. The winds had swept their tops clear of snow,
> exposing glare-ice, which glistened like giant emeralds. All
> over the pack, the smaller lumps of ice scintillated in daz-
> zling brilliance, like diamonds scattered in all directions
> as far as the eye could see ... As I turned round to face
> the ship, old *Karluk* seemed to be doing her best to outdo
> nature. Her deck covering of snow shimmered like tinsel.
> Every rope and spar was magnified by a fluffy coating of
> frosted rime.

Ice had trapped Franklin's ships just over a hundred miles
from the Northern Magnetic Pole. Irving's remains were
discovered not far from the cairn on King William Island
and were brought home to the Dean Cemetery in Edinburgh.
He was given a fine tombstone. A carved lanyard border surrounds a bas-relief of two distant ships, their sails furled as if

for winter. In the foreground, there's a sea of splintered ice, almost as regular as the cobblestones on the Royal Mile. The ice has parted like the Red Sea, forming a path down which the crew – warmly wrapped in winter coats – walk towards the viewer. Of the figures nearest the grave, one carries a spade. The next pulls a sledge. A third man stands looking back towards the ship. His eye travels that part of the image most deeply carved into the stone: the fissure in the ice that was never to come.

IV

I've been invited to show my work at an arts centre on the west coast of Denmark. In Greenland, people told me Denmark was a small country, but the five hours it takes to journey westwards from Copenhagen seem to suggest otherwise. It's a relief when the train crosses the brackish reaches of the Limfjord and draws into Hurup Thy, almost the last stop on the line. I reach up to the luggage rack and pull down my suitcase.

My exhibition accompanies a book festival called 'On the Margins', making a virtue of the fact that the town is almost as far from Copenhagen as it is possible to be. The nineteenth-century American painter William Morris Hunt called the margins 'the best part of all books', adding that a blank margin had 'the soothing influence of a clear sky in a landscape.' He could have been thinking of the clear spring skies over this waterway that runs the length of the Danish peninsula, from the small town of Agger in the west to the city of Aarhus in the east.

Mette-Sofie picks me up at the station. As we drive to the gallery she recounts a folktale about the creation of the Limfjord. In the distant past Limgrim, a witch's hog-like son, used his snout to plough a furrow through the land from east to west and water flooded in. Mette-Sofie is a rationalist, and suspects Limgrim might have been a glacier. Glacier or hog, the boundary between land and water is not clearly defined here. The land is low-lying, and the water is deep. The bedrock of the peninsula is still slowly rebounding from the weight of glacial ice. Some land has been reclaimed from the waves for farming, but the water is encroaching again – the whole town flooded last year, and roads turned to rivers. New artificial breakwaters and locks have been constructed to stem the damage to the coast from an increasingly wild North Sea.

Meanwhile, the fjord is a playground for boat-loving retirees. Lars lends me his nautical charts, but I don't use them to travel – I hang them up to block out the sunshine coming through the venetian blinds in my hostel room. When the windows warm in the morning, the charts fall to the floor as if under the weight of light. On the last Saturday in April, the boats that have rested in gardens and garages all winter are wheeled out onto the narrow jetty. The hulls have been repainted, red or black, up to the waterline. I watch as one by one *Adriane, Anni, Elfrida, Louié, Malajka, Falsang, Silver, Ballerina, Kleopatra, Laribé, Out Skerries, Inge-Marie* and *Emilca* are girdled in a belt sling and chained to the hook of the hired crane, which hoists them high and winches them out over the water. Moored in the air, the dark hulls swing uncertainly, but they touch down safely on the water and sail away up the fjord.

There's a local idiom for strolling to the end of the jetty and turning round, returning: *at vende bro*, literally, to turn the bridge. Over the years, as more and more boats have sought moorings here, the jetty has grown longer, and there are new bridges to turn. The timber extensions crook across the fjord, pinching vessels between their planks. It takes four and a half minutes to walk from the gallery to the very end of the jetty. I make the short journey several times each day. Black eelgrass sways in the water, seeming to float from the surface downwards, as well as from the sand upwards. Further out, there's a hint of eel nets in the water, a line of floats and a black flag. By the time the exhibition opens to the public, I have spent as much time looking out across the fjord as in the gallery.

The festival falls on a beautiful May weekend. Even so, Lilli Riget is red-nosed from a cold caught at another book fair in Aalborg. She rarely misses these events, Mette-Sofie tells me, touring Denmark to promote the winners of the annual Danish book design awards. I admire her continued enthusiasm for books, her lifetime's dedication to them. And I'm curious about the heavy silver pendant in the shape of an Inuit hunter that swings against her heart. Lilli starts to tell me her own Arctic story.

Many years ago, shortly after the birth of her daughter, Lilli's husband had left her, and she found work as a cataloguer for the Royal Danish Library in Copenhagen. In early 1968 a colleague suggested a transfer to the National Library of Greenland, then part of the Danish Commonwealth of the Realm. Lilli did not hesitate: she left her daughter with her ex-husband and his new girlfriend, and set off for the north.

Greenland's governors had established a small public library in a former school building in the capital, Nuuk, during the 1930s. This initiative was followed by even smaller branch libraries in towns up and down the coast. An ambitious extension of the Nuuk library was being completed just as Lilli arrived, but on 10 February 1968 a fire reduced the new building to ruins.

Lilli may have been cataloguing the collection before the fire started – or perhaps she was sent to help restock the library in the aftermath of the disaster. The chronology changes each time she tells the story, Mette-Sofie tells me later. Does a month or two matter, when these events happened almost fifty years ago? Although it's been revised over decades, Lilli's story takes place on just one night. I don't remember her exact words, which were frequently interrupted by customers wanting to look at books, but these are the pictures I see in my mind: a dark night; a flickering light visible through the broad panes of a wooden building typical of the Arctic. It's winter. The sash windows are usually shut against the cold, but someone has flung them open. Smoke pours out; pale hands appear and papers tumble from them. The fire hoses direct water through the windows, drenching burning furniture and books alike. The air grows warmer, heat dances before the glass. Papers fall like giant snowflakes onto the ice. The books that are thrown out after them are black: carbonized bindings, charred fragments of paper. Over 26,000 of the library's volumes were burnt that night and others were irreparably waterlogged. The night was so cold that water from the fire hoses froze around the debris on the snow.

It is the habit of conservators to preserve things in the

condition in which they are found, just as you do not move an accident victim if you think their neck is broken. When the charred papers were collected and flown to Copenhagen for conservation, they travelled in cold storage still surrounded by blocks of Arctic ice.

The rescued documents included some of the earliest writings on the Greenlandic language. Their author, Samuel Kleinschmidt, was born in Greenland in 1814 and trained with the Herrnhut mission in Germany. On his return to Greenland he was posted to the mission at Lichtenau (German for 'light water'), which had helped in the search for the missing woman Alinnaata and later buried her with a holy text which no one but the missionaries could read. At the Lichtenau mission Kleinschmidt was required to make his congregation recite religious texts by rote. But he didn't approve of rote learning, and he knew that the few books printed in Greenlandic for the missionaries' own use were riddled with errors. He was more likely to be found wandering the hills and talking to his neighbours than undertaking duties prescribed by the mission such as brewing and labouring. His appreciation for the landscape and its inhabitants led him to preach the very first sermon in fluent, everyday Greenlandic, rather than the outdated idiom approved by the religious community. At last the whole congregation could understand the preacher's message.

The mission might not have approved, but Kleinschmidt was dedicated to pursuing his linguistic studies. As someone who put great store by speech, it is ironic that his biographer, a near-contemporary named Otto Rosing, interprets

Kleinschmidt's character using graphology. If handwriting can demonstrate psychological traits, Rosing writes, then 'Kleinschmidt's fist shows his fine character and great sense of order'. Kleinschmidt's manuscripts are meticulous, but they were never easy to read. Despite being extremely near-sighted, he often chose to write in microscript. He was frugal with paper, which would have been scarce in a study so far from Copenhagen. He wrote using a magnifying glass, and a magnifying glass is essential to read his work.

Kleinschmidt was not alone in his fascination with Greenlandic. The first missionaries to arrive in Greenland encountered a tradition of oral literature: a past preserved not on paper but in people's memories, and passed on through song and storytelling. For the evangelists of Kleinschmidt's parents' generation, and later for colonial governors, it was not only necessary to learn the language, but also to decide how its sounds should be represented on paper. Men who had come bearing Bibles soon began compiling dictionaries. The settlers used the Roman alphabet they already knew to transcribe Greenlandic, but its letters could not encompass the sounds of the Eskaleut language family. Kleinschmidt devised a new system of letterforms far better suited to its character. This visionary orthography, published in 1851 as *Grammatik der Grönländischen Sprache* ('Grammar of the Greenlandic Language'), introduced the special character *kra* (Kʻ/ĸ), and the long vowels and stuttered consonants were indicated by means of diacritics. (Although these were clearly improvements, the system continued to be debated until the 1973 language reform, when *kra* was replaced by *q*.)

Linguistics was not the only field in which Kleinschmidt

strove for greater knowledge than was sanctioned. He sketched and surveyed the west coast of Greenland in drawings that are now being used to assess how the landscape has changed. For many years he observed and recorded a phenomenon almost as ephemeral as speech – the aurora borealis. The Danish meteorological institute curtly informed him that this wasn't necessary, that the aurora held no interest for them because so little was known about it. Yet Kleinschmidt continued to take notes three times a day, from 1865 until his death in 1886, earnestly forming his own shorthand composed of letters and numbers to record the location, orientation, shape, movement and colour of the entrancing lights in the sky.

Fire is a danger to books, but so too is water. And papers that have been subjected to both elements – first burning, then suffering the jets from fire hoses – rarely survive. Those well-intentioned people who race to put out a fire with water often succeed in damaging all they have saved. Water can stain or weaken paper, and mould will start to grow on the organic matter within damp paper in a few days. Paper made before the mid-nineteenth century can absorb large amounts of water. In a manual for librarians bluntly titled *Disaster Preparedness*, Constance Brooks, chief of the Preservation Department at Stanford University Libraries, lists supplies that every library should have on hand for the conservation of documents. She includes 'deep-freeze facilities', into which wet documents can be placed to prevent the spread of mould. At the National Library in Nuuk, these facilities were provided by the immediate environment.

The Danish conservators feared that the inks might feather

or migrate as the ice around Kleinschmidt's manuscripts melted. The manuscripts remained frozen for two years while James Flink and Henrik Høyer debated the problem and conducted experiments on modern paper samples. Finally, the documents were transferred to the Technical University of Denmark in Lyngby, a suburb half-an-hour's drive from Copenhagen, and placed in a freeze-dry chamber in the Food Technology Lab. In freeze-drying, ice is converted to vapour without passing through a liquid state; the vapour is then drawn off. The process is used to prepare many everyday consumables from instant coffee to dehydrated strawberries, and the team working on Kleinschmidt's manuscripts wanted to see whether it might preserve the water-damaged archives. Flink and Høyer pried apart the stacks of frozen documents to allow the manuscripts to dry more quickly. (It was possible to do this without causing damage to the manuscripts because paper folders had been interleaved through the file.) The little bundles of paper, 2–3 centimetres thick, were then placed on pre-cooled, porous trays and sealed in the vacuum chamber. After a day or two, the doors were opened again. Flink and Høyer found that each page separated easily from the next, and the ink had not run.

Flink and Høyer's success story has become a case study for conservators. They preserved some of the earliest written examples of Greenlandic for posterity. However, the prospect of future readers for these documents was beginning to look doubtful. A few decades later, in 2009, the Greenlandic dialects studied by Kleinschmidt were added to UNESCO's *Atlas of the World's Languages in Danger*. The words that had proved so resistant to written form were beginning to disappear.

*

I am curious to find out how much of Kleinschmidt's archive was preserved by the ice. Where are the papers now? I consult the catalogue of the Royal Library in Copenhagen (known as The Black Diamond) and find eight reels on microfilm 'after orig. in Nuuk, Greenland's National Library'. The website of the National Library in Nuuk has more on these originals: 'The main materials are now in the Groenlandica collection. These collections are irreplaceable and are kept carefully and protected from fire.' Whether this is a direct reference to the events of 1968 is unclear. The website continues: 'Groenlandica has made 2014 action year for the digitization of this collection.' There's only a week left of 2014 when I read this, so I look eagerly to see what is available online. There are a few letters to Kleinschmidt, but none from him. When I download the letters I find that most have been scanned at a resolution too low to be legible.

The online trail has petered out. It's a familiar feeling. My time in Upernavik had taught me that in the Arctic problems which seemed insurmountable from a distance were often easily resolved on the ground. It is time to return to Greenland.

The National Library is now housed at the University of Greenland campus, halfway between the city and its airport. My taxi approaches an architectural masterpiece that has been designed to look like the rocky landscape: a far cry from the gable-roofed building by the harbour that housed Greenland's first library. The glass lobby offers a view south towards the sea. Instead of ice, the water reflects a cloudless sky. On land too, everything that was concealed under the ice is revealed to me now.

The traveller who arrives in Greenland in August has already missed most events of the summer: the celebrations for Midsummer (and National) Day, and national hero Knud Rasmussen's birthday on 7 June. The days are still long and light, but an indigo gloom descends around midnight. For an hour at least, streetlamps shed their rays like the heads of cotton grass that line the dusty gutters. Most students are on vacation, and the library interior is quiet, save for the soft thud of books being re-shelved by an intern. When I explain my research to Charlotte Andersen, the director, she whispers, 'Ah, it's such a shame you didn't come last year.' In September, James Flink made the journey from Denmark to Greenland with his daughter Sofia in order to look at the important documents he'd worked on once more before he died.

Charlotte brings me a file on the conservation of Kleinschmidt's documents. I find within it printouts of emails arranging Flink's recent visit, and a series of Kodachrome transparencies depicting the manuscripts in Flink's cupboard at the Technical University in Lyngby. I hold each tiny plastic frame up to the light and examine the image. At last, a sighting of the elusive documents. It's impossible to get these copied so I will have to record what's there. I scribble descriptions down in my notebook, trying to be accurate: the binding of the books, the height of the stacks of paper. But when I come to the end of the slides, I realize I have only captured the manuscripts' external appearance.

There is only one image of Kleinschmidt's handwriting in the files. It is a photographed page of manuscript in immaculate copperplate which lists the rulers of Egypt. Its ordered approach to history reminds me of the *Stream of Time*. The pharaohs' names are transliterated into Greenlandic. The venerable names have been preserved on paper, whereas their bodies were covered in natron powder and wrapped in linen. How much does either relic convey of the living person? The elaborate Egyptian rituals of mummification remind me of the unnamed Inuit, now on display in the National Museum a few miles away. The 500-year-old grave was discovered at Qilakitsoq in 1972 by brothers out hunting for ptarmigan. Inside, the remains of six women and two children had been mummified by cold temperatures, not by a sacred ritual. The frozen water had sublimated from their bodies naturally by the same technique Flink had used in his laboratory to preserve the manuscripts.

As I leave the library I notice a box of de-accessioned books for sale at just a few kroner each. I buy an illustrated children's primer, *Vi Læse Dansk* ('Learn to read Danish') from 1971, aimed at Greenlandic children. Then I spot a sober Greenlandic grammar from 1952 that uses Kleinschmidt's orthography, including the hard К'/к and obsolete diacritics. I read the easier of the two books on the yellow bus which winds its way through new housing developments towards my hostel. I'm intrigued to find that alongside the accounts of seal hunting, shopping and snow, there's a story about a fire. The house of Anton, the tall stranger from abroad, is in flames. There's smoke coming out of the door and out of the windows. Where is Anton? 'Anton, Anton!' call the children. 'Your house is on fire!' But where *is* Anton? In the illustration, smoke billows alarmingly around a man seated, nose deep in a book. He has not noticed anything amiss. 'Anton is reading and reading.'

III

HUNTERS

THE SOUND OF A KNIFE

Ilulissat Kunstmuseum, Greenland
The British Museum, London

Memory does this: lets the things appear small,
compresses them. Land of the sailor.

Walter Benjamin, Ms. 863v

I

The director of Ilulissat Kunstmuseum, Ole Gamst-Pedersen, makes coffee and serves it with biscuits he announces with a flourish as 'Danish'. I help myself to a shortbread finger and tuck my feet up under me on the banquette while we discuss the work I plan to do during my residency. I travelled up the coast from Nuuk this morning, and the pills I took for the flight have made me sleepy.

'The museum is open to the public for three hours every afternoon,' Ole says. 'One to four. I'll be here then, of course, but the rest of the day you have the place to yourself.'

I will also have it to myself on Fridays and Saturdays, when the museum is closed all day. (This seems to preclude rather a lot of visitors. Sometimes in the afternoons as I look out the window I meet other faces peering in, travellers whose brief sojourn in town doesn't overlap with opening hours.) And it's mine all through the night too. I will sleep in a spartan antechamber off one of the main galleries, furnished with a narrow bed, a desk and a sealskin rug.

Ole leaves on the dot of four to feed his dogs, and a sensor on the door gives a little ping as his tall form passes it. I'm glad I will be able to hear if someone is entering the museum: with its maze of interconnecting rooms, it would be easy to not notice an unexpected guest. The building was once the home of the Danish governor, and there are signs of its history as the centre of colonial power. While it is small by comparison with the galleries in former industrial warehouses back in the UK, the museum feels spacious, and is a conspicuous landmark among the smaller homes and shipping containers on this outcrop near the harbour. (Shipping containers are a ubiquitous form of storage in the Arctic, as if even now people are determined to be ready to pack up and sail away.) Outside the building, two enormous flagpoles reach almost as high as the fish factory cooling towers.

Left alone in the museum, I feel as if I have inherited a stately home complete with its art collection. I wonder if I will have a favourite work by the time I leave. Many of the paintings are on a large scale, with gilded frames adding to their grandeur, but there are also intriguing sketches of ships and sounds and dog sleds. Most of the works in the museum are by the Danish artist Emanuel A. Petersen. As a youth, Petersen struggled to forge a career for himself as a painter, resisting the disapproval of his clergyman father. Since he could not afford to study fine art, he took a practical approach to his training, first apprenticing himself to a house painter and subsequently working for the Royal Porcelain Factory in Copenhagen, painting marine scenes onto vases and other luxury tableware. In 1921 he tried to secure a passage on a freighter to the Mediterranean but there were no vessels due to sail south, so he jumped aboard a ship bound for West Greenland instead.

By this twist of fate – not unlike that which had first sent me to Upernavik – Petersen became a 'Greenland Painter' (*Grønlandsmaler*), one of a group of Danish artists who travelled to Greenland during the nineteenth century and used its landscape and people as motifs in their paintings. His first journey north was followed by another, four years later, when he spent a year here in Ilulissat, sketching the waters of Disko Bay which surround the town, and the icebergs that drift across them. By this time photography had already superseded drawing and painting as a form of documenting landscape, but there was still a strong market for scenes of remote fjords and icebergs illuminated by the setting sun. A few tarnished medals in the museum testify to the worldly success that these paintings brought Petersen, an artist now almost forgotten in Denmark.

Picturesque icebergs are such a feature of this town that it is named for them: 'Ilulissat' means 'icebergs' in Greenlandic. Around a tenth of all the icebergs that the Greenland ice cap produces calve from the great glacier, Sermeq Kujalleq, into a nearby fjord. As tabular bergs the size of sports pitches shunt out to sea, they split along internal rifts into craggier shapes, scattering innumerable football-sized 'bergy bits' (that truly is the technical term) which wash up at the old harbour. There were obvious similarities between the painted views inside the museum, and those I could see through its windows, even if the old skin kayaks riding the waves had been replaced by polyethylene ones, and there were no shipping containers to be seen in Petersen's colourful settlements. It wasn't just these everyday artefacts that had changed. Petersen sketched in Greenland, but many of his paintings were completed back in his studio in Denmark. As he was relatively unfamiliar with the places he was depicting, and unable to go back to the original subjects, his canvases cannot be taken as a faithful record of the landscapes he observed. Yet I felt there was a more significant difference between what I saw on canvas and what I saw out on my walks, which I couldn't quite put my finger on. The relationship of his paintings to the topography beyond the museum walls began to puzzle me.

I lived with Petersen's work for two weeks. I passed the paintings in the twilight as I went to bed, and during the long mornings before Ole unlocked the front door and the sensor made its merry electric ping, I looked at them closely, with the kind of hunger that only the absence of any other entertainment could generate. I returned to them after my own encounters with the landscape. In Ilulissat, I delighted in discovering a freedom that had been restricted on Upernavik. It was one thing to slither around a small icy island in the dark, something else entirely to set off into the hills in my orange windproof jacket, knowing that I could continue walking until the ice sheet brought me to a halt. My retinas were scorched not by ice but by miles and hours and days of sunlit rock, the scale of which induced a kind of vertigo. I felt intrepid, but this was no unexplored wilderness. Come winter the land would be crossed by dog-sled trails.

One day, after improvising a route among the loose boulders lining the gorge and then striding out across exposed stages of gneiss, I arrived back at Holms Bakke, the barren ridge that overlooks the icefjord a mile or so south of Ilulissat. It's the kind of view tourists are supposed to take photographs of. I get out my camera. First, I tried focusing the lens on the icebergs clustered in the fjord, then on the mountains disappearing in a haze towards the horizon. A raven flew past, a tiny dark speck whose swift flight brought the magnitude of the ice into perspective. Back in the museum, I pause before Petersen's painting of the same scene, to see how he achieved the illusion of distance on a flat canvas. He only used white paint where the sun strikes the facet of the berg directly; the shadows are an intoxicating blend of blues steeped in blue. Like the melting ice itself, the painting asks the viewer to prefer shadow to sun. The cloudless sky is the least dramatic part of the image, guaranteed not to draw the eye away from the ice, and it's only by chance that I notice a couple of puncture marks in the canvas just below the edge of the gilded frame. I can tell they come from drawing pins because around one is a ghostly circle where the pinhead has been pressed down. It looks like the halo that appears around the sun when light is refracted through ice crystals in the Earth's atmosphere.

Petersen's lack of training meant that his work in oils was sometimes flawed: he failed to apply primer to his canvases, for example. (Primer is a layer of white gesso, which stops paints sinking into the canvas, allowing them to keep their colour longer.) After noticing the pinpricks, I begin to examine the effect of time and the environment on his other works. Nearly all these paintings once had to make the journey north from his Danish studio, and traces of their travels can be found on them, or signs of neglect remain from their time in private collections. The rough waters in the icefjord through which a kayaker makes his way look even rougher now the lively brushwork that represents the waves has cracked and is threatening to peel away from the canvas. Vertical cracks run the length of a colossal portrait of the schooner *Heimdal*, showing that the canvas has been rolled up; concentric lines in the sky above the eagle's nest look for all the world like the hairline cracks children create when they stamp on brittle, icy puddles. In *Sea, Ice and Mountains*, the fields of blue are interrupted at the horizon by a tiny three-cornered gash where the canvas shows through, which may have been made by another painting's frame piercing it from behind. A snow scene is dimpled where a sharp-cornered object has bashed against it from the front. In one painting, the space in an ice floe left by a piece of flaking paint has been coloured in using a blue felt-tip pen. These incremental physical changes in the paintwork seem, even more than Petersen's original marks, to express the character of ice. Step back, and the forms resolve into an ideal landscape, step in close, and you see the damage. Although the museum is sensitive to the demands of artworks in extreme conditions at 69 degrees north, and they won't deteriorate further, correcting these earlier signs of wear understandably lies beyond the budget.

Flaws develop in sea ice too. In cryologist-speak, the flaw lead is an opening that runs between ice attached to the coast (shore-fast ice) and the ice on the sea (drift ice). The flaw leads are unpredictable: during the autumn they can form anywhere in the frozen ocean where wind or currents place stress on the ice, and they often freeze over again. To find them, look up to the sky: a flaw may be indicated by steam rising from the water, or the dark reflection of the water on a cloud. Hunters often head out over the fast ice to the flaw lead in search of the mammals – seals, whales and narwhals – that gather there to breathe. With the same object in mind, polar bears will arrive over the drift ice. The flaw is an aberration, but also a rich resource; its fault line, a meeting point.

The museum is an imposing building to have custody of, and I'm glad of a break when Ole and his elegant wife Thrine invite me round for dinner. Also at the table that evening is Bendt, a scientist who has been laying sensors down on the icefjord to observe the movement of the glacier. To celebrate his return to Greenland for another season of hunting data, Thrine serves her signature dish: walrus cooked in the style of beef Wellington. Bendt asks for a large piece of the dark meat and bemoans the drudgery of the cryologist's life, in which a single light-bulb moment is bracketed by years of carrying heavy, expensive equipment across hostile ice fields, and often watching bits of it disappear into the ice it is supposed to be recording. Ole and Thrine's table has welcomed many scientists who come to Ilulissat to research the effects of climate change on the permafrost or investigate the vast crevasses opening in the ice sheet. As Bendt grumbles, I understand what has been troubling me about Petersen's paintings: they represent a romantic depiction of the Arctic, from a more innocent time, before icebergs and sea ice had become an indicator of climate change, when convention framed such a view as majestic rather than temporal or even tragic. Now any iceberg in the bay is likely to have been tracked by a data sensor before it is recorded by a painter, and artists and scientists sit at the same table.

One of the most interesting exhibits in the museum (to me) was Petersen's battered travelling trunk, which accompanied him on all his Arctic voyages, containing his art materials and presumably tobacco and some other home comforts. He must have been keen not to lose it: rather than merely tagging it with his name or his initials, he painted a scaled-up version of his official signature on each of its leather faces, as if it is another work of art. Despite the vast galleries at his disposal, Ole has placed the trunk in a corridor by the back door of the museum, next to the lavatory. This is a curatorial stroke of genius, since it seems to emphasize that the artist is just in the process of leaving, as he so often was – and as all too soon I would be too.

II

Russell Square is quiet. A sign advertising gelato still hangs outside the park café, but the fountains have been turned off for the winter and the last leaves are being swept from the paths. Rain falls in Bedford Place, where at number 21, Jane Griffin was born on 4 December 1791, and grew up with her three sisters and a governess, Miss Peltreau. It was her beau Peter Roget – a physician who loved lists of words so much he spent the latter part of his life compiling the thesaurus that bears his name – who introduced Jane to the Arctic, and her future husband, taking her in March 1818 to Deptford to see the ships *Dorothea* and *Trent*, then under the command of a young lieutenant Franklin on his first Arctic service. Jane would marry John Franklin in 1828. Now the home from which her travels began is occupied by The Penn Club, and I am staying in a slightly scruffy room on the top floor – a part of the house I suspect Jane never saw.

It's a short walk along an elegant Georgian terrace to the British Museum. I'm ushered into an auditorium in the basement, where a book launch is in progress. Shari Fox Gearheard is here to introduce *The Meaning of Ice* on behalf of her large investigative team, who couldn't travel with her. A photograph of the book's authors is projected onto a screen instead: they lie in a circle on the ice with their heads together in the centre, half-hidden by the furry hoods of their parkas. Dr Gearheard researches the relationship between humans and sea ice for the National Snow & Ice Data Center in Boulder, Colorado, but she lives and works in Clyde River in Nunavut, in Canada's far north. As a 'musher', someone who drives a team of sled dogs, she can be counted as one of the *silalirijiit*, an Inuktitut word meaning 'those who work with or think about weather'. Shari and her co-investigators are pairing local knowledge with climate science and environmental modelling to understand weather patterns around Clyde River – and the ways in which they are changing.

Shari and her fellow researchers travelled between Clyde River and other communities – Barrow, on the north coast of Alaska, and Qaanaaq in north-west Greenland – compiling traditional knowledge from those living on the 'ice garden'. She clicks through from the image of her colleagues in their parkas to drawings demonstrating how to make them: the correct ways to skin a seal and then divide the prepared skin into the panels of the coat. These techniques differ between cultures across the north, as does whether you choose to use a skidoo or dog team and, of course, the language you use to describe them.

Just as ice is formed from a single crystal and grows into a more complex structure, so the Eskaleut languages spoken across the Arctic take a root word – like *hiku*, which means simply ice of any kind, including ice cream – and add further morphemes to express specific qualities. The English definitions of the long, polysynthetic terms for ice can read like miniature nature essays. Yet some languages, such as that spoken in Qaanaaq, are only beginning to be written as well as spoken.

I slip away at the end of the talk, before the champagne and canapés. I'd love to ask Shari about her life in Clyde River, across the water from Upernavik, but I know these occasions are no place for conversation. I buy the book and when I get back to Bedford Place I draw an armchair close to the fire in the reading room. I skip to the pages on sea ice terminology, to discover what journey *hiku* might take me on. The ice conditions in Qaanaaq are closest to my own experience on Upernavik. I begin with *haard'dloq*, extremely thin new ice that cannot be stepped on without danger, and then *hikuliaq*, new ice, which is still slippery and yet can be travelled across. When *hikuliaq* is older it becomes *hikuliamineq* – you might call it old-new ice – as it gets thicker there are frost flowers (*kaneq*) on its surface; the *kaneq* mean it is no longer slippery, no longer dangerous, safe to travel across. But not for ever. When *hikuaq* and *hikuapajaannguaq* break up, they make *eqinnikkalaat* – splinters of thin ice that can lacerate skin.

Would I be able to tell the difference between *hikuliamineq* with its frost flowers and *hikuuhaq*, described as: 'old ice, which has been frozen in the same place since freeze-up, which has drifted snow cover (*agiuppineq*) or just snow.' But while that's a significant amount of old ice, it's ice that stays in one place, and I might need to distinguish it from *hikuuhaq*, 'ice that comes down from the North; very thick ice; multi-year ice'. These words not only describe visual features but also dynamics and processes, such as *tinumihaartoq* – when broken ice is moving, as it does on the waves, and makes a sound. They describe the relationship of humans, and of course dogs, to the ice. As well as difficulty, I found there were classifications for danger, such as *aukkkarneq*, 'open water in sea ice formed by fast-moving currents under the ice, open area or crack, dangerous' or *aputainnaq*, 'snow cover over open ocean; very dangerous.' There's a reason for these distinctions for sea ice – survival. And in a time of rapid climate change, survival can turn on a knife edge.

What a contrast with the World Meteorological Organization's glossary of *Sea Ice Nomenclature*. Originally published in 1970, it's available as a download for anyone with enough interest in the subject or space on their hard drive. The glossary describes ice in four languages (English, French,

Russian and Spanish) and in terms of its size and appearance, rather than how it grew and the way it might be used:

Floe giant: Over 10 km across.
Floe vast: 2–10 km across.
Floe big: 500–2000 m across.
Floe medium: 100–500 m across.
Floe small: 20–100 m across.
Small ice cake: Less than 2 m across.

The glossary contains 220 categories – and that number is growing in response to changing conditions. 'Dirty ice', 'frost flowers' and 'small/medium iceberg' were among the terms added in the latest edition, published in 2014. This dictionary is aimed at communications for shipping and submarines that are trying to avoid ice, or even break through it, rather than those travelling over it.

In the past, the Intergovernmental Panel on Climate Change, based at the World Meteorological Organization's office in Geneva, has largely relied on information from scientific studies, rather than traditional knowledge. In this, it unfortunately reflected the history of power relationships between indigenous groups and other bodies with interests in the Circumpolar North. But there's growing recognition from scientists of the insights that traditional knowledge provides. Of course, those with this knowledge never doubted its use.

'I became aware of snow and summer sixty-six years ago,' Peter Elachik testified at the Snowchange conference in Alaska in 2005, asserting his decades of experience. 'In the early 1940s, snow was very dry and you could hear footsteps thirty metres away; now because of the moisture you don't hear footsteps.' Such detailed understanding of the ice has become more critical, with an uncertain future ahead. Margaret Opie, an elder from Barrow, told others gathered at Snowchange: 'In my short lifetime, things have really changed for my community and for our subsistence lifestyle. The whaling season is stalled. There are a lot of winds; the ice is many, many miles away. We depend on the marine mammals for our skin boats. Early break-up is hazardous to us. This summer the ice was gone too early and was too far out to get the number of seals needed to replace the skin boat ... Now we see all the big swells and they won't quit until the ice is back.' As Margaret, Peter and their fellow elders shared observations of snow and ice it became clear by consensus that the fast ice on the Alaska coast was a fraction of its former extent, and therefore more easily dispersed by wind. There was more open water along the coast. The pressure ridges (high walls of ice, formed when two floes collide) were still there – but they were much smaller than they had once been.

This knowledge can't be separated from the words in which it is expressed. But, like the ice, the reach of some languages is diminishing, to the extent that the state of the language may be of as much concern as the ecosystem it describes. In 2008 the Arctic Indigenous Languages Symposium brought together six groups (the Aleut International Association, the Arctic Athabaskan Council, the Gwich'in Council International, the Inuit Circumpolar Council, the Russian

Association of Indigenous Peoples of the North, and the Saami Council) all concerned about their languages' future. A growing number of books are sharing traditional knowledge in indigenous languages such as *The Meaning of Ice* and *Kingikmi Sigum Qanuq Ilitaavut – Wales Inupiaq Sea Ice Dictionary*, a catalogue from the North Alaska–Bering Strait region. In some areas, these glossaries may be the first textbooks for a previously uncodified language.

These arc momentous initiatives as speculation about the future is unusual in the Arctic. The geographer Nicole Gombay writes about the perception of time in Inuit culture: 'The physical realities of the natural world – knowledge about its unpredictability – translate, I believe, into deeper existential perceptions about the nature of reality in general, and time in particular. Everything is in flux.' As I had discovered in Upernavik, it is hard to make plans when the weather or *hila* is constantly changing. Better not to plan to do anything, and wait until the last minute to take action. The term '*hila*' recognizes the connection between humans and their environment: it can refer not only to the unpredictable atmosphere but also human consciousness.

The names for different months reveal the importance of ice in the community's calendar. September, for hunters in Nunavut, is *Akullirut* or the waiting season. 'During this time there is snow on the ground and everyone is waiting for sea ice to form,' Joelie Sanguya explains in *The Meaning of Ice*. In October – *Amiraijaut* – when the sea ice arrives from the north on ocean currents, the hunters know that 'freeze-up' is beginning. This month, *Tusaqtuut* (November) means 'news time': the sea ice allowed people to travel long distances between camps and meet up with each other after months of separation and open water, bringing news of friends and family along with them. In contrast to the explorers for whom the arrival of the ice meant the end of their journey, the cessation of contact with their kin, for those who knew the Arctic best it was only the beginning.

III

The next day I meet a friend I haven't seen for a few years. Last time I met Bethan she had just finished cataloguing the British Museum's vast collection of William Blake prints. In a Greek café around the corner, she tells me about her latest discovery: the Dalziel Brothers.

'Who?' I ask, mouth full of spanakopita.

'You'd like them,' she says. 'They made some wonderful engravings of icebergs.'

Dalziel – there's even something icy about the name. But ice wasn't all they did – far from it. Bethan could interest anyone in the artists, according to their predilections. The wood engraving firm – the Getty Images of their day – illustrated everything from novels and theatre programmes to trade manuals. As well as illustrations for the works of Charles Dickens and William Wordsworth, they created images of flotation aids and diagrams showing resuscitation procedures for the Life Boat Institution and advertisements for hot chocolate and musical instruments. There were small decorative initials for poetry anthologies and humorous vignettes for magazines. Before each finished woodblock was sent from the engraving workshop to the printer, a proof was taken on fine paper as a record of the firm's achievement. Day after day, these were trimmed and glued into giant leather-bound albums, with only occasional notations, such as a date, scribbled alongside. These surreal scrapbooks are a Great Exhibition in miniature, reflecting the industry and ambition of the age. But in an era famous for productivity, little else has survived: many of the books the Dalziels illustrated never went into more than one edition, and only a few, like the works of Dickens, outlasted changing literary tastes. The even more ephemeral trade logos and advertisements faded as fast as the fashionable items they promoted. Even the albums kept by the firm were put aside and forgotten for many years, due to a lack of interest in commercial art. Bethan has stumbled upon a treasure trove.

She tells me that George Dalziel was the first of the family to move from Northumberland to London, travelling south by ship in 1835. His brother Edward joined him in the capital four years later. They worked together for over fifty years, seeing their firm through the many technological, cultural and commercial changes of that busy century. Their work included the production of dramatic illustrations to works of Arctic exploration for readers whose curiosity was aroused by Franklin's sensational disappearance while searching for the Northwest Passage. These illustrations enabled readers to visualize the Arctic, long before wildlife documentaries with their seductive drone footage showing icebergs from above. None of the Dalziels had seen the scenes they depicted: they worked from explorers' sketches, a draughtsman's designs, photography or their own imaginations.

'I found some images of Inuit hunters,' Bethan says. 'You should come and see.'

The following week I make my way up the north stairs of the museum to the Prints and Drawings Gallery, where an exhibition of Maggi Hambling's monotypes of the sea has just opened. The secure door to the Print Room is concealed behind an enormous Michelangelo chalk drawing. I stuff my coat, bag and water bottle into a locker, and put the key on its safety pin carefully in my pocket. Thus stripped of twenty-first-century impedimenta, I enter a chamber redolent of the Dalziel era. On every wall glass cases reach up to the ceiling, holding shelf upon shelf of grey archival boxes, which in turn hold layers of prints. The weak autumn light falling through the vaulted roof windows is supplemented by brass lamps on the desks. Books are laid out on thick foam rests and readers are studiously not touching the pages.

It's easy to spot Bethan's bright wax-print blouse in this subdued setting. She sits on a high stool, methodically cataloguing the finely burnished proofs. She heaves an album onto a foam rest and opens it at the title page to show me the copperplate legend, tidy as ship's rigging: 'India-Proofs of Wood-Engravings by the Brothers Dalziel. General Work. Various. 1865.' Underneath the date is added: 'This Book was made at the Time the Engravings were done.' Each phrase is underlined three times. Bethan turns the pages for me, pointing out how illustrations to *Alice in Wonderland* and equally fantastical works share a spread with technical diagrams and anatomical illustrations.

'Imagine having a hold on all these different genres!' she says. 'The Dalziels helped to shape the way people saw things, so they had enormous cultural power ... Yet in many ways the artists remained so anonymous.'

George and Edward were joined in the 1850s by their brothers Thomas and John, and their sister Margaret. The business grew to encompass many employees, including Francis Fricker and James Clark, who worked for the firm for over forty years. All signed their work 'Dalziel'.

'What I like about these,' Bethan says, when we reach a page of illustrations to *The Great Frozen Sea* by Captain Markham, 'is how they present the Arctic as a place of geometric shapes and really unusual light.'

One image shows a man driving a dog sled under a starry sky, another a tall ship moored among improbable icebergs. Darkness, ice, dogs: it's the essence of Greenland, although it is a bit like a dream in which everything is distorted. I am fascinated by the icebergs: one effusion looks like a municipal fountain frozen mid-cascade, another could be the turret of a chateau.

'This artist is having fun,' I say. 'Look at the icebergs! That one looks just like a lady's fan. And those lights in the sky. In all these images there's a halo around the sun, or sundogs either side of it, or something.'

'Do you think those white lines are meant to represent an aurora?'

'Could be. He's certainly packing in everything he can.'

Through this landscape bursting with archetypal Arctic marvels trek the explorers. Markham's is a dreadful story. Subtitled *A Personal Narrative of the Voyage of the Alert during the Arctic Expedition of 1875–6*, the book starts, unpropitiously, with the names of three men who died; one succumbed to 'frostbite whilst sledging', two more 'of scurvy whilst sledging'. The ten-week spring sledging expedition was designed to find the Open Polar Sea, but Markham returned with a more galling discovery – the fact it was unlikely to exist. Markham's men had to drag the sledge themselves, since their dogs had died or escaped. Their equipment wasn't fit for the terrain they found themselves navigating: 'We found the ice exceedingly hummocky, with narrow water spaces between, *just* too broad to admit of our jumping over, yet not sufficiently wide to launch the boat into ...' The men were travelling in the direction of the North Pole and they established a record of the Farthest North, at Latitude 83°20'26" N, before being forced to turn back. It was to be the last of the 'great' British Arctic expeditions.

Markham would have been trained in watercolour painting as a midshipman, so that he could record topographical details on his voyages. Some of the engravings clearly draw on sketches he made in his journals. The artist worked on the compositions to make them more suitable for Victorian tastes, bringing the harrowing narrative into a known tradition. In another album, I spot an engraving of a hunter in a kayak harpooning a seal, which uses iconography familiar from medieval images of St George spearing the Dragon.

'That seal is rather fine, don't you think?' says Bethan. 'It's much more realistic than the man.' She tells me the designer who adapted some of the Arctic images for the page, Johann Baptist Zwecker, was a specialist in animal pictures – she gets the impression he didn't much like drawing people. The hunter holds his harpoon high, aiming it at the seal over the prow of his kayak.

Wood engravers use blocks made from the wood of the box tree. In contrast to the soft brush, absorbent paper and delicate pigments used by Markham and other shipboard watercolourists, box is one of the hardest woods available, a material dense enough to record fine detail that could survive the rigours of printing. This also makes it tricky to carve. Jackson and Chatto's manual, *A Treatise on Wood Engraving, Historical and Practical*, sets out the objects an engraver would keep on their desk: 'an *oil-stone*, a *sand-bag* or *cushion*, an *eyeglass*, a *lamp*, and a *globe*.' The globe was a glass sphere filled with water, which was designed to focus light from the oil lamp or candle onto the block. Even before the artists took up their tools to create a scene on the wood, they were playing with light.

The manual describes the choice of tools available to an artist: there were gravers and tint-tools, gouges and scorpers. The tint-tools, Jackson and Chatto explain, 'are used for cutting tints or shades in which the series of lines are intended to be exactly or neatly parallel, or equidistant.' This is a precise art. As with the use of any tool, the process requires the co-ordination of the body to the task; 'leaning a little more or less heavily will make a deeper or shallower, a wider or narrower, cut or incision'. A wider incision on the block made a thicker white line in the final print. As wood engravings were generally printed with black ink, the white lines let light into the block. White is the colour of camouflage in the Arctic. Everything white disappears against the ice: the polar bear is concealed by its fur; the hunter raises a white sailcloth in front of his sledge so his approach is hidden from the seal. The Dalziels understood this balance of colour, mixing dark and light in their Arctic illustrations so the images do not disappear in a white-out on the page. They find ways to anchor the block: balancing the outlines of icebergs against dark cliff-faces; introducing calm black water to reflect stars; adding a trail of footprints to shadow the snow.

These engravings are linked with the Arctic, not only through the subject matter, but also their form. The act of engraving a boxwood block is similar to sculpture, in that both artists work in three dimensions. Carving was the traditional medium of Greenlandic artists. For a long time stone and bone were the only available materials, and occasionally driftwood washed ashore from Scandinavia. Even maps were carved, with the benefit that they could be held inside sealskin mittens on cold sea voyages, and the intricate bays and inlets 'read' with the hands as well as the eyes.

Bethan lets me out of the Print Room through a hidden door, on the other side of which I find myself – surprised as Alice in one of the Dalziel illustrations – in the galleries of Korean Art. As I walk through the museum, I pass some artefacts from the Arctic on display. Among many practical objects, such as toggles, pipes and netting needles, there are representations of the world in miniature: an intricate sled complete with a tiny dog team; little seals and birds ornamented with small black dots. The seven dots were used to indicate the seven openings of the head – eyes, ears, nose and mouth. These carvings were made by someone who knew the animals well, who had cut the flesh to release the bone they held. They knew about shape-shifting, and understood that a good story can animate an artwork. They knew a carving can be two things at once: a bone that looked like a polar bear from one angle, might seem human from another.

NANCY CAMPBELL

IV

The Greenlandic explorer and anthropologist Knud
Rasmussen is still honoured in his hometown of Ilulissat: his
birthplace is a museum, and his statue looks out over Disko Bay
from an escarpment above Ole and Thrine's house. Like the
painter Petersen, Rasmussen was the son of a Danish pastor,
but his father's parish was even more remote. He wrote: 'My
playmates were native Greenlanders; from the earliest boyhood
I played and worked with the hunters, so even the hardships
of the most strenuous sledge-trips became pleasant routine for
me'. Rasmussen would travel far by sled. His journey from
Cape York to Upernavik was the first recorded sledge crossing
of Melville Bay (although far from being the first).

Rasmussen's first ambition was for fame on the stage, and
as a young man he moved to Copenhagen to work as an actor
and opera singer. While he was resting (which was often) poet
and journalist Mylius-Erichsen persuaded him to join the
Danish Literary Expedition, which was conceived as a new
kind of exploration – Mylius-Erichsen was adamant that no
scientists would sully its artistic nature. The men left for West
Greenland in 1902 and travelled in the Arctic for two years,
meeting isolated peoples and recording their stories and songs.
In one of the stories, the shaman Kunigseq travels to the world
of spirits, where he encounters his mother. She is content to
be among the dead, she tells him, but she has one request to
make of him. 'When you return to earth, send some ice, for
we thirst for cold water down here.'

For the rest of his life Rasmussen continued to explore the
north and write about its culture. In 1910, with his friend Peter

Freuchen, he returned to Cape York and established a trading base. Even this was given a literary provenance: he named it Thule, saying it was 'the most northerly post in the world, literally, the "Ultima Thule."' The name Thule has been used by writers from Pytheas onwards to designate various islands, and was included as early as 1539 on Olaus Magnus's map. By Rasmussen's time it had become an archetypal term from the north, still resonant with all the mystery it held for earlier writers who used it as the limits of the known world. During the winter of 1916, an archaeological dig unearthed the remains of a Paleo-Eskimo encampment not far from the trading base. It seemed Thule had been inhabited for many years, by a civilization which had stretched as far as Alaska. (This ancient culture was also designated 'Thule'.) Rasmussen afterwards used Thule as a base for his polar expeditions, and in travelling eastwards to the Bering Strait he retraced the vast distances traversed by those who had settled at Thule before him. These migrations had been made in defiance of hunger and the harsh climate. In the thirteenth century, the Thule people followed bowhead whales east from Alaska along the receding sea ice margin, populating northern Canada and Greenland. These dramatic migrations were later reprised on a smaller scale in the annual movement between springtime and winter camps.

Not all such relocations have been voluntary excursions into new territory, or impelled by the desire to reach traditional hunting and fishing grounds. In Nunavut, the older generation still recall the resettlements between 1954 and 1975, when thousands of indigenous Canadians were classified as living in places 'with no great future' and moved to towns in the south with telephones, electricity, alcohol and schools where children were forbidden to speak Inuktitut. In Greenland, during the Cold War, the inhabitants of the north-western settlements close to Rasmussen's former base were forcibly relocated to clear land for an American air base – also known as Thule. A diplomatic telegram sent in May 1953 from the district governor in Thule, Egon Mørck Rasmussen, to the Danish government runs:

> for permanent under-secretary of state /stop/ village population a total of thirty families now all removed to mouth of inglefield bay staying the summer in tent camps at kanak kekertarssuak and natsilivik /stop/ the people are amply supplied from here with hunting equipment clothing provisions kerosene and medicine /stop/ the base has promised to drop kerosene for tent campers during the summer if necessary /stop/ removal began when shortly after our return we notified the population the decisions made in denmark /stop/ many people were grieved by parting with the place but everyone understood it was for common good /stop/ many hunters asked me to send their respects to permanent under-secretary of state thanking for the help already provided in form of equipment and for promise of new and good houses in compensation for those they abandoned in thule compliments mørckrasmussen

The population moved north by sleds, and Qaanaaq now lies 110 kilometres north of its original position, on a deep fjord from which glacial meltwater flows west into the Nares Strait, which in turn feeds south into the waters of Baffin Bay.

*

The sled trails across the sea ice of Baffin Bay and Melville Sound are etched in the minds of Qaanaaq's hunters. These routes are older than the permanent settlements, even though they disappear with the melt each spring. In the museum at Upernavik, I had found old photographs of hunting trips from the 1960s and 1970s. The viewpoint is that of the hunter astride a sled: looking at the back of the dog team, their traces converging on a point just out of sight below the frame, where they are knotted to the slats. The wide horizon, the monotony of whiteness, is sometimes broken by an iceberg. 'This place no longer exists,' the hunters say. Of course the physical location still exists – what the hunters mean is that this spot will never freeze in the way it once did, even in the depths of winter. It is no longer a path over the ice, or a place to set up an overnight snow shelter during a long journey. The changing climate has removed both the possibility of movement, and the promise of rest.

Rasmussen divided the long tales he was told on his travels across the Arctic for his publisher, some longer, some shorter, parcelling them up skilfully as others might divide a seal to make best use of organs, flesh, and skin. Or so it appears. You don't learn butchery from diagrams, but from watching others. And you improve only with practice.

Once there was a great hunter.
No, tell it properly.
Well then – in the beginning was a not-so-great hunter and his wife and they wanted a child.
No, tell it better.

In the beginning was a twist of grass and the berries on the hillside . . .

Never mind all that.

Where does the story begin? Rasmussen's collection of folktales is like a glacier, which has emerged from the ice cap in one great tongue and subsequently split along hidden weaknesses. One glacier makes many icebergs. Can the story of Tugto's wife and her mission to the Queen of the Sea be told without explaining how Qujâvârssuk was born? That's how Rasmussen tells it: he explains that Qujâvârssuk was a *great* hunter. That is how people knew they were in trouble, because even Qujâvârssuk couldn't catch seals any longer. Yet this is not a tale about hunters – it is about the ice. Soon, even the great hunter fades from the text, and listeners are left with nothing but the sea.

One winter the sea froze right across, and there was only a narrow flaw lead, very far out. To get to it Qujâvârssuk had to haul his kayak over the ice for several hours. By the time he reached the water it was almost time to come back. Yet he continued to make his record catches, bringing home at least two seals a day. Not everyone was so lucky. Qujâvârssuk was generous to those who came to him for food – 'as they do in such times' – giving his guests the best parts of the seal.

One day Qujâvârssuk found there was only room to lay his kayak on the narrow lead between the ice sheets, and the seals who came up for air found no breathing space, and sank back down again. That night he went home without having made a catch. If he could no longer provide food, everyone would starve.

Qujâvârssuk cut the last seal across at the middle. He took a hefty portion of the tail and a generous amount of blubber to Tugto's house. Tugto and his wife were strangers who had only recently come to live among them. It was known that they had special powers, for Tugto's wife could survive in the mountains alone, and Tugto – well, what Tugto could do is another story. Qujâvârssuk thought they would know how to remove the ice.

The entrance was so covered with snow that it looked like a fox's earth. Qujâvârssuk dropped the gifts down the passage and crawled in after them.

He got straight to the point. 'Please can you send away the ice?'

Tugto turned to his wife. 'In this time of hunger we cannot reject meat that is given to us.'

Tugto's wife blew out the lamp. She sat in darkness and called on her helping spirits. They would know where she needed to go. She saw two flames appear in the west, which took the form of a bear and a walrus. The bear took her in its teeth and flung her out over the ice. As she fell, the walrus thrust its tusks into her and hurled her even further. The bear ran along after her, keeping beneath her as she flew through the air. And so they travelled swiftly: each time she fell on the ice, the walrus was there, thrusting its tusks into her again and sending her skywards. The walrus and the bear did not leave her alone until she had passed the outermost islands.

The wind came down and with it the driving snow, and the ice began to break up. Tugto's wife caught sight of an iceberg. She had just clambered up onto it, when this too began to break up, and there was no way for her to save herself. And so, by a journey much longer than can be told here, she came to the home of the Queen of the Sea. Along the entrance tunnel a river was flowing, and the only place where she could tread was narrow as the back of a knife. She walked along carefully, using the tips of her little fingers to balance. Inside she saw an old woman lying on the bed. The woman began to curse her, then sprang to the floor with her fists clenched. They fought for a long time, and little by little the old woman grew tired. Tugto's wife noticed that her hair hung loose and was full of dirt, and she began cleaning her as well as she could. When this was done, she put up the woman's hair in its topknot.

'You are a dear little thing,' said the old woman. 'It is ages since I was looked after so nicely. I have nothing to give you in return, but why don't you move my lamp to one side?'

As Tugto's wife did so, she heard the sound of wings. A flock of birds flew down the passage and continued without stopping for a long time. 'That's enough now,' said the old woman at last, and Tugto's wife straightened the lamp. Then the old woman said, 'Why not move it a little to the other side?' And so Tugto's wife did just that. She thought she saw men with long hair swimming towards her, and as they came closer, she realized they were seals. When many seals had escaped, the old woman said, 'Now that's enough.' And Tugto's wife returned the lamp to its original place.

Then the old woman looked her in the eye, and said: 'When you go home, tell everyone they must not empty their dirty water into the sea any more, for when they do that, it all goes over me.'

It was still night when Tugto's wife came home. The next

morning, people saw that her face was horribly scratched. 'You must not think that the ice will break up at once,' she told them. 'It won't break up until my face has healed.'

The scars healed slowly, and some people mocked her as they passed her window, 'It is time the ice broke up!' She ignored them.

One day a black cloud appeared in the south. By evening there was a gale, and the storm did not abate until it began to grow light again. When people woke up, the sea was open and reflected the blue sky. A great number of birds were flying above the water, and there were seals everywhere.

I'm writing this chapter backwards, working in reverse like a wood engraver. I'd been to Ilulissat twice before my summer visit to the art museum. During my original journey to Upernavik, the weather had been so bad the plane was grounded in Ilulissat for a few days. I was put up in the five-star Hotel Arctic by Greenland Air. This brief and stormy encounter was enough to lure me back to the town. Within a few years I'd saved enough for the flight to Greenland but I had nothing to spare for accommodation, so I messaged friends in Upernavik, asking if they knew any work I could do in exchange for a place to stay. I needed someone who would invite me, tell me I was welcome. To my surprise it turned out that there *was* something useful I could do. A hunter who was working as a tour guide in Ilulissat wanted some improvements to the English text on his website.

I look up Inuit Tours. One of the activities Malik offers is 'Feeding the sled dogs':

The Greenland dogs are an ancient breed that we use north of the Arctic Circle. They live outdoors and can withstand cold temperatures. They are perfectly suited to pulling a sled and they will never be substituted by motor vehicles. The feeding ritual, with the commentary by the tour guide, shows the characteristics of the dogs and their relationship with the owners.

As Malik knows, there are a few grammatical slips which should be corrected, as they will not inspire confidence. And some parts of the website read more like a lobbyist's brief than backpacker blurb. Will tourists want a guide who comes fully equipped with his own soapbox? I email Malik and we agree that I will visit soon to give his website a spring-clean.

The hero Kiviuq is the Ulysses of Arctic legend, a man whose travels are so unrelenting that they mark him out, even in a society of nomads. No one knows when he was born, but it is common knowledge that he is still alive and travelling the world. When Kiviuq was a baby his grandmother cleaned his body with the skin of a sandpiper, whispering a charm, 'You will always be able to come home, no matter what the obstacles.' When he grew older and his first kayak was made for him, sandpiper skins were used to pad the kayak frame.

In one version of Kiviuq's tale, he is imprisoned in the dwelling of an Ikpik. This Ikpik – the spirit of the sandy place where the water folds over the land – has taken the form of a woman, who offers him a night's hospitality. However, the next morning, when Kiviuq tries to leave her hovel, the doorway grows narrower, so that he cannot pass through it. In the end, he has to call on the help of spirits to escape. He runs down to the sandy shore and scrambles into his kayak.

As he paddles away, the Ikpik emerges from her hovel and threatens him. In response to her voice the sea becomes rougher. She is holding her *ulu* (a crescent-shaped knife never far from a woman's hand) and she waves it to cause Kiviuq to capsize and drown – but he is able to right his kayak. Then she raises the *ulu* high, and calls out: 'I could have sliced you with this.' And he gestures back as if to throw his harpoon, shouting, 'I could have harpooned you!' The woman almost falls over with shock. She drops her *ulu* and it shatters with a tinkling sound. At once ice forms on the sea.

And so ice and sound are linked in early Arctic legend. Ice is not created by the cold, it is formed by the noise made when a woman drops her knife. Ice is where the water overcomes, or becomes, the land.

The seats of the plastic chairs in the airport lounge are embellished with sealskin. All the other travellers have dispersed, some collected by relatives, others taking taxis to their hotels. No one has come to meet me. Eventually I ask a Greenland Air assistant to phone Malik's number. No answer. Could they redial? No answer. The assistant offers to call me a taxi, as there'll be none waiting outside the airport until the next plane arrives, possibly tomorrow. I should learn a more Greenlandic approach to time. If a plane might be delayed for several days, why rush to meet your guest?

The taxi weaves through the snow-covered landscape I have just flown over, into the centre of Ilulissat with its pretty wooden houses, and across to the other side of town. The apartment block outside which the driver drops me is bigger than the airport terminal.

The stairwell is sprayed with graffiti – FUCK YOU – FUCK OFF – BLACK SABBATH – JACKASS – insults punctuated by a storm of question marks. Toys are scattered on the balconies. I know when I've come to the right one, without checking the number: a pair of caribou antlers hang on the wall, and beneath them are rusting secateurs, a tangle of string. A few clean bones. An empty clothes airer is suspended from the balcony railing with green twine.

The door is ajar. I can hear the TV. I muster my confidence and call inside, 'Hi! *Hae . . . Aluu?*'

'I am sleeping,' explains a man, emerging from the gloom.

I have never been in a house with so many family photographs. Framed photographs are arranged around the clock on the wall and more are propped on the shelves. Sometimes one or two photographs are stacked in front of a frame which is already filled, as if they are awaiting their turn. Photographs stuck on the fridge, of course. I try to piece together Malik's family from the images, but it's impossible – the shots are from so many different decades and the older ones have faded. Several commemorate graduations, confirmations or weddings, with those being feted wearing national dress. It seems you have to stand straight in stiff *kamiks* (sealskin boots that reach high up the leg) and beaded collars.

Having let me in, Malik lies back down on the sofa and resumes his nap. I feel I should leave him in peace, so I dump my stuff and head out to the Pisiffik to buy some biscuits.

Grethe had told me that Malik began to learn to hunt when he was twelve years old. His father was the manager of a small store and hoped that Malik would go on to be a manager like him. But Malik was determined to be a hunter, and so, as such knowledge is always handed on direct, he learnt from his uncle. And he married Sarah, a hunter's daughter. Like many others, he mixes hunting with other activities to make ends meet. Climate change has turned him into an entrepreneur. While he hunts, and hunts for tourists, Sarah works in the hotel.

When I get back, Sarah is preparing Greenlandic 'country food'. The familiar term encompasses all meat caught by hunting, as opposed to imported food sold by the supermarket, which (as I have just discovered) is prohibitively expensive. It is also unreliable – the stock depends on the supply ship being able to get through the ice. Sarah's latex gloves are covered in blood. She removes the sinew from a lump of dark meat which is bigger than the chopping board it rests on.

I am awed by her butchery. 'Who taught you to do this?' I ask.

'No one taught me,' she says. 'I just watched.'

She explains the dietary calendar. During the winter seals, narwhal and walrus are hunted along the ice edge. Hunters in north-western Greenland still rely largely on dog sleds and kayaks as they have always done. Sarah is looking forward to next month, when dovekies and ptarmigans are back in season and the summer, when they will go fishing for small halibut and capelin in the fjords. Although, she adds, she may not have enough leave from the hotel to accompany Malik on a fishing trip this year.

She continues to chop at the joint, throwing the rejected

scraps into a plastic bag in the sink, and slowly the forms of ribs emerge. Sarah is frustrated at the perception of hunters, 'We are not just killing because we want to, but because we need to – and we use everything. We are part of this land.' It's true. Greenlanders are one of the few nations that don't worry about eating fruit and vegetables as all the vitamins a person needs come from the narwhal's skin. She's upset that fewer boys are learning to be hunters, though it's scarcely surprising, when those that do face economic hardship – due to a loss of hunting grounds as well as fewer animals. Most teenage boys want status, not self-denial. Her own son, Niels, is no exception. And while keeping dogs represents the promise of hunting, the cost of feeding and maintaining working animals is leading many to reconsider doing so.

'So it's tourism instead?' I ask.

'Yes,' Sarah is excited about the idea, but an overseas company holds the monopoly, and it's hard for local operations to spread the word about their services.

Over seal soup we discuss Inuit Tours and how to tell their story on the website. I get overexcited and recommend Malik registers for eco-tourism credentials. 'Maybe,' he says, evasively. He doesn't want to commit to a definite plan.

The next morning, Sarah throws a bunch of furs onto the floor. From it she extracts a pair of black sealskin trousers. 'You can wear these, Nancy. They are mine, and they'll fit you.' Then she pulls out an enormous pair of white bearskin trousers. These are for Malik. Despite everyone's concerns about the ice vanishing, winter temperatures still reach –20°C, and we will need to keep warm.

In order that I understand their business, Malik and Sarah have decided I ought to do some of the activities. A dog-sled ride is certainly more appealing than desk work on a crisp spring day. The dogs are tethered on the outskirts of Ilulissat. A new law has ordained that they must be kept away from inhabited areas and any dog seen loose in town will be shot. Dogs will eat anything, including children, and so it is advisable to keep them out of the way of people – especially tourists, who want to pet them. On the way to the dogs we pass more shipping containers with spray-can graffiti, its message more ambitious than that in the flats: 'Live Fast Die Young'.

I can hear the dogs howling from a long way off. In many Greenlandic settlements north of the Arctic Circle, there are more dogs than people, and Ilulissat has around 6,000 dogs to 4,000 inhabitants. The dog-city occupies land out by the helicopter pad, where each hunter's pack has its own territory centred around a haphazard kennel. In winter, Malik makes some extra cash by selling dog food (fresh seal meat) to his fellow hunters. Today, his own dogs are getting frozen meat. In silence he takes an axe from his bag and begins to hack at a giant lump of seal. It has come straight out the freezer and ice crystals cover the surface of the muscle. The adult dogs squeal and fight for the chunks Malik hurls in their direction, straining on their chains. Their puppies are loose; they tumble in and out of old fish crates and scamper perilously close to the axe, until Malik bats them away.

While Malik attends to the dogs, Sarah untangles the traces and ties them to the *pituq*, a long looped rope which will be attached to the sled. The thirteen dogs will run side by side in a fan hitch, as sled dogs have always done. The design of the sled has changed little over the centuries, although wooden boards have replaced driftwood and the green nylon twine – so common in Greenland that it seems to knit the landscape together – ties down our equipment instead of sealskin thongs. The sled's joints are loosely bound to allow it to move flexibly over uneven snow and ice. It is strong enough to withstand a crash, yet light enough to travel around 10 miles per hour.

At a shout from Malik, the dogs plunge forwards and we rip away from the dog area, leaving the ordure and chicken wire behind. The dry snow flies into my face as we race cross-country towards the mountains, where the route gets precipitous. When we capsize down a ravine it is only our counterweight that prevents the sled from overturning. Malik calls to the dogs, egging them on with his voice rather than using his whip. He tells me every hunter has his own commands, which he will only share with his dogs. Their names are not a secret: Aaqqati, the gloved one; Kammak, comrade; Kunngi, the king; Rudolfi, Rudolf; Ipeq, the smelly one. The dogs say *VaaVaa*, not 'woof woof'. When we reach Nalluarsuk, they drop to the ground, panting. We sit on the sled, and Malik offers me a draught of coffee from his flask. I turn to him and see only the icebergs reflected in his aviator glasses. *From the rocky summit you will view nature at its most awe-inspiring. A huge ice-sheet lies before you and the air is charged with the dramatic sounds of a fast-moving glacial ice-stream calving into a fjord full of icebergs.* I am thinking about getting out my camera, when *hup!* Malik hoiks me up like his fourteenth dog – it is time to return.

*

Malik and Sarah have spent the last two summers building a traditional turf hut down the fjord, not far from the ancient ruined settlement known as Sermermiut. They lend me shoe chains for my boots, and we hike to a bluff where turf sods and rocks have been stacked up against plywood walls to make a squat, snug home. They plan to accommodate tourists here. While it's sparsely furnished, there's a bookshelf: on snow days campers could amuse themselves with Danish translations of Ian Fleming, Jack London or John Steinbeck. Sarah has hung a little paper cut-out of a teapot in the tiny window, and wrapped red lace around the plastic beakers which contain the white plastic cutlery. There's no room for such whimsy outside: the handles of shovels and other tools stick out from the snow that has drifted up around the building. From the doorway of the hut I can see a few metres of rock and beyond, the tips of icebergs lately calved from the glacier. It's a steep drop to the bay. I catch the whine of a dinghy's engine as it returns to the harbour.

'*Iminnarpoq*,' Sarah sighs, and smiles at me. 'It means "the air is clear, so sounds can be heard from far away".'

On the way back we call in on the older generation. Sarah's parents' home is covered in paraphernalia: a skin-on-frame kayak, parched as an autumn leaf, hanging from the wall out of reach of hungry dogs; dried fish the length of my arm, spotted like leopards, with grotesque jaws; clear plastic milk containers with green and red caps, slung on a slack rope like outsize beads. A velour beach towel, decorated with lions and baobabs, is draped over an outboard motor.

I follow Sarah and Malik into a narrow hallway, covered in cardboard – a space to take off your boots. It smells of damp fur. Although it's very dark in the house, Sarah's mother Karen is wearing tinted glasses. She brings out a soft Arctic fox skin for Sarah and Malik. The little black nose is just the right size for Karen to dangle the whole skin from her plump finger. Behind the sofa on which her husband Jonas sits, several narwhal horns are stacked. Traders once believed these pale twists were the horns of unicorns: they were used to build a monarch's throne or ground to powder to make aphrodisiacs. Sarah draws out a full-grown horn, and laughs as she waves it at Malik. Jonas looks on, smiling absent-mindedly, and occasionally picking his nose and wiping his fingers on his dungarees. By his feet a pair of the grandchildren's Action Man toys have rolled out from under the sofa valance, apparently locked in combat.

I wish I could join in the conversation. Karen and Jonas will have seen so many changes come to Greenland: the transition from a hunter-gatherer lifestyle to the job economy and welfare system under a Danish government, and more recently, Home Rule; the additions to the town of schools and hospitals and the flats in which their children live; the growing availability of material goods since the millennium. Karen brings out her box of scraps, and she and Sarah address what is to be done about a scuffed area in her *kamiks*. A summer of weddings and christenings is approaching. Sarah dips a sugar-cube into her cup and smiles at her mother for as long as it takes for the sweet cube to draw up colour from the coffee. Then she pops it in her mouth.

I walk home with Malik and head for my room, which he jokes is my Greenlandic office. What I'd give for this high-rise view over Disko Bay every day – but we both know I've only got it on loan. The room belongs to his teenage son. Niels is away in Nunavut playing ice hockey at the Arctic Winter Games. I am sleeping in a champion's bed. The Winter Games is a celebration of circumpolar sports and aboriginal culture – contests include dog mushing, snowshoeing and all the sports that can be played indoors in winter, like badminton and hockey, as well as traditional Dene games like snow snake, once used to hunt caribou on ice. However, the posters that are tacked to Niels's walls feature not Greenlandic athletes but Manchester United players. I contemplate Ryan Giggs's beauty while my laptop struggles to connect to the Inuit Tours website.

'Your tour guide will tell you many stories about the sights and local wildlife,' runs the Hiking page. 'The Inuit have lived and hunted in the surrounding areas for many centuries, and understand the wild environment better than anyone else. The tour travels along paths that our ancestors found through the scenic landscape.' The itinerary begins: 'Start at the electric power station.'

'Could we call the start point something else?' I call to Malik. 'Something more . . . ancestral?'

Each evening Malik gets the bath first, as head of the household, and I'm offered the water second as honoured guest. I appreciate such frugality: his determination to follow a vocation, despite the hardships that entails. Sarah saves the coffee grounds in the filter paper for the next morning. There's a word for this practice – *kinguneqartarpoq*, to make a second brew from old coffee grounds or tea leaves – so she can't be the only person who does it. She is creative with the resources at her disposal and has a garden on the wide living-room windowsill: a climbing ivy, a shy pair of cacti, a white orchid which may be plastic and two astonishing scarlet gladioli which are definitely not.

Malik is fond of stories which emphasize how his own life differs from that of his ancestors. One night after supper he complains of his loss of freedom: the freedom to follow a traditional way of life, or failing that, to earn a decent livelihood. The TV is tuned to the National Geographic channel; as if on cue, a programme about the Amazon rainforest is playing mutely in the background. Malik gestures triumphantly at the screen, saying: 'People should stop doing these things. Flying. Cutting down trees in Brazil. Everything. The ice is vanishing. Soon we won't be able to live here any more.'

Outside, the evening round goes on: the hunters head up the road to feed their dogs; blood and scales are scrubbed from the market stalls under fluorescent lights; the glacier calves one more berg into the darkening fjord. Malik's words caused me a sleepless night. I know tourists want an authentic experience, but he may offer them a little too much insight for comfort.

I see more of the cracks. There is a desperate energy to Malik's invention, but he seems unable to overcome the forces stacked against him. When we're not off on a jaunt on the sled, he does a lot of sleeping. Is he depressed? He seems not really to believe in the website, or the tourists it will bring. The tours Malik and Sarah plan together never take place. The copy I write about barbecues in the mountains and hikes to the turf hut and ice fishing never makes its way online. Back in the UK, I email a few times to ask what else I can do, but he seems unenthusiastic, and so I don't press him. A few months later, I check the domain. It is empty.

When I returned to Ilulissat I asked Ole about Malik, and he looked troubled. 'Oh, so you know Malik? He moved to Nuuk.' This worries me. Greenland dogs are not permitted to travel below the Arctic Circle. If Malik has moved to Nuuk, he will not have been able to take his dogs. And yet the relationship between a man and his dogs is as binding as any marriage. What could have lured him away?

'He's going into politics,' Ole says.

IV

SKATERS

TRACES

Reagan National Airport, Washington DC, USA
Kinross Curling Club, Scotland

And that the serpentine line, by its waving and winding
at the same time different ways, leads the eye in a pleasing
manner along the continuity of its variety, if I may be
allowed the expression; and which by its twisting so many
different ways may be said to inclose (tho' but a single
line) varied contents; and therefore all its variety cannot
be expressed on paper by one continued line, without the
assistance of the imagination, or the help of a figure . . .
that sort of proportioned, winding line . . . will hereafter be
called the . . . *line of grace* . . .

William Hogarth, *The Analysis of Beauty*

I

A figure approaches across the ice. Silhouetted against the only light source for miles, half-hidden by a whirling mist of diamond dust, we can't see his features. He trudges slowly, dramatically through the snow. He peers into the darkness ahead of him, as if he knows we are here. As he comes closer, we see he is dressed in white. He wears a crown of pale antlers; his faded coat is trimmed with the skins of ermines; silver tassels hang down from his sleeves, from the rim of his cap. At first he's alone. Then others step forward from the shadows. He strikes his staff on the ice sheet, and each beat causes green waves of light to ripple outwards. As the aurora disperses over the ice and appears in the sky, he points the staff at the darkened vaults and creates constellations in the shape of creatures: raven, coyote and bear. The crowd gasps.

But the shaman's magic is not all-powerful. Burning comets begin to fall from the stars and cracks ricochet through the ice on which he stands. The sections drift apart, revealing an ocean shimmering with fluorescent life. The shaman and his followers are forced to run, leaping from one ice floe to another to make their way to safety.

Grethe murmurs her approval. Everyone in Upernavik has been awaiting the 'Winter Ol' and she has invited me over to watch the opening ceremony live from Vancouver on their flat-screen TV. I lounge between her daughters on the sofa, eating Polar Ice – cheap, flavourless lollies, their tips dipped in chocolate.

The backstage is divided from the arena by a walkway half-concealed by iridescent flags of ice, shimmering like selection-box wrappers. As the athletes emerge, they are already waving and smiling. They look astonished. Amazed. Some hold a camcorder to one eye, filming the arena – and in turn, they are being filmed. The camera flashes from a million spectators in the stands add to the sensation of sparkle. The athletes and their audience are the only real thing in this arena on the edge of the Pacific. The shaman is an actor. The ice is a light effect. The giant polar bear, which balloons upwards from the rink, covered in artificial stars, is certainly not real.

Each team of athletes is preceded by a standard bearer who carries the name of their nation on a sliver of artificial ice in the form of a split pennant, as if announcing medieval jousters. The teams of the XXI Olympic Winter Games march behind them: Georgia, Ghana, Greece . . . Greenland's red-and-white flag is absent – the nation still competes under Denmark's colours. The athletes parade around the arena and up into the stands, keeping to an orderly arc by following a faint path of footsteps projected from above. Like atoms in constant motion, a troupe of dancers in white quilted jackets and woolly hats bop at the rinkside, cheering the athletes on and guiding onlookers in the use of drums, torches and other props.

The next act in the spectacle is a gorgeous fantasia on the landscapes of Canada. The arena is a screen onto which anything can be projected. Sea ice becomes wheat fields becomes forest becomes mountains, but between acts, the rink asserts itself. Dancers somersault on zip wires above it. Enormous totems that seem to be carved, not from wood, but from ice, rise from the surface, and as the leaders of the Lil'wat, Musqueam, Squamish and Tsleil-Waututh peoples intone words of welcome, dancers representing all First Nations peoples, including Inuit, whirl onto the ice. The lights in the whole arena dim, until just one spotlight covers the performers in the centre, and while the audience is distracted by their whirling ceremonial regalia, the totems disappear. When the lights come up again a pop star in a white suit stands on top of a two-tier cylinder as it rises from the rink, and tiny candle flames are projected onto the ice. She begins to sing a torch song. At the final chorus, the golden flames transform into doves and flutter up into the roof, leaving the arena dark. But the fire will come back again, in the form of the Olympic flame.

I step into the night and look down towards the harbour, trying to identify the position of my cabin. I may be experiencing a sugar rush from the Polar Ice. Where is a snowboard when I need it? It would be the perfect vehicle for this slope.

The moon is hidden by clouds and much of the island is in darkness, but I can make out a few houses where a candle is burning on a windowsill behind a lace curtain, or where eaves are delineated by fairy lights. An occasional streetlamp with its companion red bulb tinges the falling snow pink. Washing still hangs outside Grethe's neighbour's house, arranged by colour: on one line a hunter's black polo necks and underpants, on another lace table runners and striped Babygros. There's a pram parked in the driveway, full of snow as if it's been unused for days, or even abandoned, and the plastic sledge of an older child overturned beside it.

I hear a snuffle, then the clank of a chain. A dog disturbed from sleep hobbles after me a little way, without threat or even much interest, until the chain links pull taut, and it limps back to its dirty circle of snow.

A new fall of snow is blowing in sideways. The flakes cling to the drifts piled up by the roadside, nestling in the slim hollows of the cladding on the buildings, blanketing the handles of tools leaning against balconies. I am used to snow being so transient that even its arrival is instilled with anticipatory nostalgia – the expectation of its melting. But here the cold preserves what's fallen, and all human life is recorded on it. The thin line of blood that trails through the snow the morning after a hunter's return; a knot of tiny footprints near the school gates; tyre tracks stopping at the end of the pier and then doubling back over themselves: all these can be decoded. On a small island the residents know each other's business, and snow is the medium for the gossip that runs between them.

The snow on the roads has been polished by the weight of a winter of tyres in snow chains. (Although the roads are few, their existence singles the island out from the land surrounding it. The only links between one town and the next along the coast are less material routes, signalled by plane contrails, ferry wakes or dog-sled trails.) I totter on. Even with hiking boots, the road is too icy to walk on, the snow banked beside it too deep to wade through. When you are in an unfamiliar habitat, it is best to follow others' tracks. After falling several times on the ice, I stumble across a snowy expanse between two houses and sink up to my waist.

My evenings on Upernavik are more usually solitary. When I can no longer move words around on the page, I turn on the box – a far cry from Grethe's flat-screen – for a dose of

Winter Ol. I suspect this machine dates from when TV first arrived on the island, with the installation of a radio mast in the 1980s. It would have been a treasure then; it is treasure to me now. When I press the power button it makes a dull click and static appears on the screen for a few seconds. Gradually, images align, but never completely come into focus. Tonight the picture is so fuzzy, 'snowy' even, that the broadcast seems unreal; this is exacerbated by the fact that biathlon is repetitive, even in real time: over and over a small figure slaloms around a bend in the course, unstraps its rifle and aims it at the target. The Danish commentator sounds excited. The sport is my only distraction from work, so I watch faithfully – although the indistinct landscape, so similar to the ice fields which surround me, makes for an odd kind of escapism. I have been hindered by the ice: my excursions limited by its reach; my dignity compromised by falls. There is a vicarious pleasure to be gained from watching skiers and skaters, travelling with speed and grace.

My favourite programme is the weather forecast. I have no difficulty interpreting the icons of snowflakes or clouds hovering over Greenland's coast. Europe, North America, the rest of the world are off the map, beyond the edges of the screen – out of sight, out of mind.

II

A traveller who walks through Terminal B of Reagan National Airport in Washington DC, in not too much of a hurry, might notice the mural of an ice rink that hangs above Delta's and Air Canada's check-in desks. Larger than life skaters tower over the constantly changing crowds below.

These figures sweep across the ice, watched by spectators at the edge of the rink, ringed by the flags of many nations. The mural offers the traveller a view beyond the clinical space of the terminal into a mirror world, one filled with the possibility of more light-hearted, impetuous motion.

The artist Bill Jacklin RA is a connoisseur of the movement of people, the swirling currents of energy which we generate. His own life story is far from static: he relocated from London to New York in 1985, his first years in the city marked by a notorious crime wave. Jacklin discovered that his own marginal profession, that of committing images to paper, could be concealed in the action of crowds: among voyeurs and performers he was able to observe without being observed. He sketched New Yorkers on parade, at the beach, in the park. He drew labourers in the diners near his studio on West 14th Street. He drew in Frank's, the steakhouse in the meat market, and Florent, where pop art icon Roy Lichtenstein ate lunch with his studio assistants. At night he sketched travellers in the Great Hall of Grand Central Station and rough sleepers on the benches; at dawn he drew chain-gangs of prisoners in police stations. 'I always thought of New York as an arena,' he says. 'The light shining down, my spotlight.' He directed his own drama on the canvas, and his ultimate stage was the outdoor ice rink in Central Park.

Bill Jacklin tells me that he visited the rink often in winter, taking his sketchbook and later working up paintings in his studio. As he watched the skaters they seemed to form a vortex of shapes moving like ice crystals in a storm, a means for the artist to examine not just the people sweeping past him but 'the flow of forms and the play of light'. In London during the 1970s he had made his reputation as an abstract painter, a minimalist juggling squares and dots, but now people were his patterns. They provided an asymmetric motif that offered endless variation: the skaters' silhouettes, the light on the surface of the ice rink, the relationship between bodies.

Bill and I meet up at the beginning of June at the Royal Academy on Piccadilly. It's Varnishing Day, when the Academy welcomes artists whose work has been selected for the Summer Exhibition. Traditionally, the day was set aside to accommodate artists who might change their minds about their work – adding a dab of red or painting out a face, a last chance to alter their composition before the application of a coat of varnish. It's rumoured that Turner once submitted an empty canvas and painted the whole work on Varnishing Day. In some of the galleries, the presence of a scissor lift betrays a last-minute installation, but these days the works are not restricted to paintings, and few could be easily altered at the last minute – so the occasion is devoted to networking and drinking. (Any actual varnishing would probably be discreetly discouraged.) When I arrive at noon the galleries are already full of artists and the champagne is flowing.

Some of Bill's recent paintings are on the walls, including – of course – one depicting the subject for which he is famous. Search online using only the words 'Jacklin' and 'skaters' and thumbnails tumble into view from all over the web: some from prestigious auction houses and others from the Instagram accounts of fans. I stand before *City Skaters* considering the inexhaustible possibilities of figures on ice. Whereas in the airport mural the rink fills the whole frame, allowing the viewer to imagine it as being anywhere in the world, this painting unequivocally depicts Central Park: the perspective is pulled back to include a view of the Manhattan skyline, its skyscrapers brushed by cumulus clouds. A long shadow from one of the World Trade Center's towers falls across the nearest section of the rink, a shadow through which the skaters are moving, undaunted. You can tell from the streaks of paint raking the sky that it is a breezy day. The skaters seem bird-like – even fragile. One torso is just a splash of bright orange, with the leg a faint brushstroke that leaves the canvas before it describes the foot. On another afternoon the rink would be completely transformed: different people, different light, different tracings on the ice.

For his latest rink, Bill has scaled down to the size of a passport: using the restrictions of etching – the tones inherent in the black ink, the smaller frame – to create a highly charged atmosphere. The elegant skater tracing lines on the ice could be a metaphor for the artist himself, his lightness of touch matched with formidable skill. The blades score the ice as deliberately as the artist's hand passes the burin over the etching plate, leaving a channel which will hold the ink. The whole plate is inked up, then areas are wiped away with scrim, so that ice is suggested by the colour of the paper in the unmarked area of the plate. Plates and skates: thin sheets of metal, one placed down on blank paper, the other slicing across the ice. It dawns on me that the printmaker's editioning of an image, his pursuit of uniformity, is not unlike a skater tracing figures over and over again. The print run is over when, in one brutal gesture, the printer scores a line across the plate to signal the end of the edition.

Bill has flown in from the United States to help curate the Summer Exhibition, and he appears slightly tousled by the turbulence in the gallery. His mid-Atlantic accent reminds me that this city is his home too. He grew up in London during the Blitz; the first planes that he remembers seeing flying overhead were the Luftwaffe. We escape to the relative calm of the Academician's Room, and over coffee I ask him about the Washington airport commission. He relaxes, leaning back in the generous blue velvet armchair, and begins to reminisce. 'Well, César Pelli – you do know Pelli, don't you? The famous architect – got in touch when he was invited to update the airport building.' He explains that Pelli's design included a vast window overlooking the runways and the Washington DC skyline, turning arrivals and departures into a spectacle. 'When the airport was first built in the 1930s, artists had been asked to provide work for the main hall, and so when Pelli came to fill the space in the nineties, he commissioned new artworks as an echo of the original scheme.' Bill was one of thirty invited artists and, while many works referred to flight, none but Bill's depicted ice.

Ice is rarely a positive element in aeronautics. If it accumulates on a plane's fuselage it will affect the aerodynamics of the craft, lending more drag and less lift, with dire consequences. Yet there's a connection between travel over ice and through the sky: humans have to develop wings or blades to achieve take-off. Bill's work makes me think of the flight of Icarus: how it required Daedalus the craftsman to make the wings and the boldness of a youth to use them. It is no wonder that skating attracted the attention of Leonardo da Vinci, who sketched out a design for a speed-skate in 1448, before moving on to consider the possibility of human flight.

At 24 feet wide, *Rink* was the largest commission Bill had ever worked on. He was provided with six separate panels, which would be connected on site to make the interior fabric of the airport. He had to rent a bigger studio on West 26th and tenth in Chelsea to accommodate them, since they were over 6 feet high and far broader than they were tall. At first glance, the skaters' movement across the mural might appear chaotic, but the composition is cleverly controlled. Character is suggested through position and posture only; the faces are hidden. The viewer's eye is drawn here and there, as figures skate into, and out of, focus. Specific characters seem to repeat across the canvas, creating a narrative: here's a cautious figure in a three-quarter-length coat, emerging from the shadows and shuffling onto the ice. This couple can't decide whether they are doing the tango or a waltz. There's a woman in a red dress whose skates are carrying her forward too fast – she's leaning back and trying to slow down, just off-centre of the canvas which adds to the sense of drag – and there she is again, to the left: down on the ice, feet in the air, disrupting the skaters around her. *Rink* considers the sense of being on the cusp of a significant moment, as when the wheels of a plane rise from or make contact again with the ground.

The figures in Bill's painting are not trapped in one place and time. Carolyn Brown, one of the lead dancers for Merce Cunningham's avant-garde dance company (whose workshop was located near to Bill's studio when he first moved to New York), has described Cunningham's approach to choreography: 'The dances are treated more as puzzles than works of art; the pieces are space and time, shape and rhythm.' Space and time, shape and rhythm likewise lie behind Bill's way of working. Although *Rink* depicts an apparently impetuous, joyous free-for-all – not the ambitious speed of forward movement that intrigued Leonardo, or the rigid aesthetics of professional figure skating – it does so through a careful composition, using all a body's knowledge of movement.

A new airport was required for the capitol region, but where to build it? Airport locations are generally selected for their neutral setting: in this case, surveyors explored the mud-flats on a bend of the Potomac River a few miles south of Washington DC. Pilots from different airlines made test flights over the area, and the US Weather Bureau collected year-round studies of weather conditions. On Gravelly Point the approaches to proposed runways from eight directions were clear for sufficient distances to provide ideal flight angles. The only problem with the location was that most of the proposed site was underwater. On 21 November 1938 construction began with one shovelful of grit, ceremonially deposited by President Roosevelt; over the following year almost 20 million cubic yards of gravel were imported to raise the ground. The airport was an ultramodern development. Contemporaneous accounts boast of its exemplary handling of planes, air traffic and field traffic control, the fine lighting, and not least the design of its buildings, and facilities for public comfort and convenience.

It was not just the fabric of the terminal that changed during the 1990s. Originally called Gravelly Point Airport after its location, then Washington National Airport, the name was changed once again in 1998 to incorporate Ronald Reagan's, even though (as people pointed out at the time) 'Washington' was already named after a president. Regardless of these superficial changes, the pilots continue to descend from all over North America, using the river visuals of the Potomac which flows on a course it has kept to since the seas receded from the land 20 million years ago. Sometimes the air will be cold enough to show the planes' condensation trails; I wonder how Bill might depict them – surely they would appeal to his fascination for evanescent patterns.

But Bill hasn't finished with skaters. Before we go our separate ways he talks of his ambition to make a sculpture to fill the Royal Academy's great court. He imagines skaters of all sizes and shapes, cut from Corten steel – swirling in space, casting shadows on the flagstones and reflected in the windows of the grand Italianate facades of the Learned Societies. Later, leaving the Academy, I cross the courtyard that he imagines filling with his vectorized skaters. It occurs to me it's just about the right size for a real ice rink. Could Bill's imagined skaters find themselves gliding alongside real ones? Might researchers in the great double-height libraries of the Royal Astronomical Society, the Geological Society and the Royal Society of Chemistry that surround the quadrangle put down their theses at lunchtime and descend from their attics to lace up a pair of skates?

III

The summer of 2017 is the hottest on record in England. The temperature at Heathrow reaches 34.5°C on 21 June.

To cool off, I hunt down a favourite childhood story: Noel Streatfeild's novel *White Boots*, about child skaters Harriet and Lalla. It's thirty years since I've read the book, and I have to borrow a copy from a neighbour. The red cloth is faded, the corners soft and bumped. The title is gilt-stamped on the spine, but the gold has worn away everywhere but in the serifs. The pages are spotted and dog-eared, and even torn where they have been turned too eagerly. 'Please be careful with it,' Caroline says. 'I've had it since I was eight years old.' Her name is neatly inscribed on the flyleaf, together with an address in Barbados. She also read it in the sun.

Harriet is convalescing from a serious illness, and looks like a daddy-long-legs. Her family doctor recommends exercise. When she visits the ice rink for the first time the reader senses from Streatfeild's description that the encounter, though Harriet doesn't yet know it, will shape her life:

She gazed with her eyes open very wide at what seemed to her to be an enormous room with ice instead of floor. In the middle of the ice, people, many of whom did not look any older than she was, were doing what seemed to her terribly difficult things with their legs. On the outside of the rink, however, there were a comforting lot of people who seemed to know as little about skating as she did, for they were holding onto the barrier round the side of the rink as if it was their only hope of keeping alive, while their legs did the most curious things in a way which evidently surprised their owners. In spite of holding onto the barrier quite a lot of these skaters fell down and seemed to find it terribly difficult to get up again.

By coincidence, the rink is also used by child prodigy Lalla Moore for her daily practice. Lalla is not one of those clinging to the barrier, though she would have good reason to fear the ice: her parents died by misadventure while skating on a lake. She is being brought up by snobbish aunt Claudia to follow in her father's footsteps as a champion skater. The boots he wore on his final, grim excursion hang over her bed in a glass case. But the white boots of the title are not his; they are the ones that Harriet will wear.

The girls soon become friends, and Lalla enjoys sharing her skills:

> Lalla, skating backwards, had towed her into the centre of the rink.
> 'There, now I'll show you how to start. Put your feet apart.'
> With difficulty Harriet got her feet into the sort of position that Lalla wanted.
> 'Now lift them up. First your right foot. Put it down on the ice. Now your left foot. Now put it down.'

When the novel opens Lalla has just passed her Inter-Silver exam with flying colours, but as the Silver exam approaches she is distracted by thoughts of the costumes for her next gala performance and her anticipation of the press response. Wise Nana – who sits by the rink knitting woollens for her charge and does not hold with ice, 'nasty damp, stuff' – worries that Lalla is 'not a child whose work was improved by applause'.

The advanced figures of the Silver exam require a precision which the free-spirited Lalla can't quite match. Brackets are a problem, and the change edge loops are the last straw. They demand a different sort of skating: 'control, and rhythm, both of which she had sometimes, but as well they needed immense concentration ... somehow, however hard she fought to stop it, her mind would slip off what her feet were doing, and this showed on the ice in a bad tracing.'

Now I read the novel as a lesson in how to work: Lalla's ambition and imagination versus serious Harriet's application. For Harriet seems to enjoy escaping the problems of poverty by focusing on figures. Nana muses: 'Harriet was not the kind of skater anyone would think about, she never did things which caught the eye, she was always in some corner, or, when they were on the big rink in the centre, working away by herself, practising and practising, and studying her tracings.' Yet Max, Lalla's coach, is impressed by her dedication; and her quiet style is captured by a photographer from the local newspaper. The illustration that stays with me is a line drawing of the two girls standing – motionless – in the middle of the rink, holding the evening newspaper open between them. On the front page is the photograph of Harriet. Its publication marks a change in both girls' lives. Through her encounters with Harriet's family, Lalla discovers the rewards of life beyond the rink, and Harriet's talents are endorsed when she receives a pair of the coveted white boots for Christmas.

Harriet and Lalla play out between them the central conflict of figure skating in the twentieth century: between the tension of compulsory figures (from which the sport gets its name) and creative freestyle. Streatfeild's novel was published in 1951, and I like to think Harriet's introverted application to figures, her anxious checking of her traces by contrast with Lalla's extrovert passion for performance, was inspired by real debates within the sport.

In 1948 the number of figures that skaters needed to demonstrate in competition had been reduced from twelve to six. It was the first sign that the influence of figures was waning, although they still counted for a majority of the overall score. As TV coverage of sporting events grew in the 1960s, so too did the importance of free skating: the repetitive and intricate nature of figures did not make for good general viewing. Neither did the judges' time-consuming analysis. In 1980, the president of the International Skating Union, Jacques Favart, as if channelling a petulant Lalla, called figures 'a waste of time'. Worth only 20 per cent of the final score by 1989, they were eliminated entirely from international competition in 1990.

When I was the same age as Harriet and Lalla, I turned triple salchows on the living room carpet as Jayne Torvill and Christopher Dean skated their *Boléro* routine at the Sarajevo Olympics on Valentine's Day, 1984. Was anyone in England impervious to their charm? Millions of TV viewers watched as the pair performed doomed lovers hurling themselves into a volcano. They skated laps of the rink, scooping up cellophane-wrapped bouquets thrown down by fans, as the score was read out over the tannoy: a unanimous 6.0 from every judge for artistic impression, the highest score in figure-skating history. Describing the 'plot' behind the routine, Dean said: 'It was a volcano erupting and we had to climb to the very top before throwing ourselves into eternity.' His words could equally have referred to their gruelling training, and subsequent stardom.

Torvill and Dean's Face the Music tour received five-star reviews, with newspapers proclaiming 'a new ice age'. The show came to Whitley Bay Ice Rink in 1995, the year I got my first pair of glasses. I could see everything from my seat at the back of the stands: the monks' firebrands in the brooding *Carmina Burana*; the musical notes sewn onto sequined waist-coats in *Let's Face the Music*, the final number. I was struck by Dean's solo, set to the Beatles song 'Paperback Writer'. Unusually for a pop song, the subject is not love but a man trying to offer a book to a publisher. The book is not a novel but a memoir, constantly added to, about a man who is writing a book. The singer's revelations about this self-reflexive, Sisyphean endeavour run absurdly counter to the jaunty enthusiasm of the tune. For once Dean skated alone – or rather, his partner was not Torvill but a cumbersome desk complete with typewriter, which he manoeuvred around on the ice. His meticulous skating was pitted against the mess of creative endeavour as he typed pages, then scrumpled them up and threw them away. (Years later, when I saw Tracey Emin's rumpled *Bed* incongruously installed on the polished floor of a gallery, I remembered this desk.)

Many of Torvill and Dean's routines paid homage to other performance genres: sequences inspired by tap and ballet moves; the circus in *Barnum*; the musical in *Mack and Mabel*, and even bullfighting (*Paso Doble*). Surprisingly few make reference to the ice on which they skate. Their facility is in making ice stand in for something else. Look, they seem to say, loitering in matching denim dungarees in the comic piece

Low Commotion, we can saunter around on the ice as if we're in a farmyard. One exception to the rule is a major production of their professional years, the ice ballet *Fire and Ice* (1986), a kind of *Romeo and Juliet* of the elements.

The Prince of Fire has a vision of the Princess of Ice, pirouetting like a charmed dancer in a musical box, and leaves his own realm to seek her out. In the Kingdom of Ice, he finds he is cold – being naked apart from a scarlet thong, wristlets and knee pads – and he's puzzled by the way his skate-free feet behave on the strange, slippery ground. The clumsiness of the famous champion compared to an agile troupe of shimmery spandex ice spirits is played for laughs. But one experienced skater offers help: the princess twirls demurely into view and provides him with a pair of scarlet skates. She takes his hands in hers, leading him around her icy world until he grows accustomed to his blades. When her venerable father sees them skating in harmony he is furious; he imprisons the prince in a huge block of ice. But the princess's passion melts the cold cage . . . and after an apocalyptic battle between their respective armies, the pair skate off together. A happy ending, assuming fire and ice can co-exist.

Some works acknowledge the ice on which they are danced with more subtlety. The competition set piece *Oscar Tango* is skated in silence. Watching a grainy recording of the championship at which it was first performed, I sense the unease in the audience, which grows to a murmur of surprise as the performers continue unabashed – without music. Just audible over the audience reaction is a noise usually disguised by soundtrack: the scrape of the blades slicing the ice as the dancers circle, and the thud when they stamp their feet. The cold surface on which the sultry dance is conducted betrays its own nature, as well as the percussive potential skaters usually strive to avoid.

In choosing *Boléro* as a musical setting, the pair broke from convention again. Ravel's composition lasts 18 minutes, but Olympic figure skating routines must not exceed 4 minutes. An arranger was commissioned to shorten Ravel's piece, but he could not compress it beyond 4 minutes 28 seconds without cutting the fiery crescendo. However, Dean knew that the judges' stopwatch would only begin when the skaters' blades touched the rink. He choreographed several bars at the beginning of the routine in which he and Torvill would be on their knees, blades poised above the ice, moving only their arms and torsos.

As with all great artists, people said of Torvill and Dean, *they make it look so easy.* The splits, the overhead lifts that turn into somersaults, the perfect heart shape that Torvill traces with her blades in *Fire and Ice.* But break down these movements into their component parts, and they seem much more daunting. I look at the illustrations for a guide to figure skating published in 1921, three years before the inaugural Winter Olympics. The author, Bror Meyer, was a minor Swedish champion. Perhaps the earliest rumblings of changes were in the air and Meyer wished to ensure the sport as he knew it was preserved: he attempts to show readers, as if they were on the ice with him, *exactly* where to place their feet. Something of a challenge in the days before video and online access, and the wealth of detail that they offer, became ubiquitous. Meyer decided, 'after great consideration, to illustrate the work by means of photographs taken with a Cinematograph'. The images capture every stage of the skater's movement. Described on the title page as 'illustrations from motion picture photography', they are reminiscent of Eadweard Muybridge's experimental photographs of people and animals in motion from the 1870s.

I begin my lessons with Bror Meyer. *Figure 1.* The solitary skater is superimposed on a stock Alpine landscape, with snowy peaks and pine-forested slopes. In each illustration, a tiny skater progresses across the page, with infinitesimal variations, moving along a series of lines which indicate the strokes their blades have left upon the ice. Meyer explains that a figure is so called because it is based on the figure eight: two circles back to back, sometimes three. For the simplest figure, the *circle eight*, a circle is skated on an edge of the blade on one foot, then another circle is skated on the corresponding edge on the other foot. He continues: 'The change of foot at the centre is accomplished by a *thrust* from the former skating foot onto a *strike* by the new skating foot at the point of intersection of the two circles.' These elementary figure eights can be endlessly adapted by varying the thrust and strike, and dividing each circle up through different turns, such as a three turn or bracket turn at the halfway point. Meyer progresses through loops, with their *paragraph* and *serpentine* variants and the change-edge loops that caused Lalla such grief. But the text is turgid, and would be incomprehensible without the cinematograph images.

Rob roars with laughter when I tell him that I found it difficult to learn figure skating from a century-old book. After giving up on Meyer, I sent Rob an email to ask about figures.

He's on holiday, but – as if realizing the true gravity of the situation – he suggests meeting straight off his bus from the airport the following evening. It transpires he's just reluctant to go back to his cold narrowboat after a dose of winter sun. He explains that from October onwards, when you leave a boat it's a good idea to let the stove burn at a very low heat all day, so you can light the fire easily when you get back. It is counter-intuitive, he says, to leave a fire burning in a boat. But he's been away for a week and the embers will be dead.

As an athletic child, Rob accompanied his sister to the rink when she began skating and discovered an aptitude for the sport himself. His parents saved to fund his coaching, spent hours driving him to and from the rink every weekday before and after school. 'You're a teenager, your mates are at discos,' he reminisces. 'And you're stood in a freezing cold ice rink, on a clean piece of ice, wearing clothes you're not sure why you're wearing them. And you push out backwards, go round in a circle, change. Change the edge, go round the circle the other side, backwards. And the circles have to line up, perfectly, each time you do it, three times around for each one.'

He is so engaged in the memory that without thinking he gets up from his chair and sketches out the turns in his trainers while he is talking. The café manager knows Rob, and smiles at him before returning to her service.

'There is the adage that watching figures is like watching paint dry, and we'd say that doing them is *like being the paint*. It's agony. For a good forty-five minutes you just stand on the ice and go round in circles.'

When the ISU ended the requirement for figures, every

skater Rob knew was over the moon. 'But at the same time we thought, how many hours of our lives have we spent doing this?'

Rob's story began where *White Boots* breaks off: a stellar rise through British figure skating, reaching the very top for his age group. He quit the sport while he was ahead, after competing in the European youth championships at the age of eighteen. Does he regret all those hours of practice, the discos missed? Not really, he tells me. The figures not only improved his basic skating technique; they instilled the mental discipline required for other aspects of the sport. He winces as he describes the determination required to practise a jump if you have already fallen four times on the ice, and know you will fall again on the fifth. In acclimatizing the body to disappointment, figures were a good lesson for life.

How does a skater know the figures are right? Rob would take a scribe – a large compass – and spin it round to carve a line to practise on – or to check the shape of circles already skated. In competition, scribes are not permitted, nor can skaters rely on painted markings on the ice. They only have instinct. Clean sections of the rink are marked out for each competitor. The judges stand to one side, watching. When the skater has finished, the judges check the alignment of the figure from different angles, examine the tracings of the turns, and pace off the diameters of the circles to check their sizes. Are the circles perfectly round, without wobbles, flats, bulges, or any inward curl? Are all the circles in the figure the same size? Are the turns on a figure lined up with the central axis, and do the circles themselves also all line up? Are the turns symmetrical in shape and executed on true edges without scraping? Are the loops shaped like loops, and not circular or pointed? Then the next skater steps out onto the ice.

I'm still considering, after my attempt at reading Meyer, how figure skating might be notated. I ask Rob what system he used.

'But it's not really written down,' says Rob, surprised by my question. 'You might have a list of moves in your head . . . '

I think of all those routines, lost to posterity. I wonder if tracings are ever recorded before the Zamboni ice maker sweeps round and cuts the rink clean. 'Did your coach ever film you so you could watch it back to improve, or take photos of your tracings?'

'No,' Rob says. Nor was anyone watching him practise. 'You'd do it in isolation. You'd go off and do it on your own. There's a focus, and a calmness to be found in doing that. I never used to like people talking – parents coming round to speak to their child, or someone passing on information: "Your mum's going to be late tonight." A friend saying, "Hey, how's it going?" would break my concentration.'

'Were you listening to the ice, then?'

'I used to like getting the sound just right. When I pushed off it made a kind of crunching sound: *Ssssch*. I'd see how quiet I could be . . . When you start off you're more heavy-handed, and when you're doing it right, the ice sounds right as well. No one ever said to me, you must get it sounding a certain way – but you'd know, for example, when someone did a jump well. You didn't hear a big dollop into the ice. They just caught it right. The sound of skating is quite lovely. It's amazing how people can do these massive jumps and come down quietly.'

It certainly is. It terrifies me. 'What's the best kind of ice?'

'Some rinks get really cold. The ambient temperature in the rink is different to that on the ice. Sometimes I was freezing, and then I didn't feel as fast – when ice is too cold it tends to be more brittle. There'd be a sweet spot you wanted to get to where there's almost a sweat on the ice, where it's clean, and when you push out it's really smooth. I'd like to think that I wasn't too much of a diva when it came to the quality of the ice. But I really cared. Because if the ice was done just so, then you could go fast over it, without much resistance. It is dead thin: three or four inches of ice over concrete – so you want it to be really smooth. Fresh ice is beautiful. When you go to a public session, with people going round in circles, it's like a record with many grooves – you try to get across it, your foot gets caught. You go slower, and you have to work at it, because you're going over everyone's ridges. And if you fall – my God, it's like sandpaper.

'When you do figures, the ice must be absolutely clean and smooth with no markings. The Zamboni goes round and cuts but it also puts water down behind it. After a really heavy session, they'll have to cut off more than they wanted to and put down more water, and it won't freeze – so you're doing figures into wet ice. Horrible. You can't see where you're going. Sometimes you can still see marks in the ice beneath you. Or you'll find the ice hadn't frozen smoothly so there are little dimples. If you hit one of those, if there's any roughness on the ice when you're doing figures or jumps, you'd go off course.'

Rob's mention of irregular ice makes me wonder if he's ever skated outdoors, on natural ice.

'No,' he says. 'I had dreams about it. As a kid I had dreams of being able to skate through the fields to Oxford, the whole world would be covered in ice.'

'Just think,' I say, 'you could have skated downriver from Bicester to get to the rink.' Rob laughs again at that thought, and heads off into the frosty night to warm up his boat.

Talking to Rob about ice rinks reminds me of swimming pools, the everyday examples of H_2O in captivity which contribute in their small, artificial way to the 71 per cent of the world that is water. The open-air swimming pools vanish at the very same time that the outdoor ice rinks appear. In autumn, the strong winter covers are pulled back over the pool's water in parks and hotels around the world and the water level drained. Meanwhile, commercial rinks appear seasonally in the forecourts of major museums and public parks. I imagine outdoor ice rinks freezing and melting, freezing and melting, as seen from space.

One midsummer Sunday, Neddy Merrill, the protagonist of a short story by John Cheever, decides to travel the 4 miles home from a house party by swimming through neighbourhood pools. 'He seemed to see, with a cartographer's eye, that string of swimming pools, that quasi-subterranean stream that curved across the county.' He swims, and in between pool lengths he walks through hedges and jogs up garden paths and even crosses a major highway, growing impossibly weary on the way. He swims, and enters a dreamlike state: 'The water refracted the sound of voices and laughter and seemed to suspend it in mid-air'. A dry pool – 'a breach in the chain' – disappoints him. His journey creates a sense of the unreal, the out of time. A storm is brewing. He gets home to find he has aged decades, can barely stand. His home is dark, and empty – his family gone.

Could a skater travel through space and time like Cheever's swimmer? I consider the difficulties – there are fewer rinks than pools, for a start. After all, how many people have a private ice rink? But while it's geographically implausible, it would also change the tone of the story. No – the immersion of the swimmer in water has different implications. Neddy Merrill is nearly naked, wearing nothing but his trunks. The outfit, or lack of it, makes him seem more vulnerable and gives his hubris a comic edge. A long-distance skater would have to be well wrapped up and purposeful, like a Dutch champion racing along the frozen canals and rivers of Friesland in the annual *Elfstedentocht* ('Eleven cities tour'), arms swinging as the skates glide forward at high speed. A skater would not be left behind by time.

IV

The rink's surface plays a vital role in curling – a unique sport, in which players affect the speed and direction of the puck not by making contact with it, but by polishing the ice in its path. There is one dedicated outpost of this sport in England – in Tunbridge Wells – but I choose to take the train to Fife. I want to visit Kinross Curling Club, which claims to be the oldest in the world. (It celebrated its 350th anniversary in 2018.) Many of the rules of curling were laid down here in 1838. It's not the rules of the game I hope to unravel, however, but how the ice is made.

The end of October finds the season well underway, and

it seems there's barely a gap in the timetable on the rinkside whiteboards. My train pulls out of London before dawn. The city's Hallowe'en orange glow is soon replaced by darker skies over the home counties. The sun rises over late fields of blue flax as I travel north. By midday, I'm crossing the new Forth Road Bridge into Fife.

The pink-footed geese are arriving for the winter, flying south over Loch Leven in long skeins, shifting around in V-formations to catch each other's slipstreams.

The curling clubhouse is tucked away behind a grand golf hotel on the main street of Kinross. As I walk around the windowless exterior to find an entrance, I hear the soft throb of the refrigeration plant over the wind. Inside, it's a silver temple to cold – above me the huge crumpled tubes of the dehumidifier hang from heat-reflective foil ceiling panels. The rink takes up most of the floor. I've made it one hour before the Ladies Super League Championships begin, just in time to see the final preparations. At the far end of the hall I spot a figure dressed in blue, walking up and down method-ically, spraying the ice with water.

Steven Kerr has been in charge of the Kinross rink for over twenty-five years, creating the ice pad and caring for it over the season. The drops of water he is spraying create the 'pebble' effect that allows the heavy granite stone to move smoothly over the ice. The iceman's skill lies in distributing the water evenly, so that one drop lands on every square centimetre of the rink. This is done by carefully regulating his walking pace, and even the swing of his arm. Once the pebble has frozen, Steven has a few more passes to make over the rink before the surface is ready to play on. He shaves the pebble with a guillotine blade or 'nipper' which sings like hail on a tin roof as it clips the ice. After taking the tips off the pebble, he walks the rink once again, softly brushing the ice with a sheepskin to remove debris; finally, he places ten curling stones in a wooden frame, and pulls the whole rack over the ice. The principle behind this manoeuvre, also called the 'first end', is to break in the ice for the players – a philosophy akin to making, and then throwing away, the first pancake.

Steven sets the stones out on the ice to acclimatize and shows me the polished area on the base which will make contact with the rink. Tomorrow, Steven tells me, he will pare back the battered pebble to the ice pad, and begin the process again. The movement of stones, sweepers and shoes, ironically the very activity for which the ice needs to be perfect, soon destroys its patina. The iceman is constantly in demand; he must observe the rink's conditions closely. As we are talking, he checks the temperature gauge, to make sure the surface of the ice is -4.5°C. Any colder, any warmer, and the stone won't curl.

I touch the ice briefly. It feels solid as a textured glass window on a winter morning. It's hard to believe how delicate it is. Any part of the body that touches the ice will raise the temperature. The iceman learns to see activity on the rink as if through infrared thermography: a player who puts out a hand to steady themselves as they slide forward with the stone becomes a glowing field of red and yellow against a cool blue background. Even the number of players using the ice must be taken into consideration. Extraordinary to think that my presence here is a threat. 'Come and get a cup of tea,' says Steven, luring me away from the rink.

I'm curious to know how one becomes an iceman. My

state school in the Scottish Borders encouraged skiing and golfing, but not curling. Nor was ice-making among the career choices that were suggested to me (but then neither was writing books). Steven tells me that after school he began to train as an optician. Then a friend invited him to join the rink in Stirling, and he found that ice was more alluring than eyes. Does he play? Well, he used to, he says, but it's a bit of a busman's holiday . . .

The championship ladies are gathering in the bar, which is perched above the main hall in the manner of a church organ. The space is insulated to ensure that none of the dust or heat from our bodies reaches the ice. There's no sense of claustrophobia, since a window runs the length of the bar, looking down on the rink with its red, white and blue targets or 'houses'. The ladies sip tea and catch up on the news. There's little time to waste. Some are already zipping up their gilets, or digging out footwear. They show me the smooth Teflon sole that enables them to slide across the ice, and the single slipper with grips (a 'gripper') that is worn over it on just one foot, to control their movement. At the bell they move downstairs onto the ice. 'After you, Maggie.' 'Thank you, Sheila.'

One woman remains in the bar. Jean has recently retired from the game, and volunteers to tell me what's going on down below. Her accent thickened by a cold, she explains that the match is divided into eight 'ends' in which players aim their stones into the house. 'The idea is to get a number of stones right in the centre of the house. It's a bit like bowling,' Jean continues. 'But it's a very strategic game.'

I remember reading that curling has been compared to chess played on ice.

Jean points out the four players in each team carefully: 'The first person to deliver the stone is called the Lead, then the Second, then the Third . . . then the Skip. The Skip goes up to the end towards which the stones are aimed, and she dictates the tactics of the game.'

I'm already confused. 'So the Skip's at the far end?'

'Well, some of the stones are at that end, and they're playing down the way,' says Jean inscrutably, taking a sip of Merlot, 'and some of the stones are at this end and they're playing up the way.'

I see now: the ice is like any pitch, with a goal at each end. The Lead releases the stone so that it glides across the ice; as it travels the Second and Third sweep ahead of it with their brushes. The stone makes me think of a child potentate: everyone's eyes are on it, and its apparently independent movement is cleverly controlled. The degree to which the Second and Third remove frost on the surface of the ice will alter the stone's course. I watch it move gracefully between the slow-sliding Lead and the frantic sweepers, before it meets other stones in the house with a percussive knock.

'This curler here, she's going to try to read the ice . . . '

'Here! Here!' shouts the Skip. The Lead almost does the splits as she slides forwards with the stone.

'. . . Oh, it's on the heavy side,' says Jean, with disappointment. 'It's going to go right through the house I think. That hit nothing – it's called a "fresh air" shot. You should be able to read how much of a swing there is in the ice, and then you've got to adjust your brush accordingly to give an adequate amount of ice for your stone to curl back in.

'Now they are going to try and hit the red one right in the

middle, and as it comes back, it will clip the other red one, and the two of them will split and go out. That's if she plays the shot right. If she doesn't, she'll push the red onto the yellow, that's a tricky shot. She fresh-aired her last one so she can't afford to make a mess of this one. Oh! She's a touch wide. You see how it's not coming over the centre line? And she's heavy. So she could just fresh-air this. Oh, and she is. Oh, Lizzie . . . She will *not* be happy.'

Light reflects differently off ice that has been abraded by the stone or scuffed by the players' feet. Grey marks are beginning to appear on the surface of the rink. 'Do you have to make allowance for that as the game goes on?' I ask.

'Well, the ice gets keener, it gets quicker. Just with the wear on the pebble from sweeping and the feet sliding up and down. Most of the game takes place on the central area – so that ends up being keener, and if you want to play a stone slower you can do so on the outside . . . Good shot, Maggie!'

'Have these players come from all over Fife?'

'Oh yes indeed, the girl on the right is through from Linlithgow. Her sister who's standing beyond her lives in Milnathort. There's one from Braehead in Glasgow, one from St Andrews. This is a league that's played all over.'

Between matches, I walk down to the shore of Loch Leven. It's a bright day, and at the jetty a few visitors are boarding a boat bound for one of the loch's seven islands. Their tour will take in the castle where Mary Queen of Scots was imprisoned – and from which she later escaped. I'm more intrigued by St Serf's Inch, an island at the far side of the loch. The monks of its priory are credited with the invention of curling in the sixteenth century, though I suspect this story should be taken with a pinch of salt. But on a cold day like today, it's easy to imagine the lake iced over and the Augustinians making their own entertainment on the short winter days.

Over to the north lies the village of Kinnesswood, where the father of meteorology, Alexander Buchan, was born in 1829. Buchan grew up to become a teacher but, unable to raise his voice due to a weak throat, he soon had to change career. Instead of holding forth to his pupils, he began to map the movement of the winds across the surface of the planet. In the autumn and early winter of 1863 he observed how weather systems travelled across Europe and drew up detailed charts. In a *Handy Book of Meteorology*, published a few years later, he traced the route of a storm across the Atlantic from America to Northern Europe, using it to demonstrate his discovery that points of equal atmospheric pressure could be connected on paper, forming lines like the sinuous contours on maps. Buchan was the first person to use these isobars to forecast future weather conditions, as meteorologists still do today. Another of his theories, the Buchan Spells, has been discredited. He proposed that the smooth transition of tem- peratures through the year was subject to nine predictable interruptions, which he attributed to changing pressure pat- terns at certain times of year. The first Buchan Cold Spell is supposed to fall during the week before Valentine's Day; the first Buchan Warm Spell is in the second week of July. I check his chart: the next spell on the cards is a cold one, between 6 and 13 November. I mark my calendar, and sure enough, I draw my curtains on 7 November to see the first frost.

*

Curling ice comes and goes according to season, just like natural ice. Outside the eight-month curling calendar, which runs from September to April, many players defect to the golf course. Meanwhile, the iceman cleans the empty rink. He switches off the refrigeration system. As the ice melts he removes the slush from the concrete pit. He checks the gas supply and cleans the fittings, and carefully repairs any chips in the paintwork.

Then the ice pad is built up again. The iceman pumps glycol from the refrigeration plant through pipes hidden under the concrete floor, cooling its surface to -4.5°C. These pipes are the iceman's secret accomplice, and will keep the ice pad frozen for the remainder of the season. Then the water is added. Although the official term is 'flooding', the iceman does not merely stick a hose in the pit and wait as water gushes in. This is a task which requires great patience and precision; the water must be added in increments and the level checked as each layer freezes.

'When we flood,' Steven informs me, 'we are governed by the amount of water coming out of the mains. I have always planned to increase this but it's more difficult than it seems. We have a flow rate of between 1 cubic metre and 1.75 cubic metres per hour,' he continues, as if posing a primary school maths problem. 'Let's say we flood for one hour at a flow rate of 1 cubic metre per hour, we would put down 220 gallons of water. When frozen, these 220 gallons give 2 millimetres of ice.'

It's not just number crunching. Ice management requires human judgement, just like the sport itself. The first layer of water, a light spray to provide the initial 2 millimetres, will be followed by around ten successive floods over five days. When the ice pad is almost complete, it will be painted with three coats of water-based ice paint. The markings are laid out: black wool stretched taut across the ice for the guidelines; the red and blue circles of the houses measured with pinpoint accuracy and painted on by hand. Then the whole rink is lightly sprayed again before flooding to level, about eight floods. The whole procedure takes around three weeks, and by the time the rink is finished the iceman will have walked a total of 50 miles.

Steven sends me a link to a website for curling ice professionals, run by an organization known simply as The Circle – the acronym for The Curling-Ice Research Centre for Leisure and Excellence. He's on the committee, along with fellow ice-maker John Minnaar, and has helped to write the definition of curling ice which was adopted by the World Curling Federation. This website is home of the ultimate ice information, but there are caveats for those experts who grow too confident of their skill with this slippery substance. Minnaar writes: 'Not everything in curling or curling ice can be explained, and history has left a burden of many misconceptions that science cannot yet answer.' Indeed, he sees the site as a space to publish reports 'that ask questions to which there are no real answers'. In one such report for The Circle simply entitled 'Good Ice', Minnaar captures the irresistible magic of the icemaker's art:

That curler, who slides so gracefully towards the brush and releases his stone with that little push on the out-turn that ensures his stone is already a foot off the line, is a valued customer and a competent curler, and there is definitely a funny line just there, but otherwise the ice is good. And that curler, who applies handle at the last moment on the inturn to fling his stone wide by at least two foot, knows very well that the ice is not good, because the stone never drew an inch. And that visiting team, well used to playing on frozen water needing strike weight to reach the hog, cannot ALL be wrong, the ice is simply too keen because all their stones are out the back . . . Good ice is true and consistent. It is silky smooth under the slider, but not slippery. It feels gentle under the stone with no roughness transmitted to the handle, yet it is so sensitive that the smallest flaw in delivery will affect the stone. The sweepers will know that the stone will glide rather than plough, and with their sweeping they can take it exactly as far as they want to and as straight as they need to for perfection. The skip will know he can trust the ice anywhere and call all the crazy shots, the freezes, the angled raises, the gentle splits and the triple tap-up killers.

The modern game is a version of the outdoor matches which have been played since the sixteenth century, since the monks of St Serf's first spun a stone onto the loch. In Kinross, curling became a sport for farmers, merchants and masons – and especially suited farmers, who had time to play during the quieter winter days, leaving the farm in the charge of hired hands while they headed to the loch. Looking through some 1950s archive photographs, my attention is caught by a woman wearing a sensible plaid skirt – she could be an aunt of one of today's champions. She's using a broom to sweep the ice and a large wooden pepper pot as the house.

Today's players are not immune to the romance of natural ice. I ask Steven what it is like playing on the loch. He admits that the ice is okay but the wind can be variable, and that affects the game – hard when you're aiming into it, easy when you're not. He tells me that the circles of the house aren't painted on the ice in primary colours, as they are at the club – they're just shovelled out, so you can barely see them. He laughs. Such a game isn't really about hitting the house at all – just keeping warm, and drinking whisky. After all, one doesn't take the score so seriously when a match can be discontinued at any moment by the umpire, if a sudden thaw strikes, a snowfall threatens, or darkness starts to fall.

The annual Grand Matches or 'bonspiels' arranged by the Royal Caledonian Curling Club between the North and South of Scotland – in which over 2,000 curlers take part – are still held outdoors, when there is enough ice. Loch Leven is one of the traditional locations. It takes at least two weeks of cold weather for the loch to freeze and, if the ice holds, a committee bores through the ice to check that it is the requisite 9 inches for safety. It rarely is. Grand Matches are usually held indoors these days, but everyone I speak to concurs they're not quite the same.

Over the years there have been changes to the game, not least the developments in ice-making technology that allow players to improve their technique indoors, but the changes the Kinross curlers notice most are that the club membership is lower, the bar quieter, and the roster of matches more empty. Unlike golf, a Scottish sport that has become international and mainstream, curling remains niche. However, I'm struck by the warm camaraderie of this cold activity. There are handshakes before the game begins and conversations among teams in the bar afterwards. There's even a note to this effect in the Royal Caledonian Curling Club rulebook: 'The spirit of curling demands good sportsmanship, kindly feeling and honourable conduct.' A true player, it says, would rather lose than win unfairly. The next day, I defer my trip to Edinburgh and return to the upstairs bar to watch another match, purely for pleasure. This time, the teams are less experienced, and seeing their uncertain steps on the ice, their wide shots, I realize how much skill lay behind the apparently effortless performances I saw yesterday.

I order a cheese toastie from the bar, which comes with a crisp salad on the side. Jim Steel, a member of the ice team, ambles over to check I've got everything I need and stops for a chat.

'What makes Steven such a good iceman?' I ask.

'Experience,' he says, adding, after a moment's thought: 'And curiosity. Because there are so many things that can change the ice: the outside air temperature, the humidity, the number of people on the rink. And whenever there's a problem, Steven will always investigate until he has solved it. He will examine all the variables until he finds out what is the cause. And he's not proud – he will pick up the phone and ask other people's advice. He knows icemen all over the world.'

I have an image of an optician testing the eye, said to be the human body's most complex organ. He looks beyond the firm white sclera containing the iris and pupil, to the structures that lie behind it, the rods and cones that process light and colour. He offers the patient innumerable options, twisting and turning different combinations of lens, until the solution for perfect vision becomes clear.

Before I leave Scotland, I visit a curling rink constructed long before the game moved indoors, and without the benefits of refrigeration technology. I take a train from Edinburgh to Glasgow and get off at a deserted station halfway between the two cities. The hawthorn hedges are bare of leaves, revealing the grey lichen on their branches; only the gorse is still in flower. I wait by the roadside for a bus.

'You want 'Syth, pal?' asks the driver. It must be a popular destination.

According to Wikipedia – and its own homepage – Kilsyth Curling Club vies with Kinross for the title of oldest in the world. It was founded in 1716. The pond that was created at the Colzium Estate for its players is probably (there are a lot of uncertainties in the history of curling) the world's oldest man-made rink. The story of this area is one of building and transformation – from the ruins of the Antonine Wall that run from coast to coast a few miles away, once the northern frontier of the Roman Empire, to today's new housing developments. The captivating names of the latter fail to disguise their insidious creep across the Lanarkshire greenbelts. The as-yet-uninhabited homes of Bonny Side Brae, their windows dark and empty against the immaculate pebbledash, tumble down the steep hillside like boulders left behind by a glacier.

The Colzium Estate, formerly a private residence, is now a public park, approached down an avenue lined with mature yew and beech trees. A sign at the edge of the woodland forbids the burial of pets. Another sign, complete with graffiti, indicates penalties for misuse of the children's playground, which seems to be the main attraction this afternoon; it is being used entirely appropriately. Beyond the playground is a picnic area, and beyond that, a further sign indicates, I will find the pond.

The pond must always have been shallow, but now grass is growing up from its bed. So a lot of the pond is, in fact, not a pond. The eroded edges have been recently repaired with rocks held in place with wire. A duck island is moored in the middle, but since the grasses have grown right up to the island and the water level has sunk, this island is now joined to the 'mainland'. Gulls wheel over the puddles, fighting for scraps. A figure in a pink tracksuit is speed-walking around the circumference. Beyond there's a row of trees, and beyond that, a line of young saplings which haven't yet appeared above their plastic wrap – and then the long view: the houses in one of the new developments built up against the old estate boundary. The saplings may have been planted so that one day the houses won't be visible, or perhaps so their residents have some privacy from day-trippers like me. Later, reading more about the area, I realize the development was controversial: it's built on land at risk from flooding. 'Cavalry Park' is also an unmarked burial ground for those killed at the Battle of Kilsyth in 1645, in which Royalist forces destroyed Scotland's last Covenanter army.

The first curlers would not have been caught up in the action. But given the fate of the battlefield next door, I wonder for how much longer the historic but disused pond will remain? Kilsyth Curling Club moved to the indoor rink at Crossmyloof in Glasgow in the 1970s, and now its curlers play up the road at The Peak, Stirling's purpose-built sports hall. I wander back to the bus stop along a millstream which runs around the hillside. From the path I can look down on the neat ice-tray housing estates, and the bowls club where a gardener is raking the day's leaf fall from the neatly mown bowling green.

V

'It may be gold: it may only glitter. I can't tell,' wrote the inventor Geoffrey Pyke. 'I have been hammering at it too long and am blinded.'

Pyke was proposing that a giant iceberg should be used as an aircraft carrier in the middle of the Atlantic Ocean. During World War II, the Allied forces needed a staging post for planes, which couldn't fly long-distance without refuelling. Why not use a material that could be found on the ocean, which had the advantage of natural camouflage? Why not create a 'bergship'?

This 'Mammoth Unsinkable Vessel' was approved by the top brass and given the codename Project Habakkuk – after the Hebrew prophet who had transcribed God's words: 'regard, and wonder marvellously: for I will work a work in your days, which ye will not believe, though it be told you.'

When did Pyke's superiors stop believing in his bergship? Not, it would seem, after early investigations showed that icebergs would be unsuitable for holding aircraft (too little ice above water). Nor when it was established that ice floes would not work either (they were too thin). Nor even when it was suggested that an artificial iceberg was needed (this would take some work). Experiments on a lake in the Canadian Rockies resulted in a prototype weighing 1,000 tonnes and measuring 18 metres in length. This monolith was found to be too weak, but work on Project Habakkuk continued.

The bergship was not Pyke's first engagement with ice. While working on Operation Plough, an Allied plan to attack a hydro-electric target in German-held Norway or Italy, he had investigated whether troops could be hidden within glaciers. At the time he'd made enquiries of Max Perutz, a biochemist and expert in crystallography who had studied the transformation of snow into ice in Swiss glaciers before the war. Now Pyke commissioned Perutz to investigate whether a new, durable form of ice could be created.

Perutz knew of research being done in America on making plastics stronger by reinforcing them with cellulose, and he believed this method could be applied to Pyke's enquiry. In his fascinating memoir, Perutz describes how he was given a laboratory which met both his specifications and the stringent security requirements: 'Combined Operations requisitioned a large meat store five floors underground beneath Smithfield Market, which lies within sight of St Paul's Cathedral, and ordered some electrically heated suits, of the type issued to airmen, to keep us warm at less than 0°C temperatures.' Concealed behind a screen of animal carcasses, with some young Commando officers as his technicians, he built a large wind tunnel in which he planned to mix water and wood pulp. The scheme was so secret that even Perutz was unaware of the material's intended purpose. He sawed the pykrete (named after Pyke, of course) into blocks: 'When we fired a rifle bullet into an upright block of pure ice ... the block shattered; in pykrete the bullet made a little crater and was embedded without doing any damage.' He found that ice made with 4 per cent wood pulp was as strong as concrete and had a relatively slow melt rate.

Of the many curious stories that have gathered around the enigmatic figure of Pyke and his inventions, the one I'd most like to believe was revealed by Lord Mountbatten in an after-dinner speech following the war. He had gone to deliver a block of pykrete to Chequers, the country house of the prime minister, but an aide warned Mountbatten that Churchill was in his bath. Realizing this would be the ideal setting to demonstrate the properties of pykrete, Mountbatten charged in. Churchill was, allegedly, delighted with the pykrete, which acquitted itself famously, floating without melting even in his warm tub. More easy to verify is Mountbatten's mission across the Atlantic to the Quebec Conference which Churchill, Roosevelt and other leaders attended in 1943. He decided to demonstrate the resistance of pykrete to the delegates, as Perutz had done – by shooting at it. The bullet ricocheted off the block of ice and sped narrowly past an admiral before disappearing into a wall.

Despite the demonstrable strength of pykrete, the bergship was never completed. The costs of Project Habakkuk kept rising, and even before Perutz's experiments were complete the flying range of aircraft had improved enough to close the mid-Atlantic gap. There were criticisms of the design: for example, the amount of wood pulp required would have reduced the supplies available for paper production, meaning a shortage of wartime books. But Pyke was not disheartened. He continued to concoct golden and glittering schemes, and grew interested in the possibilities of supercooled water – that is, water which is cooled to below freezing without turning into a solid. He claimed it could be used as a weapon of war: pumped from a ship it could instantly form bulwarks of ice or could even be sprayed directly onto enemy soldiers. Perutz treated such impractical ideas with disdain. Pyke's behaviour grew increasingly erratic after the war, and he was to take his own life in 1948, leaving his name to a material that had yet to find its function.

New uses have been suggested for pykrete which look further afield than the Atlantic: the insulation of spaceships, and even sustainable architecture for colonies on Mars. Some proposals, like the Mars Ice Dome, draw on the design of igloos, but use pykrete-filled inflatable structures in place of snow blocks. There is abundant water just below the surface of Mars to fill such structures, and its cold climate provides the perfect conditions for ice. The fibre used to reinforce the material could be sourced from the planet itself or provided by recycling lander parachutes. NASA even suggests that the hydrogen in water would provide a shield against what its website describes as 'galactic cosmic rays'. Pykrete would also have aesthetic benefits in space; as the principal investigator of the Langley Mars Ice Home, Kevin Kempton, told NASA: 'All of the materials we've selected are translucent, so some outside daylight can pass through and make it feel like you're in a home and not a cave.'

Back on Earth, pykrete has been used in the realization of a design for a bridge first sketched by Leonardo da Vinci in 1502. The artist had envisaged a stone structure spanning the Bosphorus, creating a route between Europe and Asia, high enough for ships to sail beneath. At the time, it would have been the longest bridge in the world, but the plans were rejected by Sultan Bayezid II and lost until 1952. In December 2015 a recreation was attempted in Finland by researchers from the Eindhoven University of Technology. The bridge collapsed the night before it was opened to the public.

With a few hours before catching my train at Edinburgh Waverley station, I head into the New Town to find a bar. Inside The Globe, one wall is entirely papered in a reproduction of an antique map of the world. From where I sit, I can see the North Atlantic Ocean and its bordering lands: Newfoundland and Greenland with 'Disko I.'. This version of Greenland is a distorted version of the nation I know from modern maps, its uncertain margins marked by a dotted line.

The original 'Chart of the Magnetic Curves of Equal Variation' was issued as a plate in a popular Scottish atlas of the world. Charles Black of Edinburgh and his uncle, Adam, founded their publishing firm in 1807. As well as Walter Scott's novels, they published atlases throughout the nineteenth century, the engravings in each edition altered to incorporate surveys from the latest expeditions. This chart marks the Northern Magnetic Pole at Boothia Felix (now the Boothia Peninsula), based on Sir James Clark Ross's voyage to the region in 1831. Due to changes in the Earth's core, the position of the magnetic pole changes over time. In 2005, it was estimated that the Northern Magnetic Pole was positioned to the west of Ellesmere Island in Canada.

The magnetic curves sweep out from Boothia Felix over the entire world. They swerve around the map, as if it were an ice rink and these were the skaters' traces. They lead down in an elegant arc from Washington to Antarctica and up in an ellipse to South Africa – Natal – then rise again to roam to the Persian Gulf. Some parts of the world (the Americas, Greenland) are covered by these lines – others (Asia, Russia) are completely blank. Britain looks complicated, an island too small for its outline to be drawn with much accuracy. Its outlying islands have atrophied.

The map identifies various countries, cities, rivers and an assortment of additional topographical details. How odd it looks, with its obsolete magnetic pole, its doubtful shorelines and names that have long since been supplanted by others. I wonder how soon the maps of today will look strange to future readers and drinkers.

V

PHILOSOPHERS

UNDER THE GLACIER

Gunnar Gunnarsson Institute, Iceland
Vatnajökull, Iceland

Tears fall in all the rivers. Again the driver
Pulls on his gloves and in a blinding
   snowstorm starts
   Upon his deadly journey; and again the writer
   Runs howling to his art.

W. H. Auden, 'Journey to Iceland'

I

'One should simply say and do as little as possible. Keep your eyes peeled. Talk about the weather. Ask what sort of summer they had last year, and the year before that,' the Bishop of Iceland tells a young theologian, whom he is sending to a remote village in the shadow of Snæfellsjökull. He adds, 'Don't try to put anything right.'

The bishop is perturbed by rumours he has heard about the parish: the church is boarded up, and there is talk of heathen rites and a woman's corpse buried within the glacier. The pastor hasn't drawn his salary for twenty years and won't reply to the bishop's letters. Halldór Laxness's late novel *Under the Glacier* examines how the religious certainties of Reykjavik unravel when confronted by a pagan nature cult.

The bishop has no choice but to investigate Pastor Jón and, since he requires a detailed report, he selects as his emissary a man with some skill in shorthand. The young man, who calls himself a 'priestling', has reservations about the mission: in his eyes, shorthand is no qualification for disarming a cult, and a tape-recorder is no part of the armoury of faith. 'I'm not cut out for derring-do,' he says. But the bishop reassures him that he merely needs to observe, take notes and record: it will not be his job to resolve heresies. The style of the report is very important: 'Don't be personal – be dry! ... Write in the third person as much as possible. Be academic, yes, but in moderation.'

Thus instructed, the emissary catches a bus to the glacier, with his notebooks and tape recorder in a duffel bag. The bishop has not given him any advice on buses. He discovers that his fellow travellers are as 'commonplace' as he himself, 'they sidle off the bus at unexpected places and vanish into the moorland as if they lived in some bog there, or else the driver pulls up at some unaccountable point in the middle of nowhere, and tosses out of the window some trifle, which usually lands in a puddle.'

The emissary describes his journey to Snæfellsjökull as if he is travelling to the back of beyond, but it's not so very far: the snowy peak can be seen from Reykjavik on a clear day. Perhaps because of its proximity to the capital, it was the first Icelandic glacier to be included on maps. In 1539 Olaus Magnus noted '*iokel*' over a spit of the west coast on his *Carta Marina*. *Iokel* or these days *jökull* (glacier) is a diminutive of *jaki*, and originally meant 'icicle' – it is related to the Anglo-Saxon *gicel* (as in *ís-gicel*). But the word came to denote something much larger. The cartographers Mercator and Ortelius also marked Snæfellsjökull on their maps in the sixteenth century. The glacier acquired a role in fiction too, when Jules Verne used it as a portal to the centre of the Earth in his novel of 1864.

Other Icelandic glaciers are more elusive, including the one I have come to see. Vatnajökull doesn't appear on early maps, even though its ice cap once covered at least one-tenth of the country. It doesn't even feature in the cartographic classic *Chorographica Islandia*, published in the early 1700s, which provides a register of several glaciers. It wasn't until Sveinn Pálsson's treatise on glaciers was completed at the end of that century that surveys of Vatnajökull were published, and the names of its outlet glaciers recorded. As the Little Ice Age drew to a close, more cartographic expeditions could take place; ironically, it was as world temperatures began to rise that the mapping of Vatnajökull began. Despite its retreat, this ice cap is still the largest in Europe. From above, it looks like a comic strip splash of spilled milk, its outlet glaciers seeping between spurs of rock. Glaciers are often named after their shape or location, or a feature of the local landscape. *Vatna* – of water, of rivers. Little did I know how watery my journey to Vatnajökull was to be.

*

I sit dejectedly in the petrol station with the other passengers, two elderly women and their friend, a confused man with bruises on his scalp. Two hours from Reykjavik, the driver has tumbled us out in the village of Vík, and announces he won't drive any further that day. We all need to get to Höfn, the last stop on this route, and six hours' drive away, but our protests make no impression on the driver. High winds and heavy rains are forecast. It won't be safe to travel the south coast road. Wait and see if there's another bus tomorrow, he says. The doors sigh shut, and the coach disappears back around the mountain towards the capital.

One of the women gives me a handmade card on which an Icelandic prayer has been stuck down and adorned with silver stickers. 'I think you need this,' she says, in careful English. I pocket it gratefully. We occupy the makeshift coffee bar by the cash register. Whenever a car stops for fuel, we take it in turns to dash outside, splashing through the puddles on the forecourt to ask the driver where they are going. Of the few vehicles, none is planning to make the long journey. An hour later I smile goodbye and good luck to my comrades and shoulder my rucksack again, puzzling over the shifting logistics of my journey. There's a hostel on the hill, but the road that leads to it has turned into a river.

My dorm is empty, except for Mildred, a frail nomad from Vermont, who tells me she comes back to Vík every year. She stares intently past my shoulder and out of the window, into the night; it takes me a while to realize that she can barely see. I throw my books onto the bunk above Mildred's, climb the ladder after them, and lulled by the rain dripping from the gutters, I begin to read about how the world was created from the Élivángar, three rivers of ice.

Gylfi, the earliest known Scandinavian king, is curious for knowledge about the gods worshipped by his rivals – in other words, the secrets of power. He travels to their great hall in disguise as an old man, and begs for a night's lodging. One of the three rulers, Hár, offers meat and drink and asks what more he can give the traveller. Gylfi requests stories: first he asks Hár and his companions to explain what the world was like before humans existed. And Hár tells him that there was no world at first, just rivers of ice: 'The streams called Ice-waves, those which were so long come from the fountain-heads that the yeasty venom upon them had hardened like the slag that runs out of the fire, these then became ice; and when the ice halted and ceased to run, then it froze over above. But the drizzling rain that rose from the venom congealed to rime, and the rime increased, frost over frost, each over the other, even into Ginnungagap, the Yawning Void.'

Glaciers are still officially defined by geologists as 'dynamic rivers of ice'. While the northern part of the Yawning Void, 'filled with heaviness, and masses of ice and rime', seems to suggest glaciers, its southern aspect is reminiscent of volcanic action. Jafnhárr, the second ruler to speak, describes the south as lit by 'sparks and glowing masses'. Just as the rivers of ice and 'all terrible things' had their source in the grim cold of the north, says Thridi the third king, the south infects everything with its heat. These two opposing forces, heat and cold, met in Ginnungagap, where the climate is 'as mild as windless air'. From this meeting Ymir, the first frost giant, was created by a process akin to condensation: 'when the breath of heat met the rime, so that it melted and dripped, life was quickened from the yeast-drops, by the power of that which sent the heat, and became a man's form.' From Ymir in turn, the world as we know it was formed: his flesh became the earth, his sweat the sea.

Each of Gylfi's questions leads to another, and by the hundredth page the three kings (who know very well he is not really the old tramp he appears to be) show signs of exasperation. Finally, they take the easiest escape route. Gylfi hears 'great noises on every side of him'; and on looking around finds that 'lo, he stood out of doors on a level plain, and saw no hall there and no castle. Then he went his way forth and came home into his kingdom, and told those tidings which he had seen and heard; and after him each man told these tales to the other.'

The story of Gylfi opens the *Prose Edda*, an anonymous work which survives in seven manuscripts; no manuscript is complete, and each has variations within it. Three are fragments. Its compilation is attributed to a thirteenth-century scholar, Snorri Sturluson, but its origins go back much further. This *Edda*, and other works of Old Norse literature, are the tales people told each other, shaping the way they saw their world in words, just as the Earth itself had been forged by heat and cold. It is these fragmentary texts echoing earlier tales that we rely on for the history of the first Icelanders.

I am back at the petrol station an hour before the bus is due, with an explanation ready for yesterday's ticket. I find Mildred there, helping herself to another coffee from the flask on the counter. Strange – she was in bed when I checked out of the hostel. The rain is still falling. A rainbow hovers over the forecourt, one end rising from the petrol pumps, and disappearing over the mountain. When the bus arrives, it is in disguise: another company's vehicle with the Strætó logo on a laminated sign taped to the cracked window.

The bus drives east though the wide Mýrdalssandur estuary. Rivulets of glacial water, swollen with rain, twine through the black sands. A van has parked off the road, and where the great rock of Hjörleifshöfði rises from the flat land, a woman in a periwinkle blue dress is preparing for a photoshoot.

The word in Icelandic for an estuary, or the delta of a river – a spot where one river becomes many or many become one before entering the ocean – is ós. Back in Reykjavik, I'd met members of Ós Pressan, a group for writers working in any language who have chosen to live in Iceland. A multilingual literature group needs a name that can work in more than one language, as Ós Pressan's website explains: 'Move the accent and, in English, O's becomes the sound of delight and surprise upon discovering something new. Accent to the right again and it becomes Oś, the Polish word for axis.' Iceland is a nation that is wary of including loan words in its language. In place of them, there's a tendency to revive existing Icelandic words that are falling out of use. Thus *sími*, a Norse word for 'thread', became the official term for 'telephone'; a mobile telephone is *farsími*, or a 'travelling thread'. Surely a nation of such linguistic playfulness appreciates how Ós Pressan's puns enrich the concept of an estuary: the shifting accent an expression of multiple ideas.

Each side of the bus gives a view of a different world. The road squeezes between shore and mountain scree. Sheets of rain cross a streak of yellow sky, falling from the grey clouds to the grey sea. Clouds over the sea and fog over the mountains. Basalt cliffs and straggling white waterfalls. More mountains. More waterfalls. The hours pass. I am lulled into a similar lassitude to that which creeps into W.H. Auden's voice in the recording of his poem 'Journey to Iceland':

> . . . the issue of steam from a cleft
> In the rock, and rocks, and waterfalls brushing the
> Rocks, and among the rocks birds.

The rocks are evidence of Iceland's transformation by the forces of fire and ice described in the *Prose Edda*. The road crosses the Mid-Atlantic Ridge, one of the few places in the world where this submerged mountain range rises above the water. It marks a boundary between two tectonic plates which pull a little further apart each year – a movement no bigger than the width of a postage stamp. Where the continental crust stretches beyond its limits, fissures begin to appear on the Earth's surface. Magma surges through these cracks, sometimes taking the form of volcanoes. This district has been named Öræfi, 'the wasteland', ever since the Öræfajökull eruption of 1362 destroyed an entire community. From the north-western rim of the summit crater of Öræfajökull rises Iceland's highest peak. I know the mountain is there, but the peak is lost in clouds; beyond it, to the north, lies the icy mass of Vatnajökull. The wipers are working at their highest setting over the cracked windscreen.

The last few passengers get off the bus at Skaftafell, a lonely hotel and visitor centre, and George, the driver, invites me to occupy the jump seat. He tells me he's from Transylvania: 'Ha! Ha! Dracula!' He makes the joke quickly, before I can say anything. The mountains loom ahead in the last half hour of daylight, and between their jagged peaks a glacial outlet slumps towards us. George deftly changes down the gears, in anticipation of the approaching uphill bend; it seems as if he will drive up onto the ashen tongue of ice, intending to use it as a road, as people did in the old days, walking miles from the north wearing nothing but sheepskin on their feet in order to trade with German merchants on this coast.

The road turns sharply, just before we reach the mountains, and the bus edges round their base. George has been working this route for a month: he used to drive buses in London, he tells me, but he loathed the Saturday night shift. He likes it here: generous holidays and plenty of time to read the spy novels he enjoys. ('John le Carré?' I ask. 'Who?' says George.) We pass signs of abandoned efforts at construction – scattered bits of piping, a Portakabin and a half-built bridge which points across the sands into nowhere, with no water flowing underneath. Further on new, unbridged streams have formed from water running off the glacier. We approach a lagoon, in which icebergs are gleaming faintly like floating candles in the dusk. It is the tourist hub of the glacier, but there's no one in the car park today. George stops the bus. 'Jökulsárlón. Five minutes,' he says. He gets out, and lights a cigarette.

Five minutes doesn't seem long enough to wander across the rough moraine to the water's edge. I hang out by the bus with George. He gestures moodily towards the lagoon. 'Seals. See?' I see no seals. Then he points out Diamond Beach, named for the chunks of ice which wash up on the sands. There is more than a visual link between glacial ice and gemstones. It was once thought that minerals were created by cold temperatures. Pliny the Elder wrote in the first century: 'Crystal is formed by a very strong congelation and can only be found in regions where the winter snow freezes with the greatest intensity. It is with certainty an ice, hence the name the Greeks gave it, κρύσταλλος, ice'. The belief was still held in Elizabethan times, with the natural philosopher William Gilbert stating that 'Lucid gems are made of water.' He explained that this occurs 'just as Crystal, which has been concreted from clear water, not always by a very great cold, as some used to judge, and by very hard frost, but sometimes by a less severe one, the nature of the soil fashioning it, the humour or juices being shut up in definite cavities, in the way in which spars are produced in mines'. (Gilbert's studies of electricity have stood the test of time better, and he is credited with coining the term 'electric force'.) It's understandable how these theories arose, as gemstones and ice do both have a crystalline structure.

Five minutes is up. Crossing the rickety one-lane bridge over the mouth of the lagoon, the bus takes a punch from the wind and veers towards the suspension cables.

'I wonder,' I say, 'what this road will be like in winter?'

'Me too,' he replies. 'I am little bit scared.'

We have exhausted our conversation, or perhaps George is embarrassed by this admission, and he turns on the radio. The soft, confiding voices of the Icelandic presenters are incomprehensible to us both, but it's reassuring to know we're still in reach of human society. Two words I recognize – 'Culture Club' – and a song comes on about doing time and loving and losing. George hums along.

There have been few cars on the road, but we come up behind a cautious queue of tail lights. George puts his foot down. 'Black clouds. Storm ahead,' he announces, tonelessly, and overtakes everything. Visibility is poor, but the bus presses on into the storm. With darkness the deluge comes, and our headlights bore a path through the raindrops bounding back from the asphalt.

Höfn is out on a spit of land, and as the approach is circuitous, I see its distant glow long before we reach it. Between the darkness of sea and sky its line of lights on the horizon is as thin as the scales on a strip of smoked fish skin.

II

Like the bishop's emissary, I am weighed down with recording devices. Notebooks, camera, laptop, Dictaphone. As for my Bible, I have a copy of *Iceland Breakthrough* by Paul Vander-Molen which I discovered six months ago in a house-clearance shop. In the book, the British engineer and explorer describes his expedition to Iceland in 1983. He planned to land on the south coast, cross the ice cap and travel the length of the river Jökulsá á Fjöllum from its source in the ice caves beneath the glacier to the Greenland Sea on the north coast. His team would use daring contraptions to navigate the waterfalls and rapids in the second half of their journey: part microlight, part kayak. Travelling solo, I have chosen Paul and his team as my companions, and hope to follow their footsteps, where I can. I won't worry about the rivers yet, I tell myself – just the ice.

Our paths have already crossed once. After a passage across

the North Sea, Paul's chartered boat arrived at Diamond Beach. His team of twelve men included a film crew, and I watch their documentary in my hotel room in Höfn. The expedition cannot properly be said to have disembarked, as they got straight from the boat into kayaks, and paddled upriver to Jökulsárlón. (They claim to be travelling in the wake of the first settlers, but I'm not sure this is true.) Their scarlet hulls nudge around the icebergs, which are floating in the opposite direction, from the glacier to the sea. This scenic paddle was just a warm-up for their next challenge: climbing onto Vatnajökull. They choose to start their traverse of the ice cap on Breiðamerkurjökull, one of Vatnajökull's biggest outlet glaciers. But once they reach it, there are arguments. How, for example, will they land the microlight on the ice cap, which is covered in snow? Jerry, the pilot, is incredulous that they could even consider it: 'It's like World War III up there.' In the end Paul's determination wins out, and Jerry removes the microlight's landing gear – and ropes on a pair of skis in their place. 'The Wright Brothers had nothing on me,' Jerry brags, strapping down one of the skis. 'They were just amateurs.'

As he takes off, the mike catches his words, blown back on the wind: 'God, I hope this works.'

Now that more people travel in these regions, getting onto the glacier shouldn't be so hard. The Visit Vatnajökull leaflet lists tour companies: Glacier Walks; Glacier Jeeps – ice and adventure; Glacier Journey – snowmobile and super jeeps; Glacier World – 'where the nature nourishes your mind'; Glacier Trips; Glacier Adventure. But the weather is against me. By Saturday, heavy rains have damaged the roads. One of the bridges George drove across has washed away, and the water level has increased by 2 metres in the rivers of the south fjords. It looks as though the only part of the glacier I may ever encounter is the 6 tonnes of ice lifted from Jökulsárlón and preserved with cooling aggregate that the artist Olafur Eliasson exhibited in Berlin as *Your Waste of Time.*

Two intrepid guides from Glacier Adventure, Haukur Einarsson and Sindri Bessason, come to my rescue. We drive back in the direction of Jökulsárlón until their ATV turns off the road and bumbles through potholes and across streams towards Brciðamerkurjökull, pinning me to the back seat like an astronaut in an accelerating centrifuge. *Breiðamerkur* means broad forest. 'There's no forest here,' Haukur points out, unnecessarily, 'but in the Viking period, there was a great birch wood. Back then the climate was warmer and the glacier was smaller than today. This was the best farmland in the south-east!' The descriptive names glaciers were given are now clues to the climate of the past. I wipe the conden- sation from the window. The sparse patches of vegetation are growing smaller, with more barren ground in between. Soon there's not a single plant.

'We just missed the crowberry season,' Sindri says, braking in front of a moraine.

I open the door and jump out. Right into a puddle.

Since we do not have skis, snow-cats adapted to carry tonnes of equipment, microlights or kayaks – just ice pick and cram- pons – our ascent of the glacier will be much easier than Paul's. After days of travelling, it feels good to abandon my rucksack in the car, and step out more lightly. Good, also, to walk without consulting a map, as no map would have kept me safe from precipitous crevasses anyway; I leave the choice of direction to Sindri and Haukur, who know the undulations and ogives of the ice by heart.

I step off the moraine and enter a world in which the ground is translucent, where depth is measured by light. I need to learn to walk again. Sindri shows me how to stamp down firmly onto the ice in my crampons, bounce a little even. With these metal claws strapped to the soles of my boots, I place my feet more slowly, trying not to stand on hollow ice which might collapse, or twist my ankle on a hummock. I keep my eyes down as I walk. I learn the glacier's character through the contact of crampon teeth on its surface. Ice is less receptive than the earth. The shock each step delivers makes me aware how vulnerable my joints are, how fragile my body.

Those who walked here before me have left no footprints, only constellations of blistered stars where their crampons pricked the ice. I remember something I once read about Antarctic explorers' footsteps: the snow that they stepped on, compressed by the weight of the body, would remain fixed in place as the lighter, unmarked snow around them blew away. These pillars of ice were visible from far away long after the explorer had passed on.

As snow falls on Vatnajökull it accumulates and grows denser, turning to firn even without the aid of human footfall. The glacier is a thousand metres deep at its centre. There is ancient ice here that formed while the *Prose Edda* was being written and has endured through all subsequent tellings and retellings of its tales. No wonder the story of ice, and how people survive it, has obsessed the country's writers.

Here at the edge of the glacier I know there is between 200 and 300 metres of ice below me. Although I have researched the statistics, when I look down into the ice I cannot judge its depth. Even a few millimetres are hard to measure by sight, but tiny specks of ash or air bubbles guide the eye down. We stop whenever we see something extraordinary, which is often, given this is a barren desert without plants or animals or flies. (What are we doing here, foolish trespassers in our colourful jackets and jangling harnesses?) We see cliffs of ice imposing as Mount Rushmore, which seem, like that monument, to have human profiles; we see a black mound of ash like a troll's hat, which prevents the ice beneath it from melting; we see fallen chunks of ice, crumbly as detergent tablets and similarly flecked with blue; and peering deep in a crevasse, I see a dented bruise of ice that gets deeper and bluer the further into it I look. Blue ice has no bubbles, making it the hardest of ices (it is chosen for runways in Antarctica). But it is no more blue than the blue sky is blue. The colour is just the result of how the rods and cones in my eyes perceive the passage of light over and into the ice.

It is September, the month when the year's melting culminates. Water is everywhere. It trickles across the enamel curve of the horizon and circles into cavities. The water will seep beneath the ice cap, feeding into Jökulsárlón and other watercourses. Among all this water, I feel thirsty. I place my ice axe down across a gully, and using its handle to support me, I lower myself until I can dip my face into the freezing stream. I open my mouth and let the glacier run into me.

*

Paul had intended to cross the ice cap, a journey of over 50 miles. He had wanted to prove all kinds of things. He lists his expedition goals in a hollow voiceover. However, it is 'the worst summer ever' in Iceland. This ice cap is so vast it creates its own weather system, and the one it shows them is not pleasant. After five days on the ice, Paul explains, 'we were proving nothing and getting very cold in the process'.

The film crew captures an altercation between two men, whose faces are completely hidden by protective clothing, about the logistics of brewing tea. They shout to each other over the wind, but their words can barely be heard. 'Ice formed like armour plating on our clothes,' Paul recalls, 'yet the snow remained too soft for tent pegs.' They use their increasingly versatile skis to support the tents instead. When the tents collapse under several feet of snow, it is the last straw; they have a schedule to keep to and rivers to kayak. They make their retreat in a brief lull, with force 12 gales predicted.

The cameraman must have tired of filming white-outs. Cue a bridging shot, with an animated red dotted line heading into the centre of Vatnajökull – and then turning back.

The best explorers know when to give up. The Swedish geologist Hakon Wadell, an honourable precursor of *Iceland Breakthrough* on the ice cap, showed the risk of not doing so. Wadell made an expedition to map the central snowfield in the autumn of 1919. At the time, Vatnajökull covered an area of about 9,000 square kilometres – much of which was scattered to a depth of 10 centimetres with black, sulphurous ash from a volcanic eruption the previous year. Wadell was studying the causes of volcanic phenomena in the surrounding

THE LIBRARY OF ICE

snowfields, those that had led, for example, to the violent and terrible eruptions of Öræfajökull. Where a glacier fills a volcano's calderas, the ice will melt suddenly as it erupts, causing catastrophic floods. Such floods are so common here that the Icelandic word for them, *jökulhlaup*, has been adopted as the official international term. Wadell particularly wanted to study volcanic eruptions around the neighbouring outlets of Siðujökull, Skaftárjökull and Skeiðarárjökull, as he had noted some confusion among 'authors of recent times' who used the names interchangeably.

Leaving base camp at the end of August, Wadell spent a couple of weeks on the ice cap taking measurements with a dioptre and a barometer, and he found the huge crater basin he had been looking for. Following his investigations, Wadell made his descent from the glacier through 'moving and gently fissured' snow. Then inexplicably, on 18 September, he decided to go back. He writes: 'the expedition was overtaken by a snowstorm and had to spend two days and nights on the ice under disconcerting circumstances. Two of the four horses were lost and the greater part of the equipment and also a collection of materials which was very important for scientific investigation.' He did, however, return safely to publish a beautiful map of the now-vanished glacier outlets. They show that the terminus of Breiðamerkurjökull once reached within 250 metres of the sea, and ice covered the barren area over which Haukur drove the ATV.

When glacial ice melts faster than it is replaced, the outlet glaciers begin to lose mass and retreat inland. In the 1980s Vatnajökull still covered 12 per cent of Iceland, but that figure has now shrunk to 9 per cent. No one needs data sensors to observe the change on Breiðamerkurjökull.

'Last year, our crampon station was over there,' Sindri laments, pointing to a ridge now much too far from the terminus of the glacier to walk in crampons.

Paul's team were standing where we are now when they began their retreat. This is not to say we are anywhere near as intrepid. We turn and begin to make our descent and, in place of the dazzling ice cap, we see what the melting glacier leaves behind. The tip of its grizzled tongue lolls in the dull mud. It stretches thinly across the valley it carved out in its stronger days, from Fellsfjall – its summit seething with mist – to the lagoon. A dribble of water on the moraine reflects the sky, grey as mercury in a mirror.

Sindri's neighbour, a farmer in his eighties, has witnessed Breiðamerkurjökull's retreat. His sheep once grazed the mountains that tower above us, and he crossed from one peak to another using the glacier that lay between them as a bridge. Now the ice is gone; there is only a deep gorge in its place. The ridges on the mountains all slope upwards towards the coast, showing how deeply the weight of ice inland depresses the crust of the Earth into the mantle.

'Sea-level rise doesn't worry me so much,' says Haukur when we talk of the consequences of climate change. 'I'm more concerned what happens with the tectonic plates. They are going to rise up when the ice melts.'

The rain rattles on my helmet. I shiver as I take my last steps from the ice to the moraine. I'm cold, and I've only been on Breiðamerkurjökull five hours, not five days.

*

The priest in Laxness's novel *Under the Glacier* has an excuse for not preaching: the glacier is silent, he says. The lilies of the field are silent.

The bishop's emissary wants to hear more about the lilies of the field. He needs some reassuring doctrine to counter the strange cult he has encountered. 'Are you sure the flowers are silent? if a sensitive enough microphone were placed beside them?' he asks. (He is a believer in modern technology.)

'Words are misleading. I am always trying to forget words,' Pastor Jón responds. 'If one looks at the glacier for long enough words cease to have any meaning on God's earth.'

Not everyone would agree that the glacier is silent, but it is certainly speaking a different kind of language. When the mass of an ice cap increases, its weight forces ice out across the landscape. As these outlet glaciers creep forward, any rocks frozen into them will gouge the bedrock below, leaving tracks or 'chatter marks'. As the ice retreats, the rocks themselves are left behind. The larger boulders, known as 'erratics' (from the Latin verb for 'to stray') may well be unlike the rocks native to the place where they have fallen: they are very noticeable. The glacier's chatter and its rocky remains have provided clues to the history of the Earth.

The radical nineteenth-century geologist Louis Agassiz was the first to popularize the idea of a relatively recent Ice Age. Through his observation of mountains in Scotland, he found evidence of glacial action and claimed that 'great sheets of ice, resembling those now existing in Greenland', once covered parts of Europe. This theory was opposed by many natural scientists, who preferred to believe glacial landscapes were caused by a biblical flood. Geological research began to shape debates about the world's origins and challenge conventional Christian beliefs. Eventually, Agassiz's interpretations found acceptance. They now underlie our understanding of climate science. In the words of Pastor Jón: 'The church is closed but the glacier is open.'

Nature became the newest religion, as well as the oldest. During his *Travels in Alaska* in 1879 the Scottish naturalist John Muir perceived the mountains through the lens of his lapsed Calvinism as 'Nature's Bible' in which 'icy cañons opened to view and closed again in regular succession, like the pages of a book.' Muir depicts himself as a pseudo-pastor, ready to interpret the wonders of nature by 'preaching glacial gospel in a rambling way' to his fellow travellers on the steamship. Muir's doctrine was silver-tongued scientific interpretation, while Pastor Jón was silent with awe.

On the drive back, Sindri and Haukur try to remember all the films that have used Vatnajökull as a location. Sindri lists them laconically: '*Batman Begins, Interstellar*, those adverts for mints.'

'Over there, in Kálfafellsdalur, Walter Mitty was in Nepal!' Haukur jumps in. 'He also hung out in Höfn. And *Mitty* was actually using Iceland as Iceland sometimes, not another planet or the end of this one.' This glacier has also seen two Bonds: *A View to a Kill* (Roger Moore's stuntman leaping on skis down crevasses as Russians fire explosively after him) and *Die Another Day* (Pierce Brosnan's absurd car chase across a frozen Jökulsárlón). Lara Croft was here too, in *Tomb Raider*, following the same route as Paul over the glacial lake and onto the ice cap, despite being warned of danger by a mystic child.

It's easy to see why the glacier has been used to depict other places and other times. The speed of its retreat creates a vertiginous sense of time's advance. It's not only Hollywood that has taken advantage of Iceland's characteristic otherworldliness. The rocky terrain north of Vatnajökull was used for moon landing practice by Apollo missions during the 1960s, and astronauts refined techniques for lunar exploration and geological sampling. As the Earth changes, this rocky landscape may hint at humanity's future, as well as its past.

III

Haukur drops me off in a farmyard, saying he'll pick me up in a few hours. Meanwhile, he suggests I visit a museum dedicated to a local writer. It is housed in a former sheep barn. Along one side of the building the corrugated iron is clad with giant book spines, representing the complete works of Þórbergur Þórðarson.

It's an impressive output. I wonder what influence growing up in such harsh conditions in the glacier's shadow would have on a writer. The title of one of Þórbergur's only books available in English translation, *The Stones Speak*, reveals his sensitivity to the mountains. In such a desolate place, with so little entertainment, a rich imagination was necessary: 'Here and there on the sills, ledges and crags there were certain outcrops that resembled cones, knobs and pegs ... the rocks were teeming with silent, unobtrusive life. – They were no longer rocks. They were a giant art gallery.'

Visitors to this museum must use their imagination too. 'We don't have many artefacts from Þórbergur's early life,' explains the audio guide, 'so we are celebrating his *intellectual* heritage.' I peel off as many of my wet clothes as seems decent and hang them above a portable heater near the door. I shiver as I enter the gallery, where water trickles over a diorama of synthetic rocks. I can feel wet gravel through my socks. It turns out that a little further in, there's another water display, this time inadvertent: rain is dripping through a gap in the rusty roof. This museum visit is an immersive experience.

Before the arrival of the wireless, families huddled in the *badstofa* would keep boredom at bay on winter evenings by reading, repairing tools or working on embroidery. Þórbergur often played a game of jacks using the bones of small animals. Such entertainments were known as the *kvöldvaka* or evening wake (as in 'staying awake'). Þórbergur's mother had a talent for reading aloud, and the volumes she read from survive. There are devotional and patriotic books: a Bible; a hymnal; and an edition of *rímur* (a strict form of traditional verse) belonging to Þórbergur's uncle, with notes scribbled in the margins. These books were as hard-worked as their owners. A copy of *Njal's Saga* is falling to pieces. The signatures are coming away from the spine, and the pages are crumpled and chipped at the edges. It's inscribed on the flyleaf with the names of the four farmers, including Þórbergur's father, who saved up to purchase it together and shared it between them.

The books from the twentieth century are less worn: they are Þórbergur's own. He left home aged eighteen, and worked as a fisherman and itinerant labourer, before settling as a teacher in Reykjavik. When he published his first book, *Letters to Lara*, it was hailed by literary critics as a masterpiece, but its experimental style and socialist views cost him his teaching job. He was radical, too, as a nature writer – an ecologist who ascribed animate thought to nature:

> One should always treat stones with courtesy. This one has undoubtedly stood here in the district for a long age. It has endured all the hardships of the ice age and all the battering of the Atlantic since time out of mind. It remembers the last bird to crap on its head before the ice-age glacier engulfed it. And how could it forget those tedious times when the seals used to bask on its head after the land started to rise from the sea?

The mountain companions of Þórbergur's childhood had given him a respect for geological time. He collected watches and measuring instruments which he used to chart his own, comparatively modest, experience of time and space. On his travels he kept a compass strapped around his wrist, and stowed more devices in his pockets – a small barometer, a thermometer, an elegant silver stopwatch, a pedometer and a device for measuring distances on maps. Perhaps this helped him to ensure he was going in a propitious direction. 'It affected you differently whether you walked west or east on the path along the mountainside,' he wrote of Helguhóll Hill. 'There was more beauty heading west, and nature had more to say to you, stranger things had happened there and your thoughts grew deeper. It was as if you were never moving alone there.' However, if you continue to walk west and not east, you will circle the world before you reach home again . . . Þórbergur settled in Reykjavik and didn't come back to

Suðursveit for a very long time. When he finally did so, he confessed that he felt he had been living in the wrong place for fifty-two years.

There's a recreation of Þórbergur's Reykjavik study in the museum: his neat manuscripts, written in fountain pen, are stacked on the desk. The bookshelves hold not only the Icelandic classics, but also the *Communist Manifesto* and Arctic explorer Peter Freuchen's memoir *From Thule to Rio*. Between 1925 and 1936, Þórbergur dedicated himself to the international language Esperanto and compiled an Icelandic-Esperanto dictionary. He carefully recorded every word on an index card, building up a collection of more than 20,000 cards. This self-taught radical stylist of Icelandic began to advocate one of the world's newest languages, which held the promise of easy international communication. For Þórbergur, writing was always a way of escaping, as well as recording, his surroundings.

Cumulus clouds are gathering on the horizon. The hay bales have already been brought in from the fields and wrapped in blue plastic; they are stacked in a pyramid in the yard. When rocks fell from Gerðistindur peak behind the farm, Þórbergur wrote, it always rained later in the day. I look hopefully across to the other peak, Fosstorfutindur, for 'if a rock fell from thence, a dry spell would come'.

The rain has continued overnight, and motorists are being warned not to travel. The bridge that washed away near Jökulsárlón is being replaced, but meanwhile there is a breach in the ring road that circles Iceland. As there are no roads across Vatnajökull, it goes without saying there will be no buses. It seems I will get to know Höfn better than I intended. The breakfast room in the hotel faces towards Vatnajökull, but clouds have come down over the peninsula and our view back to the ice cap is lost in mist. Now Höfn could be any town in Iceland, with its bungalows of concrete and corrugated iron, their windows uniformly decorated with a crystal lamp or a lace curtain. The bare shrubs that mark each garden's boundaries will soon be under snow. I chew at a slice of melon.

'I hate this hotel,' a guest says to her companion at the only other occupied table. I wonder why she feels so negatively about a place that is protecting her from the elements? I think of the communal room, the *badstofa*, where, less than a hundred years ago, visitors to Suðursveit would have sheltered with the family: heat and sounds rising from the restive cows below, the floor raked with ash to minimize the smell. I'm quite happy with this hotel.

What to do in such weather but stay in and write? There's an Icelandic idiom for ruminating on something, *að leggja heilann í bleyti* – to soak one's head. I decide to go swimming, hoping immersion will help me fathom the vast scales of time and space that are making my brain spin. The pool is just two streets from the hotel, but the rain is driving sideways, and my head is soaked before I even get there.

I have the pool to myself. Rain strikes the steaming surface of the water. Occasionally, as I raise my head to breathe, the icy drops prick my face, or worse, my eyes; later, in the sauna, I notice they have broken the skin on my arms. I run back outside and jump into the ice bucket, displacing a satisfying amount of water onto the already wet concrete. Back in the warm pool, when my limbs grow too weary for another length I tread water, aware of the depth beneath me, and remembering standing on the glacier.

As I shower, a woman enters the changing room, and we start talking about the awful weather. She tells me that Icelanders believe that different elements carry different kinds of knowledge. 'The wind brings urgent messages, those that must be acted on instantly. This is why its noise blocks out all other sounds,' she explains. 'The water brings information that you can send away again on the next tide. But it may return to you – the sea allows dialogue. A rock brings a slower understanding: you live beside it, or carry it in your pocket, and the knowledge it holds will be revealed over time.'

To resolve their unforeseen difficulties, the *Iceland Breakthrough* expedition split. Most of the team set off in trucks with the heavy equipment, travelling overland around the glacier, while Paul and Jerry plan to fly the microlight across it. It will only be an hour-long flight, compared to their companions' three-day journey.

I also need to get to the land just north of the glacier, where I have arranged to spend a month at the Gunnar Gunnarsson Institute, a cultural centre in the former home of one of Iceland's best-loved novelists. There's a bus that heads up the coast. Its winter schedule is online but it's impossible to find the location of the bus stop. I ask at the petrol station which sends me to the swimming pool for information, the swimming pool sends me to the campsite, the campsite to the other petrol station, where someone suggests the airport. The airport is so small I don't hold out much hope it will be open. I'm no stranger by now to the vagaries of travel in the north. Given my previous experience with buses, I decide to hitch, and so I end up speeding along the coast road with a young car mechanic called Birna Dogg. She navigates the vertiginous turns without fear, driving into the setting sun keeping an elbow on the wheel, while texting her boyfriend and rummaging in the glove compartment for chocolate-covered liquorice drops.

Paul and Jerry have almost completed their flight across the glacier when a severe storm heads them off. They have to divert around the coast. Then the exhaust shears, and the microlight tumbles out of the sky and crashes into a moun-tainside not far from my own destination in the Vatnajökull National Park. The others wait on the glacier for five days, fearing the worst. (This must have been one of the last expeditions without the luxury of mobile phones.) But then the microlight descends on them like a pterodactyl, and Paul and Jerry explain that they were sheltering under the microlight wing, eating their survival rations and making repairs to the crumpled undercarriage so they could get airborne again.

The source of the Jökulsá á Fjöllum lies many feet below them, in a huge cavern of ice. Geothermal heat rising from the Earth's core has melted this cave from the ice cap, and then forged a steep chimney or *moulin* up to the surface where the explorers stand. Mick Coyne, a former Royal Marine, twists screws into the *moulin*'s smooth walls, and Paul and his team abseil down, then lower their kayaks gingerly.

The expedition's acetylene lamps illuminate the cave. The men take their first bath in three weeks, stripping off their wetsuits and wallowing in the thermal spring, before setting off on the next stage of their journey. The river is shallow at first, but by the time the kayaks nose out from the ice cave into daylight it has become a torrent. The water is full of fine sediment known as rock flour or glacier milk, formed as the glacier eroded the bedrock over which it passed. The waves roll over each other, thick as concrete being churned, splashing up great gobbets that fall back heavily into the surge. Soon the river banks are a mile wide in places. Steep volcanic rocks cause rapids and waterfalls, over which the microlight soars triumphantly. Sealed into their kayaks with spraydecks, the team bounce down the turbulent river, sometimes hitting 'a stopper' that holds them underwater and won't let go. There are breathtaking rescues, a hole in the inflatable dingy carrying their supplies, and, as Paul says, 'the real disaster, the sad loss of our last can of beer.' In September they reach the sea. They have all made it, despite capsizes, despite the terrifying experiments with the microlight. Despite, no doubt, many things that didn't make it onto film. Handshakes all round.

I wonder whether Paul was feeling the symptoms of his illness as he led the terrifying descent of the rapids. He was to live another two years, undergoing treatment for the leukaemia which had been diagnosed not long after his return. He had time to see his film win awards at the French Film Festival and to complete the last draft of the book, with his father's help, from his hospital bed.

IV

Around midnight Birna drops me like a suspicious package at a petrol station.

It's the day of the autumn gathering in Fljótsdalur, when

sheep are brought down from the mountain to the safety of winter pastures. The Gunnar Gunnarsson Institute has closed so that staff can climb the hills to look for their livestock. Skotta has spent all day out in the rain herding sheep and sorting them according to markings cut into their ears. Now it's time for her to gather up the rogue writer. As we drive through the night she informs me that there will always be bloody-minded sheep that stay out on the mountains, endangering their lives in the harsh storms.

An old ewe freezes in the headlights. Skotta brakes and curses, and it scrambles off into the darkness.

The electricity at Skotta's farm has been down since the rains began. When we arrive at the museum, even though the lights are working, she is careful to show me where the candles are kept.

The next morning I'm relieved not to have to venture outdoors. I draw the curtains late, to find sheep grazing below my window. These must be the obedient ones.

As an ambitious young man Gunnar moved away from this valley of sheep farmers to Denmark. In the early twentieth century neither Iceland nor its language were considered a route to a literary reputation. He wrote his first bestseller *The Family from Borg* and the books that followed in Danish. Nevertheless, he set them in this landscape, the rural Iceland of his childhood, full of snow-capped mountains and glacial rivers. *The Black Cliffs* is even credited as being the first Icelandic crime novel. One entire room in the museum is dedicated to editions of Gunnar's works, from the early novels in Danish dust-wrappers to the Icelandic translations that were published later in formidable sets bound in black leather.

There have been several paperback editions since his death in 1975. I pick out a slim volume illustrated with wood engravings from among the English translations and take it upstairs to my apartment. I wrap myself in a blanket and begin to read.

It's Benedikt's twenty-seventh winter looking for sheep in the snow on the mountain slopes along the glacial river. He takes pride in recalling previous years when he's set off on this same mission, with his faithful dog Leo and the ram Eitill, who can persuade any stubborn sheep to follow him. Benedikt's journey will lead him through the uninhabited uplands, but he's quite happy alone – more so, in fact, than with the few characters he meets along the way.

He breaks his journey at the last farm before the highlands, where he is given a supper of smoked meat and potatoes. Leo is fed and Eitill is supplied with hay. During the evening three shepherds blunder in, and ask Benedikt to help them look for their flock, which they neglected to gather weeks before. Although time is precious to a traveller out in 'stormy moor, stone and sleet', Benedikt agrees to help. He sets off early the next morning, accompanied by his irresponsible friends, and they sing to encourage themselves on through the miles of snow. When Benedikt reaches the shelter of the bothy at last, he must pick the snow off his animal companions, then the ice out of his own beard, before lighting the primus stove and filling the kettle with snow for coffee.

A new day and another distraction. Benedikt helps a young farmhand, Jon, look for his colts. Then the postman arrives, carrying mail to be ferried across the river. (It seems to me there's a lot of traffic in this wilderness.) The postman persuades Benedikt to come home with him for a night's rest and some grub. But the postman's home is a long way off, and to get there they must row across the glacial river. The boat is almost swept away by the strong currents: 'It was like reaching another country, almost another life ... how would one ever go back?' After this enforced river adventure, Benedikt is at last free to get on with his task and is drawn back to the mountains, to the 'stony moor, storm and snow'.

He plans to search the farthest valley. Five hours there and five hours back – even though he'd rarely found a sheep there, he needed to check. He puts on his skis and glides along in moonlight over the frozen land. 'The snowy mountains seemed so low and far away in the moonlight,' Gunnar writes, 'and here and there the stars glinted in the dark blackness of nocturnal ice. Such a journey was like a poem with rhymes and lovely words, it stayed in the blood like a poem, and like a poem must be learnt by heart.'

Although it's prose, Gunnar's tale of a man who endangers his own life in order to save sheep is so well-loved by Icelanders that it is often learnt by heart and quoted from memory. Benedikt's own powers of recitation are limited, since he has to chip away his frozen beard with his knife in order to breathe: 'the ice cap that was about to close his mouth'. If his beard has gone over to glacier, it looks like the rest of his body may soon follow. He makes a snow cave, where 'he rested as well as he could, and dozed, but saw to it that he did not quite fall asleep, for if a man sleeps under the snow, hungry and exhausted, it is probable that he will never wake again in this life ...' The myth of going to sleep in the snow is a potent one. Dr Elisha Kent Kane, the senior medical officer of the Grinnell Expedition of 1850–51 which discovered Franklin's final winter camp, writes of that 'pleasurable sleepiness of the story books':

> I will tell you what this feels like, for I have been twice 'caught out.' Sleepiness is not the sensation. Have you ever received the shocks of a magneto-electric machine, and had the peculiar benumbing sensation of 'can't let go', extending up to your elbow-joints? Deprive this of its paroxysmal character; subdue, but diffuse it over every part of the system, and you have the so-called pleasurable feelings of incipient freezing. It seems even to extend to your brain.

The trope of braving the elements perhaps never to return is common in Icelandic literature (the memory of a boy lost in a snowstorm is what motivates the detective Erlendur in Arnaldur Indriðason's crime novels). Happily, Benedikt does return from his mission – although he finds he has missed Christmas Day.

Benedikt was based on a local shepherd, Benedikt Sigurjónsson, whose story Gunnar read in an Icelandic magazine that reached him in Denmark. Whether sheep had been in his dreams already, or Benedikt's spirit somehow summoned him, by the time *Advent* was published in 1936, Gunnar was making plans to return to the remote Fljótsdalur valley where he had grown up, and keep sheep of his own.

There's often snow in September on the distant mountains. Not these mountains, but the ones beyond. Skúli, the director of the Gunnarsson Institute, tells me that ten years ago, there would have been snow here too. There's no snow yet, but the persistent rain continues. Within a few days, even a stranger like me can see that all is not as it should be. The fields across the valley are under water. The river grows, until it runs from one side of the wide valley to the other. The flood becomes critical. The waters rise too quickly for farmers to rescue their sheep. This year, the flock might have been safer up in the hills.

Gunnar bought farmland at Skriðuklaustur in the valley where he had been born and commissioned the architect Fritz Höger to create his dream home. Höger modelled his designs on the solid farmsteads of Germany, a far cry from the valley's other buildings with their red roofs. Gunnar had imagined an even grander project – the blueprints show enough barns and steadings for 1,500 sheep. He drew up plans for a farm of the future in the same way he might have plotted a novel. But the future was changing in ways he could not control. War in Europe had brought social change: labourers were moving to Reykjavik, food prices were rising, and there were restrictions on the import of building materials. The influence of the war is apparent in the fabric of the building: the basalt rocks on the exterior walls were sourced from a nearby waterfall.

Still, it is an impressive building, with an elegant arch over the recessed doorway and a majestic balcony supported by sturdy pillars. At the bottom of the stairway leading to my apartment there's a framed photograph of Gunnar dressed in tweeds at lambing time. He seems taken by surprise, wind-swept and leaning back slightly from the camera, his smile blown off course but genuine, unlike the studied frown of the literary portraits. He looks happy. But he was mistaken to think he could combine work as a sheep farmer and author; he wrote little, those first years back in Fljótsdalur. (The only manuscripts on display in the museum are his account books.) In a glass case in the library I find proof copies of his works in translation, each open at a page spread which shows his notes in the margins, with suggestions for improvements. I ask Skúli if I can take a closer look. He unlocks the case, and takes out the English edition of *Ships in the Sky*. He leafs through it. 'Well!' he says, surprised, then passes it reluctantly to me. Gunnar's corrections only cover the first two pages. The sheep were certainly a distraction.

Gunnar gave Skriðuklaustur to the state in 1948, and moved to Reykjavik. He spent his final years translating his own works from Danish into Icelandic. (Many people believe the original translations by his contemporary Halldór Laxness are better.) When the Nobel committee decided to bestow the 1955 prize for literature on an Icelandic writer, it was Laxness they chose – although Gunnar had been nominated in the past and there had been rumours the honour might have been jointly awarded.

Is the literary legacy of Gunnar, although carefully man-aged by the estate at Skriðuklaustur, receding like the glacier beneath which he farmed? Skúli tells me that writers live through their books, and thus he is dedicated to keeping Gunnar's books in print, his words in circulation. Gunnar's works were translated into many languages in his lifetime. Today a few books are available in English in scholarly edi-tions, but only *The Good Shepherd*, his slimmest volume, in paperback. Will his fame be restored by the rumoured Hollywood film?

The Skriðuklaustur building was designed to last and has outlasted its purpose, gaining a new one as a cultural centre. As well as housing his literary archive, Gunnar stipulated that the double walls of basalt and the turf roof should offer shelter to visiting writers.

Gunnar was not the last writer to live in this valley, nor was he the first. The grounds at Skriðuklaustur once supported the last Catholic monastery in Iceland. Bishop Jónsson of the Augustinian order founded the building around the year 1493. For just sixty years it was a centre for worship on the road north – with the Reformation in Europe, the building fell into disrepair and was soon forgotten. Because *klaustur* means 'cloister' people suspected there had been a religious building here. A recent archaeological dig uncovered the double dry stone wall that protected the holy inhabitants from the cold and a graveyard for the community they served. Some had been buried with books open across their chests. The skeletons have all been removed now, taken away to be used for research into medieval disease, but Gunnar's sheep would have grazed above them.

On the first day of sunshine after two weeks of rain, I walk down to the faint line of stones and close-cropped grass that indicates where the monastery walls once stood. The few fragments of stained glass that have been found here (one piece has a man's face painted on it) suggest the monastery was as ambitious in its own time as Gunnar's house. Only five monks' names remain in the record, but the community would have included lay helpers and the sick they cared for. The refectory very likely provided better, more nutritious food than the local people were used to – though I doubt as good as the cakes Elizabet in the museum café bakes. Looking back towards Gunnar's house, I realize with a shudder that it is completely hidden behind the slope. The twentieth century has vanished.

I stand for a few moments on the spot that was the calefactory, one of the few heated areas in the monastery – a place for activities that could not be safely done in cold conditions, such as blood-letting and (apparently) writing. I pay silent tribute to my forerunners, imagining the dedication that would have led them to work in this isolated place.

At the head of the valley is (another) Snæfell, an extinct volcano whose peak reaches high above the snow line. Small cirque glaciers pocket its slopes. One morning as the sun is rising I cycle up the valley, following the river's course towards its source in the Vatnajökull highlands. I know I won't reach Snæfell in a day, but at least I'll get closer to it. Where the valley forks I pass Valþjósstaður, the small farmstead on which Gunnar grew up, voraciously reading every book the pastor lent him. In the soft dawn light, the long spur at the head of the valley seems to be emerging from another element, like a submarine surfacing, the sea still streaming from its sides. After a few miles the road becomes a dirt track. Snæfell's peak disappears from view as I get closer to it, and other mountains tower over me. A journey planned by looking ahead soon lengthens. I think of Benedikt's words: 'All directions so high up in the mountains are "in along", towards an unknown goal that retreats as one advances, but still remains and is the ultimate end.'

At noon sunlight reaches down into the valley, gilding larch needles and drying matted grass which has snagged on the fences as flood waters receded. I rattle over a wooden bridge, the first chance I've had to cross Jökulsá í Fljótsdal, intending to cycle back on the opposite side of the river. I take out my map. Individual farms are usually named, even on Iceland's national maps, since they hold as much significance as markers in the landscape as towns do elsewhere. I've passed all the inhabited farms, but this map also notes in ghostly grey the names of abandoned farms of which only a few stones remain, several of which lie ahead of me up the valley.

The maps of Iceland are changing, and not just to incorporate abandoned farms, new data on glacial retreat or islands created by lava bursting from the sea bed. Icelanders, with the stubborn spirit demonstrated in the sagas, have begun to sculpt the land. Since the millennium a dam has been constructed across the Jökulsá á Dal and Jökulsá í Fljótsdal. (There were protests against this movement of rock and water. All Iceland's musicians up in arms.) If Paul and his team kayaked down either of these glacial rivers from Vatnajökull today they'd enter a reservoir the size of Manhattan, and at its northern tip find their way blocked by the tallest concrete-faced rockfill dam in Europe. Below the Kárahnjúkar Dam the rapids are much reduced. The river's discharge has been halved, now that it flows only with water from its tributaries. Any overspill is diverted through a concrete chute to the canyon edge, where it tumbles 100 feet. This huge man-made waterfall, high even by Icelandic standards, is not named with the traditional -*foss* suffix. Instead, it is called Hverfandi – the Vanisher.

And it does vanish. For most of the meltwater from the glacier that fills the reservoir is diverted away, running through underground tunnels and down a 420-metre vertical penstock towards a power station constructed deep within the mountain, where it rushes through turbines to create electricity.

While the first part of the *Prose Edda* is an introduction to how to worship the gods, the second part explains how to write poetry. Poetry is not just an instinct that runs in the veins of mountain shepherds like Benedikt. It was originally distilled by dwarves from honey and the blood of a wise man, and so has liquid form. The *Edda* relates how Suttung the giant took this mead and hid it deep inside a mountain. Odin, the god of death and also of victory, longs for the mead, which turns everyone who drinks it into a poet or scholar. He bargains with Suttung, promising that he will do the work of nine men all summer for one sip. Giants are devious creatures and, when the summer is over, Suttung refuses to pay Odin. Another giant, Baugi, offers to help Odin steal the mead, and he begins to drill into the mountain. When Baugi declares that the tunnel has reached the cave, Odin sends a puff of breath into the entrance to test it. Splinters of rock fly back in his face – it does not lead to an opening. Odin realizes that Baugi is Suttung's accomplice and plans to imprison him in the mountain. It is an unwise giant who tries to trick a god. He demands that Baugi continue drilling. When he reaches the cave at last, Odin turns into a snake and slithers in to drink the mead.

*

The switchgear house is camouflaged by a traditional turf roof, and emerges from the hillside in such a way that it would be almost invisible to a passenger on the daily flight from Egilsstaðir to Reykjavik. But within this mountain, the giants of the twenty-first century have been working. I imagine the blast routine: drill, insert dynamite, retreat, detonate, return, clear rubble, drill.

I get off my bike and rest between two pylons. There's a persistent thrum from electrons drifting along the wires. Only here, where they leave the switchgear house, are the massive transmission lines in proximity. The electric current is so strong that the two lines must be run through different valleys for safety. But they are both heading for one destination, an aluminium smelting plant on the fjords. Aluminium is a soft, silvery-white, lightweight metal. The name is derived from the Latin term for alum, *alumen*, meaning bitter salt. It is used for many things, including aircraft fuselages and the shiny case of my laptop. It is also the only material humans – at the time of writing – can currently use to read quantum information. It seems an appropriate, if controversial, future for those silver glacial waters.

The water that has been discharged down the tailrace spews from a small tunnel into the Jökulsá í Fljótsdal. As the river grows wider it flows more calmly, leaving its silt in the valley. From my position under the pylons I can see both Skriðuklaustur and the switchgear house, as well as the great mass of mountain between them. The mountain glows with the autumn colours of crowberry and blueberry leaves. It dwarfs everything beneath: the sheep, the farm buildings, the road that travels along the river. I consider the turbulent water, generating power deep in the rock behind my home. What urgent messages is it carrying? Will anyone hear them? The pylons march upwards and away, above the river, above the forest of larches. I stand in awe for a second, then (the default reaction of every tourist) I take out my camera. The view is too wide for the frame, so I borrow a technique from Levick, the photographer who documented Antarctica's Admiralty Range. Instead of taking a single shot I move the camera sideways: snap, and snap again, five times.

Since Gunnar's house is now a historic building, it has a conservation programme. Hjörtur comes every morning to repair the walls, where the concrete surrounding the basalt stones has begun to crack after nearly eighty Icelandic winters. This old man with watery eyes delicately chips away the crumbling concrete, and applies fresh mortar. It has taken him three summers to work halfway round the house, since he works only when the weather is dry. In my study on the other side of the wall, I am finding writing equally slow work. I build up an edifice of words, whittle them down, then add some more. The monks writing in their calefactory are long gone, so I think of Hjörtur as my accomplice instead.

The day before my departure as I am heading out for a walk, I see Hjörtur packing up his scaffolding. He has finished painting the section restored this summer, and the white paint gleams around the dark rocks. The building will look its best in the snow, but Hjörtur and I will both have moved on to other employment and won't be here to appreciate it. He hooks a cart laden with scaffolding poles to his van, and it bounces along after him down the driveway. We haven't spoken a word, just given an occasional nod of greeting. All the same, we understand each other. I'm sorry to see him go.

It was frosty this morning and the scree on the hillsides has a titanium sheen – a foretaste of the snow that will cover it a few weeks from now. I follow the narrow paths the sheep have trodden through the fields. Where they wandered too close to the cliffs above the waterfall, I detour and find my own way over the tussocks, the grass crunching beneath my feet. Mushroom caps glisten with rime. From the abandoned farm on the crest of the hill I can see down to the river in the next valley. The water appears to catch the sun, even though at noon it should lie in shadow. As I draw closer the steady gleam around the rocks resolves into sheets of ice that have formed overnight. The river usually billows so swiftly here its currents are hard to read, but now the ice gives away their pattern. Here a curve where the soft ice edge is continually nudged by the flow as it rounds a bend; here an ice-free channel formed by a persistent eddy. In the shallows by the bank, splinters of new ice as thin as larch needles are spreading out over the water. Under the ice the river continues to flow towards the valley, as dynamic as the ice is still, and yet where it moves most quickly it is indistinguishable from the ice in colour – tumbling over the crest of the waterfall, sending up white drops of spray.

There is only one gravestone now in the small burial ground surrounding the cloister. It is carved with the name Jón Hrak. This well-known vagrant features in folk tales from many parts of the country – a fact which may indicate the extent of his wanderings. One poem goes:

It is cold at the choir's back, there lies old Jón Hrak.
Everybody is buried lying East and West,
everybody but Jón Hrak, everybody but Jón Hrak.

Sure enough, the stone indicates that Jón does not lie east to west, as is customary here, but south to north. Maybe he died in midwinter, when it was too troublesome to bury him in the proper manner. Or perhaps those who buried him didn't want him to come back to them from the dead, so they turned him in the wrong direction.

Merchants walking across the ice cap to trade on the south coast; novelists who can't decide where their home lies; shepherds astray in the mountains – Icelandic culture is infused with stories of travel. When names were needed for modern machines, the technology that enables our imaginations to travel, words were chosen that centred on the quality of roaming. Thus the neologism for laptop is *fartölva*, formed from the verb *far*, meaning to migrate, and *tölva* – 'migrating computer'; its companion, the external hard drive, is a *flakkari*. The latter word can also mean 'wanderer' or 'vagrant'. In the end, it's the wanderers we rely on.

The visitor centre for the Vatnajökull National Park is a short walk from Gunnar's house, along an avenue of balsam poplars. I've saved a visit here for my last day. The leaves still give off a sweet smell although, midway through October, they are turning yellow. As befits its mission of conservation, the visitor centre is a pioneering eco building, the latest ambitious project in a valley that seems to attract them. The sharp angles, the fusion of concrete and copper surfaces, the floor-to-ceiling window, wouldn't be out of place on London's South Bank. Alongside these elements, the architect has employed traditional features – larch cladding and a turf roof – and the manager points out a waterwheel installed in the fields below, which turns as it catches the cold springs running down the mountain. It is a reproduction of one that was created by a farmer at Skriðuklaustur in the nineteenth century. Revolving constantly in the steady stream of water, the farmer's wheel ground grain night and day. His neighbours called it the 'Wheel of the Universe', because it reminded them of the dependable nature of the sun, moon and stars. Now, just over the mountain, the vast Kárahnjúkar Dam powers the electricity on which people are equally dependent.

As the night flight from Egilsstaðir levels and sets its course westwards for Reykjavik, I open *Ships in the Sky*, which Skúli has given me as a parting gift. In it, Gunnar tells the story of his childhood and his evolution as a novelist. He continued to transcribe the rhythms of his first influence: 'from the deep places of my sleep a voice came to meet me, which I instantly recognized. It was the glacier river speaking, stern and stimulating, fascinating in its rude relentlessness.'

VI

GAMBLERS

BREAK-UP

Jan Michalski Foundation, Switzerland
South Tyrol Museum of Archaeology, Italy

We need not destroy the past. It is gone.

John Cage, 'Lecture on Nothing'

I

I wasn't the only person on a quest to understand ice. I heard of sound artists who were making field recordings in extreme environments: Lake Baikal in Russia, Cape Farewell in Greenland, and even Antarctica. Then Scottish artist Katie Paterson, whose many remarkable works on time and space already included the mapping of all the dead stars, made the sounds of Vatnajökull accessible to anyone who dialled a specific telephone number. This reached a mobile that was connected to the glacier via a microphone submerged in Jökulsárlón. The fact that Vatnajökull had its own phone number somehow personified it, while the possibility of strangers dialling and always getting an answer made me think of the speaking clock, and even of chat lines. (There will inevitably be someone, somewhere who gets turned on by glaciers.) A glacial *sími*, an invisible icy thread.

Reykjavik's domestic airport is built on the marshes. The runway ends in a nature reserve where Arctic terns over-winter. There are little wooden bridges so pedestrians can cross the waterways, and great concrete bridges over the dual carriageway that leads to the city centre. Each time I pass through the city I come for a walk here, often when leaving or arriving, often inappropriately burdened by luggage, to be reassured by the proximity of other travellers: planes, birds and cars. If I have enough change I stop for a coffee in the Nordic House, which looks out over the marshes. The building was designed by Finnish architect Alvar Aalto late in his career, and its long blue tile roof is shaped like a shadow of Mount Esja on the horizon.

This morning I'm here for a conference, so the coffee is free.

Artists and scientists, lighting designers and filmmakers have gathered to discuss the dynamics of darkness in the north. Presenting her work at the same session as me is Carmen Braden, a composer whose music responds to the environment around her home in Yellowknife in Canada's Northwest Territories. Around 11,000 years ago a large part of the area was covered by Lake McConnell, a giant lake created by glacial melt; its influence still abounds in this lacustrine landscape. Here in a region Carmen identifies as 'the taiga, the boreal', the lake ice has different patterns of behaviour to the sea ice of the High Arctic. It undergoes a seasonal cycle of freeze-up (in October) and melt (in June), rather than cataclysmic change. Carmen has studied ice at different stages of this cycle, producing instrumental works and songs such as *First Frost* and, most recently, *The Ice Seasons*, which follows the growth and decay of ice through the year.

Carmen has inherited ideas from the acoustic ecology movement which began to chart the relationship between humans and their environment through sound in the 1960s. She enthuses about the pioneering work of R. Murray Schafer, whose *Snowforms*, an a cappella work for child singers, drew on his memories of the 'soft foldings of snow' around his home in Ontario: 'he used glissandi and humming techniques in the voices to create a sculpted, glowing soundscape evoking the snow'. The score of *Snowforms* is a beautiful object. Rather than a conventional stave with black notes on white paper, Schafer notated the fluid voices using white streaks and stars on a rich blue background. A series of looped lines cascading down the page bears the instruction: 'chromatic descent, one voice after another, like snowflakes'. How much simpler this is to interpret than the traditional score – for its original child singers, and for someone like me, who doesn't read music.

Carmen does not only use voices and instruments to recreate the sounds of her environment, she also allows it to make its own music. In a resonant, calm voice she describes the 'cracks, booms, pings, bangs, sniffles and shots' emitted by the ice of the great lakes – and how she 'harvests' them by immersing hydrophones deep beneath the frozen surface. She presses a key on her laptop and the noise of ice in conversation, its shards chinking and clanking, sporadic yet melodic, transforms the atmosphere in the wood-panelled room. Her recording demonstrates that a frozen lake is far from being a static, silent space. She's coined a term for the sounds made by ice: *cryophonics*. 'I believe the ice has a voice,' she says, 'and the sounds it produces in its natural state are an ongoing, ecological form of music. My approach to the use of these sounds is a borrowing or re-performance of this music.'

Gathering ice voices requires a pragmatic attitude as well as technical prowess. Setting out in her recording uniform of bobble hat and headphones, carrying a hydrophone and Zoom H4n field recorder, first Carmen must judge whether the lake ice will support her weight. The standard safety recommendation is 6 inches of ice. Carmen studies the ice thickness figures compiled weekly by the Yellowknife fire department, but ice can be unpredictable. Sometimes unexpected areas of thin ice are reported, and it is important to respect the potential dangers. Once Carmen is on the ice, she needs to get the hydrophone under it; her equipment also includes an axe and a hand-powered augur with which she can drill up to 1.5 metres through midwinter ice.

The act of recording has intensified Carmen's relationship with her surroundings. She has had transcendent experiences while working on the exposed lake in temperatures of -30°C, huddled against the wind, tucking the field recorder inside her parka so the batteries don't freeze:

All of a sudden I was aware of how cold the water might feel if the ice opened beneath me, how the wind blew ancient and new all at once, how alone I was, how alive I was. As my heart slowed, I realized that I was getting cold.

Heat was leaving my body and moving into the snow, into the ice, into the air. Sound was still leaving the ice and moving into the water, into the hydrophone, into my ears. At this moment, I felt I was growing roots down into the ice through my boots.

Just as ice affects the composer's body, so the body can affect the ice. Carmen uses her knowledge of ice behaviour to 'play' it, even before downloading the sound files from the field recorder onto her laptop. She might choose the location and time of day to get a particular effect, or even manipulate thin ice with her weight to generate percussive sounds. Yet she prefers ice unmediated by human influence, emphasizing that the best results are down to chance:

> The degree of unpredictability in individual cracks, booms and clatterings is one of the main qualities that has fuelled my current fascination with ice sounds. These sonic events are repetitive but their recurrences are constantly varied and without pulse. However, I think that ice sound patterns approach an organic logic, as if the repetitive quality of these sonic events has a way of working that is structured at some level, but which is so complex that, from my personal experiences of listening to them, I am left with an impression of a pattern that blurs randomness and predictability.

The previous spring, Carmen had recorded the sounds of candle ice. At the end of May, the ice on Great Slave Lake grows thinner and gradually breaks into huge free-floating pans, which in turn splinter into long shards of ice. During their brief existence, Carmen explains, 'these crystalline shapes are pushed by the wind and waves to jostle against each other, creating beautiful masses of sound or delicate individual sound-events with a glassy or metallic timbre.' Of course, the precise sounds the hydrophone picks up will be down to chance. Back in her studio, Carmen selected some of the sound files using a digital audio workstation, keeping the integrity of the ice's voice by editing as little as possible. She then combined these electro-acoustics with a score for piano, violin and cello. There is a difference between the sounds made by movement of ice against ice, and that of hair on gut and felt on wire. So that the audience can appreciate the subtle music of the ice, there are moments when the sound files are heard alone, or the other instruments play only very thin textures over them.

I'm curious about how Carmen outlines her intentions for the musicians. The score of *Candle Ice* places the electro-acoustic track, described as 'unprocessed candle ice sounds' on a fourth stave below those of the piano, violin and cello. In contrast to their dynamic notation, the 'ice track' appears as a continuous, bold wavy line. A performance note for the first movement reads: 'Candle ice begins to float free'. It opens with the clear ice track, somewhere between a glockenspiel and a tambourine, like the noise of distant stars. Then the piano comes in, a few hesitant notes, and the inquisitive strings. The three musicians are instructed to play in a 'shimmering' and 'shining' manner. The score builds to the intense energy of the third movement, in which 'wind and waves begin to move the ice' and the penultimate movement, 'in agony – the death throes of the ice!' These dynamic sequences express the great amount of energy the ice requires to change its physical state. *Candle Ice* concludes with a 'quiet melt into lake-water'. Ice clinks resolve into lapping water, the jagged line on the score becomes smaller, lighter – and fades out.

Carmen explains how she 'translates' the wider ideas associated with ice in her music. In both *Candle Ice* and *The Ice Seasons*, the six-part structure of the works reflects the symmetry of ice. Specific playing techniques can be used to express the ice's physical qualities: in *The Ice Seasons*, she stipulates spiccato, jeté and pizzicato with their 'dryer, pointed timbres' to evoke the tiny ice crystals. As well as transcribing the sounds she hears, Carmen sometimes uses digital analysis. She describes the creation of a sonogram from three seconds of a field recording of candling ice: 'I chose nine prominent frequencies made by individual pieces of ice clinking, and moved these to the closest equal temperament pitch. I reduced this to the pitch collection C#, D#, F, G, G# and A#.' Carmen's use of technology in her composition is as bold as that of scientists investigating the possible future phases of ice.

Our coffee breaks take place in the corridors of the Nordic House. Daylight tumbles down the long shafts of Alvar Aalto's cylindrical skylights, as if we are standing under holes drilled through midwinter ice. (I remember that the poet Goethe called architecture 'frozen music'.) As the voices of other delegates echo round us, I ask Carmen about her archive of ice sounds. She records the environment wherever she travels, she tells me, but ice is her longest-running sound collection, and the audio files, photographs and videos run to many gigabytes.

'I have several backups. My system is pretty rough – usually based on the date and where I was, and sometimes what the ice activity was at that point.' Field recording helps preserve soundscapes that are rapidly changing – or even disappearing, but most practitioners are adamant that it is not about building a library for its own sake, but about listening, learning and passing on.

In the spring of 2014, leading up to the premiere of *Candle Ice* by the Gryphon Trio at the Ottawa Chamber Music Festival, Carmen kept a video 'ice diary' of Great Slave Lake. I watch it online after the conference. In late May, as the ice broke free from the shore, she waded out into the lake to investigate the floating ice pans. The following day, the ice has dispersed further, forming an opaque mass in the middle of the lake. She has to canoe out to reach it and, dropping her hydrophone into the water, she experiences a new sound: 'air bubbles (trapped in the ice all winter) are floating free to the surface all along the pan's edge, making beautiful, gentle pip-popping sounds – like the lake is raining air'. The little bubbles rise rapidly from the ghostly cloud of ice. As Carmen puts it, spring is 'winning the battle'.

II

It was strange to talk about Greenland at the conference in Iceland: the two countries are very different but people often confuse them. At least my audience in Reykjavik knew that they were not in Greenland. As I began to introduce my work, I wondered what would have happened had I stayed in Upernavik when Grethe had asked me to. Might I have become like that mysterious Frenchman, whose name and history no one knew, who lived on a small island up the coast and appeared in his dinghy every month to stock up on beer and batteries? Would I have witnessed extraordinary things, or been consumed by boredom?

Some people did seem to think I had relocated to the far north.

'I thought you were . . . somewhere cold?' friends would say vaguely when they encountered me at events in London. This was sometimes followed by the question, 'What is it about you and cold places anyway?' Around this time the poems I'd written in Upernavik, and later while missing Upernavik, were published and the book's existence confirmed people's belief that I was elsewhere – somewhere cold. It dawned on me that I had almost managed to achieve what I'd once dreamed of: I had imagined my way back to Greenland.

What is it about cold places, anyway? I needed an answer to the question that didn't require an all-night conversation over several glasses of wine. Was my obsession the sum of the snowy walks in Scotland I had taken as a child? Or was I drawn back to cold places for even more distant reasons, because I was born during a snowstorm, in the winter that became known as England's Winter of Discontent due to the strikes and bad weather?

I never did achieve my dream of a dandelion-clock paper-weight, but when I was six years old I was given a snow globe with a pine forest in it and a log cabin, and an old woman picking up sticks to take into the cabin to light a fire. When I shook it, disproportionately large flakes of snow fell very slowly through whatever viscous liquid the globe contained.

I could watch them for hours: a quick shake of the wrist, then a slow storm.

My father was often away during those years. Once, having returned from a particularly long trip, he told me a bedtime story in countless instalments about how my toys were lost and trying to find their way back home; they had become separated from each other, as well as from me. I don't remember the plot, or even whether the toys found each other again as the nights passed – though I'd like to think the whole point of the exercise was that they did. I only remember one episode clearly, which must have pleased me more than the others: my pale Pierrot was walking through a white-out, with no sense of where he was, when he saw a shadowy figure emerging through the snow. It was an old woman, and she was gathering firewood.

What puzzles me about this story is that the sad clown seemed to be glad that he had stumbled into entrapment within a snow globe. Was this my objective too? As the years passed, the glass dome had developed a crack and air bubbles entered. They floated to the top whichever way I turned the globe, limiting the performance of the falling snow, and bringing my suspension of disbelief in the old woman's world to an end.

I can't give this as an answer.

In October 1917 a group of railway engineers were building a bridge across the Tanana River at Nenana in Alaska, some miles upstream from the point at which it joins the Yukon River and flows onwards into the Bering Sea. They watched the river waters freeze over, and bet $800 on the exact date and time that the ice would break up. A hundred years later, the Nenana Ice Classic competition has become an institution. Every spring a tripod capped with a scarlet flag is planted deep in the ice. It is connected by a cable to a clock on the shore that stops when the tripod tumbles into the water, and gamblers still bet on the day, hour and minute it will fall.

Those who are serious about their stakes in the Nenana Ice Classic competition will research past break-up records carefully. Figures indicate that the ice begins to disperse between 20 April and 20 May. While the average date of break-up is 5 May, the results are becoming more random. But the odds of winning are probably still better than a slot machine – and as Alaska law doesn't allow lotteries, this is the only occasion where residents are encouraged to bet on anything.

There are two ways the river might break up. The first is referred to as a 'mush-out'. It occurs when the ice rots and snow upstream melts gradually into the river, so the water flow increases. This is most likely to happen when temperatures rise above freezing during the day, followed by a freeze at night. The second eventuality is more dramatic. The volume of water flowing downriver increases rapidly, lifting the ice and smashing it. This will happen when there is a sudden warm period in late April or early May, and is more likely after heavy snow.

The annual collapse of the Tanana River tripod has left an uninterrupted record of Alaska's spring climate, a rare resource in a science that needs years of data to draw conclusions. Researchers at the National Snow and Ice Data Center study the charts created by the gamblers. Tanana's results are not unusual: records from a number of northern lakes and rivers (including lakes Baikal in Russia, Kallavesi in Finland and Suwa in the Kiso Mountains of Japan) show significant trends towards later freeze-up and earlier break-up.

I watch the centenary of the Nenana Ice Classic ceremony online, flipping between short home movies of an event that actually lasts hours, even months if you count the anticipation that starts the moment the tripod is first hoisted onto the ice in early March. At nearly 7 metres high, the efforts of many of the town's three hundred inhabitants are needed to erect it. (At least they are already acquainted with the ice on which they'll be putting their money.) The crucial cable that connects the tripod to the clock is festive with bunting so that viewers can see it clearly from the shore. Water has been visible in the centre of the Tanana for several hours before the ice on which the tripod stands starts to edge downriver during the afternoon of 23 April, and crowds begin to gather.

I enjoy Caleb's video most of all those I watch. It has an irresistible exuberance. His camcorder pans the shoreline, filming the backs of other amateur filmmakers also documenting the occasion. 'I'm recording!' his commentary begins. 'There she goes,' he shouts, 'the 2016 ice!' Over the shoulders of onlookers, we see the tripod making stately progress on its pan, but the black-and-white beam stands tall. It looks as though it may be another mush-out year. 'There we go!' Caleb says again, but more doubtfully, as the tripod stalls but remains upright, showing no sign of tripping the cable. There are mutterings from the crowd, most of whom have paid $2.50 to place a bet in the hope of winning the $300,000 jackpot. Is the system fair? Some people claim the ice had already broken up, since everything but the pan the tripod stands on has been swept away. The tripod has almost reached the bridge where the Alaska railroad crosses the river when the bunting tenses and rises from the water, and the ruby pennant flickers in the wind. The tripod begins to tip away from the pan in which it was embedded and – Caleb's video cuts out. I have to turn to another source to discover that at 3.39pm Alaska Standard Time, the tripod sank into the water.

Further south, Thoreau recorded the weather at Walden Pond from 1846 to 1860, and noted that break-up dates varied from 15 March to 18 April. 'This pond never breaks up so soon as the others in the neighborhood,' he wrote, 'on account both of its greater depth and its having no stream passing through it to melt or wear away the ice. It indicates better than any water hereabouts the absolute progress of the season, being least affected by transient changes in temperature.'

When the Massachusetts ponds were 'over-hung by oak woods and solemn pines bent down with snow or bristling with icicles', he got out his skates. Ice created a shortcut. Distances changed. In an essay published in 1843, two years before Franklin set off on his final expedition, Thoreau wrote that Flint's Pond was almost unrecognizable under snow, 'unexpectedly wide and so strange' that it bore comparison to the Arctic, and he imagined the fishermen to be 'sealers or Esquimaux'. A winter walk became an expedition:

> Before night we will take a journey on skates along the course of this meandering river, as full of novelty to one who sits by the cottage fire all the winter's day, as if it were over the polar ice, with Captain Parry or Franklin;

247

following the winding of the stream, now flowing amid hills, now spreading out into fair meadows, and forming a myriad coves and bays where the pine and hemlock over-arch . . . No domain of nature is quite closed to man at all times, and now we draw near to the empire of the fishes. Our feet glide swiftly over unfathomed depths, where in summer our line tempted the pout and perch, and where the stately pickerel lurked in the long corridors formed by the bulrushes. The deep, impenetrable marsh, where the heron waded and bittern squatted, is made pervious to our swift shoes, as if a thousand railroads had been made into it. With one impulse we are carried to the cabin of the muskrat, that earliest settler, and see him dart away under the transparent ice, like a furred fish, to his hole in the bank; and we glide rapidly over meadows where lately 'the mower whet his scythe', through beds of frozen cranberries mixed with meadow-grass. We skate near to where the blackbird, the pewee, and the kingbird hung their nests over the water, and the hornets builded from the maple in the swamp.

Everything Thoreau mentions – with the exception of the muskrat – is a vanished memory of summer. Even the cranberries frozen beneath the ice are already part of the past.

Towards the end of his life, Thoreau read John Evelyn's *Kalendarium Hortense; or, the Gard'ner's Almanac*, first published in 1664, which details garden activities by the season. In addition to his prose writings, he began to consolidate his observations in lists and charts that he too called his 'Kalendar'. The residents of Concord have continued Thoreau's tradition, taking their own annual readings of the environment. In recent years, the break-up of the Walden ice has occurred at least two weeks earlier than in Thoreau's day.

III

I travel to Switzerland in November, and make my way along the shores of Lake Geneva to the Jura mountains. The train passes through vineyards between Bière and Apples, in which vines have been pruned back to their stems, with just one shoot left on each plant for next spring. The train makes a request stop every few minutes; there appear to be no plat- forms: passengers step down onto the tracks and vanish over the fields, muffled up against the snow.

Where the slopes of Mont Tendre begin to climb from the valley, covered in diminishing ranks of conifers, stands one of the world's newest libraries. The architects of the Jan Michalski Foundation envisaged the buildings as an extension of the forest, with concrete pillars leading up to a concrete canopy. The writers who spend time here are accommodated in 'treehouses' hanging from the canopy. These comfortable cabins – each designed by a different architect – are as unlike the haphazard treehouses of my childhood as the concrete col- umns are unlike trees. They call to mind Greenlandic homes, which perch on stilts above the permafrost.

My own cabin is coated in a steel shell, half a centimetre thick, and painted white. From its peak to its base, this metal is punched with an abstract pattern of dots and dashes. It is the only cabin facing the mountain; the four other writers staying here have a view of the Alps.

I break up my working days by exploring the forest. During the first week I begin to map the slopes in my head. The wide lanes which run around Mont Tendre for the loggers' trucks are intersected by footpaths. These steep tracks are barely trodden; on mild days a coppery carpet of larch needles and beech leaves gleams through the snow. Stacks of logs or neat woodpiles help me to keep my bearings. Occasionally I come to a tarmac road and follow its zigzag course up or downhill for a while, taking care not to slip on black ice. The sun never reaches me when I am on these trails, and I only rarely glimpse the landscape beyond the trees. When I return to my cabin and look up towards the woods I have no sense of where I have walked.

At six o'clock each evening the lights in the library are switched off, the staff go home, the writers return to their cabins. Only one figure remains in the courtyard outside the library: a life-size man sculpted in metal. He kneels on the flagstones, looking out over the valley to the horizon where clouds reflect the lights of Lausanne. *Le voleur de mots* by Jaume Plensa is composed of letters, his body a mesh of capitals. They are arranged with deliberate randomness, so that they won't spell any words in any language. Inside his skin, the thief of words is empty. During the night the sculpture is lit from below, projecting faint sans serif shadows onto the surrounding concrete.

The Foundation was built in memory of the man whose name it bears, a continuation of his life's work in literature. As I walk the concrete paths, I think about the dedication to a loved one required to see this project to completion. It will not have been easy to plan: to erect the pillars, to cast the panels of the canopy, to engineer cables to suspend all the pods safely. Just as heavy buildings are designed to seem weightless here, so every burden is taken from a writer's shoulders to enable them to work. My feet rarely need to touch the ground. I am using the time I have been given to finish an English translation of Greenlandic songs collected by the French anthropologist Paul-Émile Victor in the 1930s. The songs were performed at feasts, accompanied by drumming and dancing. Some were used in shamanic rituals to cast spells or cure illness. The spare, repetitive forms were never intended for the page. The singers often introduced the song by expressing a determination to tell the truth in the face of criticism, an attempt to find the right words: saying *imaartiinngilanga nipaartiinngilanga* or 'I will not be silent, I will not be quiet.'

Victor was born in Geneva and grew up in the Jura. It is pure coincidence that my work on the texts he collected should bring me here. I am growing accustomed to a life parcelled into short residencies in other places. To arrive as others depart. I adapt quickly to new living arrangements and new companions – or a lack of them. I don't mind making up a bed another writer has slept in. I travel with only my laptop and a notebook, a power adaptor, a few changes of clothes. I have learnt to operate on Arctic time, living mostly in the present. Being in a place for only a month or two to create and finish new work brings focus; as does becoming acquainted with a new landscape then leaving it behind.

At night, when the winds rush through the mountain dwelling they play an eerie tune on the cavities in the concrete, somewhere between a whistle and a bluster, and an underlying whine like a glass harmonium.

Five huge lamps shaped like clouds are suspended in the library atrium. Based on a design by Frank Gehry, they have been constructed from crumpled sheets of paper. However threatening the storms outside in a winter that is being described as Northern Europe's darkest, the weather within the library is dormant. Paper clouds and secure sprinkler systems. It seems appropriate that the lampshades should be made from the same material as the books we read by their light.

I pick a couple of Hemingway's novels off the shelf. I've heard that Papa created a style which is known as the Iceberg Effect, and I'm curious about how the metaphor manifests itself in literature. Hemingway claimed to have developed the theory in 1923, when he decided to delete the death at the end of the short story 'Out of Season'. He saw books as a contribution to the 'total knowledge' passed on from one generation to the next, and yet that knowledge is sometimes best conveyed by an ellipsis. In *Death in the Afternoon*, he wrote: 'If a writer of prose knows enough about what he is writing about he may omit things that he knows and the reader, if the writer is writing truly enough, will have a feeling of those things as strongly as though the writer had stated them. The dignity of movement of an ice-berg is due to only one-eighth of it being above water.'

This style was influenced by Hemingway's early experience as a journalist, which called for clear reporting without interpretation or flourishes. But his fiction is far from reportage, although he used his own experiences as an ambulance driver during World War I in the classic *A Farewell to Arms*, published by Scribner in 1929. Italy had entered the war on the side of the Allies in May 1915, with the aim of claiming 'unredeemed lands' on its border: the provinces of Trentino and the neighbouring South Tyrol, along with Trieste. The Italian Front stretched west from the Julian Alps to the Ortler Massif near the Swiss border, almost 250 miles. The landscape through which Hemingway's characters march could be the Bernese Alps I see from my desk in the library: 'I looked to the north at the two ranges of mountains, green and dark to the snow-line and then white and lovely in the sun. Then, as the road mounted along the ridge, I saw a third range of mountains, higher snow mountains, that looked chalky white and furrowed, with strange planes, and then there were mountains far off beyond all these that you could hardly tell if you really saw them.'

Snow-line, ice-berg: Hemingway likes breaking up words.

The action of the 'White War' was barely covered by journalists, so inaccessible were the peaks from which Italian soldiers fought to dislodge their Austrian counterparts. In winter, the temperature sometimes fell to -40°C, and the daily snowfall reached at least 6 feet. Both sides employed new approaches in this high-altitude war, such as using cables to transport troops' supplies to the mountain stations. The Austrian Corps of Engineers dug an entire 'ice city' – a complex of tunnels, camps and storerooms – out of a glacier in the Dolomites. Despite such ingenuity, snow sometimes cut off communication and led to poor supplies. Snowblindness was a danger, as were avalanches – known as the 'White Death', and with good reason. During December 1916, heavy snowfall followed by a sudden thaw weakened the snowpacks. On St Lucia's Day an avalanche fell onto Austrian barrack buildings on the Gran Poz summit of Mount Marmolada, and many combatants were buried. Thousands of troops were lost that month in avalanches, some of which may have been deliberately triggered by enemy artillery fire.

After four years of war Italy was victorious at the Battle of Vittorio Veneto, and in 1919 the Treaty of Saint-Germain-en-Laye awarded the contested lands to them. Almost a century on, as glaciers retreat, reminders of the conflict are revealed. In September 2013 two young Austrian men who had been shot on the Presena glacier were found. Their comrades had buried them head-to-toe in a crevasse. A photoraph from the Office for Archaeological Finds shows the two bodies before they were lifted from the ice. The precision with which the ice has been chiselled away contrasts with the disordered bodies merged now in a single mass, the identity of skeletal arms and legs confused by twists of cloth. After the discovery of the unknown soldiers, five hundred people attended a service of memorial in Peio at which their aluminium caskets were placed in unmarked graves. The men's bodies remind me of the spindly sculptures of Alberto Giacometti, who was born just over the border in Switzerland in 1901; he would have been the same age as these soldiers when he left home to attend the School of Fine Arts in Geneva. In sculptures such as *L'Homme qui marche I* (1961), which is engraved on the Swiss 100 franc banknote, Giacometti reduced his models to their sparest elements. So thin are the limbs that in places the armature can't be distinguished from the material it supports, yet the feet are often distorted, heavily pinioned both to the ground and to each other. These figures do not feel slight, the material is rough and richly textured. Giacometti claimed he was trying to represent not human beings, but the shadows they cast.

You could hardly tell if you really saw them. Sometimes light cloud or a heat haze is sufficient to obscure the mountains, but today when I look across the valley from the library they are tinted pink by the setting sun. This weekend the snow will be gleaming on the slopes at Les Diablerets, although it has been a bad year for the ski industry in Switzerland, with predictions from the Institute for Snow and Avalanche Research that snow cover will disappear from the Alps by 2100. Without a snow coating, glacier ice is directly exposed to the sun – and melts quickly.

Last summer the *New York Times* reported an unusual find above Les Diablerets. A ski-lift technician checking the slopes saw a clump of black rocks exposed by the glacier and went to investigate. He soon found they were not rocks. Forensic police specialists were called in, and DNA tests revealed the bodies of Marcelin and Francine Dumoulin, who had left home to feed their cattle on 15 August 1942 and been lost ever since. After their disappearance, rescue teams searched the crevasses for more than two months but found nothing. Their seven children were split up across a number of families, and over the years lost contact with each other.

Images of such sensational finds are swift to appear in the newspapers and on social media. The Tsanfleuron glacier which held the Dumoulins had moved slowly, so the mummified bodies were relatively intact. The photographer has chosen an angle that makes the mangled remains look as dignified as possible. The shoot might almost be promoting the new season of an avant-garde fashion house. Fine auburn hair is sheltered by a hood; the face is in profile, just a gaunt cheekbone visible; indistinct bundles of black cloth are pinioned in dirty ice onto which a fresh layer of snowfall is seeping. Especially poignant are the hobnailed boots, carefully laced up – Marcelin Dumoulin was a shoemaker. The limbs are set at unlikely angles. The photographer has foregrounded the items the couple had with them: a book, wrapped in cloth; a green glass bottle – no longer containing water, wine or milk – and a pocket watch. The Dumoulins are presented in the midst of their lives, with everyday possessions on them, rather than grave goods selected for the afterlife. It is ironic that bodies snatched by the glacier are often better preserved than those prepared by humanity for eternity.

The discovery was a blessing to Marceline, the Dumoulins' daughter, now seventy-nine years old. She was only a toddler when her parents went missing, but she had climbed the glacier three times in later life, always looking for them. She told a reporter from *Le Matin* that it was very important to her to be able to bury her mother and father. She would not wear black: 'I think that white would be more appropriate. It represents hope, which I never lost.'

In 1917 the poet Giuseppe Ungaretti wrote of funerals, following his experience in the White War, 'Snow is truly a sign of mourning; I don't know why the westerners wear black ... Black makes me feel mystery, fear, the absolute, infinity, God, universal life; but white gives me the sense of things ending, the iciness of death.'

The glorious weather soon fades. By midweek, the grey wisps of cloud that have been drifting around the Foundation have transformed into a chill fog. As the cloud thickens I realize how isolated one can be in the hills. I stand on my balcony looking towards Mont Tendre, but even the closest trees can't be seen. A faint smell of woodsmoke comes from the village down in the valley. Without a view, the top-of-the-world feeling soon fades. However, the disappearance of the surroundings brings me a strange calm. Instead of admiring the mountains, I turn my attention to work. Once the snowstorm blows in, I don't go further than the courtyard where the thief of words casts his distorted shadows on the fog.

I'm not the only one keeping close. For two days the blue tit doesn't come to the seedball I've hung up on my balcony. On the third morning it flickers back.

After the storm the paths in the forest are silent and free of footsteps. Snow bends the branches of the fir trees, and even the young beech twigs support at least an inch. I walk much further than I intend to, and it is a while before I realize that snow has completely obscured the paths. What I had thought was a route between trees is just a glade that leads me into a tangle of saplings so I retrace my steps, and begin again. Eventually I sense the track ascending and around a corner the slope falls away so steeply that I am almost level with the summit of the pines. I no longer know where I am. I am amused to think that after all my travels I should get lost in – Switzerland. A flurry of snow falls from a branch, and startles me. I realize that wherever one is lost, it's not a good position to be in. Am I even on the same side of the mountain as before? I know once I reach the valley I'll be able to find my way to the Foundation, or at least shelter, so I turn back and keep selecting descending trails. Far off I can hear a power saw whining – perhaps someone is surreptitiously collecting their Christmas tree. The sky begins to lighten and I sense I have reached the fringes of the forest. I clamber over a fallen tree trunk. The path ahead of me is little used and uncharacteristically dark where meltwater seeps across it. From the angle of the sun I try in vain to work out where in the valley I might be. A few more steps bring me to the edge of the trees, and I emerge right beside the Foundation's pale concrete pillars.

It could be a game of Cluedo. There's a victim but the crime has yet to be solved. The initial police report declares: 'judging by the equipment, this was an Alpine accident going back many years'. On 20 September 1991, the day after the body is found, a criminal investigation is set in motion. The charge is against U.T. (*unbekannte Täter*, persons unknown), and the case is assigned to the judge responsible for all cases in which the names of those concerned begin with the letter 'U', Dr Günter Böhler.

A number of people were alone with the corpse before the police arrived to guard it. First, of course, someone had to discover it: this role was played by the hikers Erika and Helmut Simon. A leathery skull and skeletal shoulders emerged from a glacier in a gulley on the east ridge of the Fineilspitze. The holidaymakers used the last frame in their camera to take a photo in case the body couldn't be found again and descended to the Similaunhütte, a nearby mountain refuge, to report it. Within hours, word spread and others climbed up to see the corpse for themselves: the chef from the refuge; the famous mountaineer Reinhold Messner, who just happened to be walking in the hills that day; Markus Pirpamer, the young man who ran the refuge, and even his father Alois, who had run it before him, now a hotelier down in the valley. A helicopter brought archaeologist Dr Konrad Spindler and forensic expert Dr Rainer Henn. Later, there was the press. The isolated slopes were unusually well-trodden.

The lower half of the body was embedded in the ice, but the glacier melted rapidly. In the 24 hours after the body's discovery, a further 10 centimetres was revealed. During the short hours of daylight there were several unsuccessful attempts to reclaim the corpse, which now lay in meltwater. A pneumatic chisel of the kind used by the mountain rescue service to free people from the ice was worked around the pelvis, but the tool slipped and entered the flesh, damaging it further. The ice seemed to want to reclaim the corpse and froze around it again. Although the mountaineering season was over, Pirpamer kept the Similaunhütte open as Police HQ. After four days of work in harsh blizzards, the corpse was free. It was placed in a transparent body bag within an orange recovery bag, suspended from a helicopter and flown down the mountain to the resort of Vent. There it was transferred to a wooden coffin and driven by hearse to the Institute of Forensic Medicine at Innsbruck University.

I read Konrad Spindler's account of the days following the discovery, in which the learned professor of pre- and proto-history examined the corpse. The objects found with the body suggested it was not contemporary: a fur quiver and feathered arrows; a sloe berry; a white marble bead. There was a grand axe with copper head and yew handle; a birch-bark pannier containing charcoal wrapped in maple leaves (still green), used to carry a light carefully from one fireplace to the next. A couple of ibex bones indicative of a last meal.

What if a storm in the Sahara had not scattered dark yellow dust across Europe, covering the white snowfields and causing them to absorb the sun's warmth? What if the fine weather that warmed the glacier had not also decided Erika and Helmut Simon to change their plans and spend a second day in the mountains? What if they had not detoured from the recommended route that September morning? The body would never have been found. It would have decayed swiftly in the sunshine, while fragments of birch bark and cinders blew away on the wind.

After weeks of enjoying an empty diary, my only commitment putting words on paper, I have an appointment with the Foundation's photographer at nine o'clock on Tuesday morning. I find Tonatiuh Ambrosetti standing in the sunny courtyard, holding a demitasse and looking towards the mountains, which are once again shrouded by mist rising from Lake Geneva.

He asks where I would like my portrait to be set. 'Where are you most comfortable? Where do you spend your time?'

'The library,' I say. 'Actually, no. The forest.'

I don't like having my photograph taken. Worse, overnight a spot has appeared on my philtrum. Tonatiuh senses my discomfort. 'People think a photograph has to be everything, it has to be forever. But it is acting. It is just this moment: an illusion you and I will make together.'

Like an actor, I have brought props — a hat and a scarf. Tonatiuh insists on carrying them for me, even though he's already burdened with his case and tripod. He tramps ahead through the snow to select the best spot. I confide my adventure in the forest to him.

'You should always have a map with you.' He looks serious, but maybe he's just considering the composition as he sets up the tripod. He indicates that I should move slightly to the left, by holding his hands just so. I double-check I have understood him before I move. Once he is happy with my position, he holds the light meter against my cheek and my chest.

'Woah! It is like a sunny day at the shore.' As he walks back to his tripod he says, 'This sun will cast good shadows. The shadows will be strong but that will be interesting.'

I stand very still, and focus on a distant larch tree, its golden needles blazing among the dark conifers. The thaw has begun, and there is an occasional flurry as saplings that were weighed down by snow spring back up.

I can hear a woodpecker drilling dead wood. 'I'm looking for the woodpecker.'

As the sun rises in the sky it passes behind the tree trunks, meaning the seaside light doesn't hold for long. My hands are still cold, and getting colder.

'Pretend you are walking towards *that* tree,' Tonatiuh peers round the camera, 'and you suddenly hear the woodpecker *here*.'

'You are the woodpecker?'

'Yes, I am the woodpecker.' He smiles.

He doesn't warn me when he is going to take a photo –
there's no countdown, no 'cheese'. Although I'm looking
away, after a while I find I can predict the moment from the
tiny sounds I hear in the stillness – something inserted into the
folding camera, something removed. Pause. Click. This capture of the body reminds me less of a theatrical performance
than of a medical test – I recall a CT scan of my brain, sliding
head-first on an examination table into a tunnel. No, don't
think of bad things, it might show on the film. I raise my chin.

The mist is coming more strongly now up the path, as if it
is chasing us into the forest from the valley.

'Mist, fog, what is the difference?' he asks. 'Fog is polluted?'

'Well, sometimes. But mainly, it's about their . . . thickness.
Polluted fog in a city is smog.'

'Smog.' He tries out the word. 'Thank you.'

He is silent between shots, and I try to concentrate on looking natural. 'We will take one last one in the mist,' Tonatiuh
says. 'You will be in shadow – but I think it will be good.'

As we walk back to the Foundation, I ask if I am free to
use the photos.

'Yes of course, there's no point taking photos if no one
sees them.'

Once Spindler confirms the age of the body – 5,000 years –
it is no longer treated as a crime victim. More paperwork is
required. The body becomes a 'national monument'. The
iceman is older than the pyramids, older than Stonehenge, and
his mummified flesh becomes a kind of protected landscape. A
monument needs a name, and archaeological finds are usually
named after the place of discovery. But here the archaeologists

filling in the forms face a quandary: the place the corpse was discovered had no name on the maps. It is decided to call the glacier find '*Homo tirolensis* from the Hauslabjoch', although it is now acknowledged that the glacier was not quite on the Hauslabjoch – it was nearer to the Tisenjoch. Next, how to describe the object for the 'find category' on the form? The archaeologists settled on 'glacier corpse'. Of course, unofficial names were bandied about – the French media called the iceman 'Hibernatus', after the film in which an old man who has been frozen in the ice at the North Pole comes to life again. The name which stuck was coined by Viennese reporter Karl Wendl, who arrived at it through a contraction of Ötztal (the region) and 'yeti'. 'Ötzi' was first used in a morning edition of the *Vienna Arbeiter-Zeitung* on Thursday 26 September. Ötzi had been a week above the ice.

As archaeologists know, once you excavate a site you alter it forever. The glacier corpse has been preserved, conserved, carbon-dated, rehydrated. It has been X-rayed and displayed. Researchers have analysed Ötzi's genome sequence, his fertility and his propensity to tooth decay. The only source of information on Ötzi's story is his own body and the artefacts found with it; and since his are the only remains surviving from that millennium, he is also fated to be the example by which all life in that era will be judged.

Grains in his clothing suggest Ötzi left the valley following a harvest, meaning he was buried by the ice around the same time of year he was discovered. He was walking the main route across the Alps, coming from wooded settlements, where he collected the leaves in his fire-lighting kit. His heavy cloak and grass shoes imply his ascent into the mountains was planned. For as long as anyone can remember, the shepherds of this region have taken their flocks across steep couloirs and snow fields to the mountain pastures in June, and at the end of the summer they bring them down from the hills. Ötzi carried a shepherd's tools. But his stomach was found to contain layers of pollen characteristic of different mountain elevations: hornbeam, then conifer, then hornbeam – showing that he had climbed up then down the mountain in quick succession, before his final ascent.

Why would a shepherd who had brought his sheep down from the hills at the end of the summer go back into the mountains in poor weather, especially when weakened by injury? (A few days before his death, Ötzi had sustained a deep cut to his right hand.) Perhaps Ötzi had encountered conflict on his return to the valley and was retreating to a known place of safety. It was originally believed he had been overtaken by a storm and frozen to death, but there is evidence that he was confronted by an enemy in the mountains. In 2001 a scientist looking at an X-ray noticed a white blotch on the film, a sign of something denser than bone. A flint arrowhead was embedded in Ötzi's shoulder; it had been fired by someone standing close behind him.

The elements of his last meal – einkorn wheat and ibex meat – reflect that Ötzi lived at a time of great change. As well as hunting animals as they had always done, humans were beginning to farm grains. Farming would one day lead society to increasing conflict over land and resources, but for Ötzi the only borders would have been those created by impassable mountains or seas. If the high mountains were a neutral space in 3300 BCE, they were not by the twentieth century. When the border was drawn up between Italy and Austria following the Treaty of Saint-Germain-en-Laye, the watershed was used to define the frontier. However, this ridge lay under a glacier, making it impossible to determine its exact location. Over time, as the ice dispersed, it transpired the border had been drawn too far to the north – although it remains valid to this day under international law. The gully in which the iceman was found lay on the Austrian-facing side of the Alps, but an official investigation of the area concluded that he was on Italian territory. 'In the high mountains, who cares about the exact line of the frontier?' Konrad Spindler asks, before recalling how fiercely the two nations competed for ownership of the corpse.

From the moment the iceman emerged from the glacier he was a media star. The corridors of the department of Forensic Medicine at Innsbruck University were packed with journalists and reporters in the first days of the find, and its telephone switchboard broke down. Better communications were required: more telephones were ordered, more fax machines, more photocopiers. In addition to the newspaper reports and cartoons about Ötzi, children's stories were published, and books claiming it was all a hoax. Two years before the millennium, the car manufacturer Suzuki created 'the Vitara "Ötzi" for all those valuing independence'; the vehicle promised to be 'as weather resistant, as unaffected by sun, rain, snow and ice as Ötzi'. Recently an asteroid has been named after Ötzi. Asteroid No. 5803 in the great asteroid belt, which is invisible to the naked eye, travels the sun at a slightly elliptical orbit, taking 4.3 years to complete its trajectory.

Ötzi's mummified body is now on display in the South Tyrol Museum of Archaeology in Bolzano, a museum dedicated to him. He rests on a glass shelf in a cold cell, behind glass. The public view him through a small window, about the size of the *Mona Lisa*. Only one person can look in at a time. He lies face up, but the viewer cannot quite see his face. It is theatre of course: the light that shines on him is no ordinary fluorescent bulb, but reminiscent of a cool blue glacier. He lies on precision scales at -6°C and at 99 per cent humidity. He is regularly sprayed with sterile water to prevent loss of his natural moisture.

He is such a popular attraction that a new museum is under construction to allow for more visitor capacity and, twenty-five years after the find, a feature film is due for release. 'Neither scientific research nor archaeological investigation have so far been able to explain what exactly happened before his death, and why this man, who 5,000 years later was to be named "Ötzi", was murdered,' intones the press release. 'The film *Iceman* fills in the missing pieces in the story of a dramatic event which took place on the Tisenjoch one day in early summer some 3,300 years BCE.'

The film premiere is 30 November. Tomorrow. Living in central Europe rather than on the margins must have gone to my head, for I consider making a trip to South Tyrol to attend the screening. I type the address of the cinema into a search engine and look for directions from Switzerland to Bolzano. I'd have to travel across the Alps. A six-hour drive, via Milan and Verona – but I can't drive. I click on the pedestrian icon. Walking, 108 hours, via Bern: 'This route includes roads that are closed in winter'.

I will have to wait for a wider release to see actor Jürgen Vogel's interpretation of Ötzi. But there are other manifestations. The South Tyrol Museum commissioned a life-size model of the iceman. Now, there are two Ötzis in the museum – the original and a recreation. The full-length figure uses the latest in forensic mapping technology based on three-dimensional images of the skull, as well as infrared images. The reconstruction shows a prematurely old man, with deep-set eyes, sunken cheeks, a furrowed face and ungroomed beard and hair. It is one thing to show features, but quite another thing to capture a character, as this statue has managed to do.

The exposure of Ötzi, like the photography of the other bodies which have emerged from glaciers, makes me uneasy. What are the ethics of displaying human remains, long hidden from the world's view, without consent? What can be learnt from such voyeurism? I remember the Greenlandic mummies at the National Museum in Nuuk. 'They're my relations,' Thrine had said, possessively and with sadness. She won't visit the museum: one visits living relatives, and respectfully buries the dead. The clinical context in which Ötzi rests now would surely be alien to him. Scientists have discovered much about this Neolithic man (even his DNA has been extracted from his bones and sequenced in a Boston lab) but what beliefs he may have held remain a mystery. Would the procedures enacted on his corpse fit in with his own view of an afterlife?

It's not surprising that there are rumours of an Ötzi curse. Since that palindromic discovery date (19.9.91), five of the men who worked on the body have met unfortunate ends.

Forensic expert Dr Henn, who placed the corpse in a body bag with his bare hands, died in a road accident on his way to a conference at which he planned to discuss Ötzi. Kurt Fritz, the experienced mountain guide who had led Dr Henn to the peak, died in a freak avalanche in 1993, the only fatality among his group. In October 2004 Helmut Simon failed to return from a hike and was found eight days later; he had fallen 300 feet to his death and his body was frozen under a sheet of ice. Even Konrad Spindler, after writing many accounts of the iceman, dies – although from a medical condition. Isn't the truth that those who walk in the mountains are statistically more likely to die in the mountains?

Ötzi would have been unaware, as he died – with no one to bury his body – that he wouldn't be forgotten. Today a cairn marks the gully in the mountains where Ötzi's body was discovered. A cairn of stones is a sign of achievement for climbers. Yet in the Arctic it has a different significance. There, where the ground is too hard to be dug, on account of permafrost or rocks, it is the traditional means for making a grave; a mound of stones both conceals the remains and memorializes the dead. The structure is also seen in the *inunnguaq* – a stone monument which evokes the shape of a human body. An *inunnguaq* can be placed on a headland to mark the disappearance or death of a person. Knud Rasmussen describes an Inuit community's response to a drowning: 'The men ... sorrowed so deeply over the loss of their women that they built cairns up on the shore, just as many cairns as there were women lost. They did this because they wanted the souls of the drowned women to be on dry land not out in the wet sea.'

IV

It used to be that the only red buildings in Greenland were those of the church and the traders: the infirmary was yellow; the salt house was white. The wooden buildings erected by Danish missionaries were painted with pigments mixed with seal oil, and over time a colour code was established, which made it easier to find one's way around in poor visibility. The tradition continues at Aappaluttoq mine, which opened its red buildings in 2017 on the ice cap near Nuuk. Prospectors extracting drill cores from the hard grey rock at Aappaluttoq have found rubies and pink sapphire running through the mica and amphibole. The transparent pink crystals may be the oldest rubies in the world. It's safe to bet they won't stay in Greenland for display.

Yet it is too early to know if the rubies will be a going concern. Mines come and go more swiftly than one might expect in Greenland. Many enterprises fail due to lack of investment or disappointing prospects and even successful mines are tapping finite resources. A gold mine which opened to great excitement at Nalunaq closed, after only a few years' operation, in 2013.

Other materials such as lead and zinc and the seventeen rare earth metals may be less romantic than gold and gemstones, but as competition for the world's resources hots up, they have the potential to be equally profitable. Not long ago, after an event at a literary festival, an elderly gentleman handed me a slip of paper before excusing himself modestly. Back in the hotel I unfolded the note and found a map of Greenland, with an 'X' marking a spot south of Upernavik and the name

---

'BLACK ANGEL MINE'. There was an email address. Who wouldn't respond to such intrigue? I sent an email, and I was invited for lunch.

Tom turns out to be a Geordie geologist, eager to compare notes on the north. Once we've covered our shared fondness for Newcastle-upon-Tyne, the conversation turns to the Arctic. He tells me that his very first job after graduating in the 1970s was at the Black Angel Mine, named for an angel-shaped zinc outcrop high on the mountain. The Pouilly-Fumé pairs perfectly with the goat cheese tart as Tom reminisces about the extreme conditions in which he worked, and the challenge of getting building materials from the port in the fjord to the drilling zone using cables and a helicopter. The mine was active for seventeen years. Now under new ownership it has reopened using a Greenlandic name, Maarmorilik. It remains 'a geologically favourable target area', according to a new promotional film made by ARC Arctic Resources. I can understand Tom's love of rocks and minerals and his fascination with the deep time which forged them. I'm also impressed by his pragmatic approach to the world.

Greenland's warming temperatures make underground exploration increasingly viable as the permafrost – soil that has been frozen for thousands of years – begins to melt. Mining and drilling bring new opportunities to the Arctic, money that might enable Greenland to achieve financial independence from Denmark at last – although the country's fortunes would then be tied to the vagaries of multinational corporations instead. In 2013, the government granted four times the number of exploration licences approved a decade before. The same year, after a debate that divided the country, parliament voted narrowly to repeal a 1988 ban on uranium mining. (Uranium is a radioactive metal mainly used for nuclear fuel and weapons.) The repeal has allowed an open pit mine sourcing uranium at Narsaq in the south of Greenland. There was outrage up and down the coast; Ole even went so far as to wear a button badge. Protestors fear that as well as bringing welcome jobs to areas that are suffering economic hardship, open source uranium mines will generate radioactive dust which could spread over land and sea.

One secret of successful gambling is to bet low. Another is to play a predetermined number of wins. Never forget that everything that's won can be more easily lost.

It takes me a few weeks to realize that the irregular perforations in my cabin wall are Morse code. I decide to translate my home. I stand outside in the snow, jotting down the sequence of dots and dashes. I look up a history of Morse in the library to get a crib sheet for the code and I discover that it was not originally sent as short and long tone pulses over radio. The dots and dashes were punched onto paper tape, the intention being that they would be read. The system only became sound-based when telegraph operators noticed that they could transcribe the clicks made by the apparatus directly, making the tape unnecessary.

The letter-by-letter decoding of Morse is much more laborious than the work I've been doing on the Greenlandic songs. There is no punctuation; I don't even know where the gaps between the words fall. Gradually I impose order on the stream of letters, spelling out a quotation in French. I realize it's a translation of a work originally in English, although were it to be translated back again, it would only faintly echo the original. The dots and dashes spell out Thoreau's words, written in his own cabin beside Walden Pond: 'The very simplicity and nakedness of man's life in the primitive ages imply this advantage, at least, that they left him still but a sojourner in nature. When he was refreshed with food and sleep, he contemplated his journey again.'

Epilogue

THE ICE-HOUSE

Walden Pond, Massachusetts, USA
The oceans

Íss er árbörkr
ok unnar þak
ok feigra manna fár.
glacies jöfurr.

Ice is bark of rivers
and roof of the wave
and destruction of the doomed.

Old Icelandic Rune poem

'We sure as hell are screwing up this planet,' says Abigail Rorer, driving her SUV along the leafy New England lanes to Concord. Sometimes Abigail likes to talk like she's from a fictional Wild West, not genteel Philadelphia. I've heard that a few generations back there was an opera singer in her family. Yet if this artist has inherited anyone's mantle, it is that of the Dalziel Brothers. A wood engraver who spends hours each day hunched over a magnifier in her studio, she's also a dedicated observer of the natural world. Years ago Abigail fell in love with Thoreau's descriptions of his environment, the ponds and vernal pools of her adopted Massachusetts and she too, 50 miles west and 150 years in his wake, has been recording the wildlife – not in words, but in images.

I have been working with Abigail in her studio for a couple of weeks. She's making a wood engraving of a fox to illustrate Thoreau's account of a winter walk. My job is to set his words in metal type, then print the work on a handpress. As I fit the tiny lead letters into the composing stick, tight enough that they will stay true when the ink rollers pass across their faces, I consider the course the words have taken to reach this point. Our publication may be printed with the same technology used in Thoreau's own time, but we've sourced the text from an online edition of his work.

As a reward for my labour Abigail is taking me on a jaunt to Walden Pond, so I can see where Thoreau lived and wrote. Now the only trace of the cabin is a circumference of stones among the trees – his home would have been almost the same dimensions as my Swiss treehouse, but rather less well-equipped.

This idyllic spot, now protected, was once exploited. As we walk along the shore, Abigail tells me that it wasn't just wild-life Thoreau saw from the window of his cabin. During the winter of 1846–47 he was surprised to observe on the pond 'a hundred men at work like busy husbandmen, with teams and horses and apparently all the implements of farming'. They were cultivating the ice. At the turn of the nineteenth century, the entrepreneur Frederic Tudor had realized that the ponds around Boston froze quickly due to the brisk autumns and cold winters, and he decided to 'farm' the ice while the real farmers rested at their firesides. He created a business based on the scarcity and desirability of ice in the days before artificial refrigeration; Thoreau found himself living in the heart of an ice factory.

Thoreau wrote of Walden: 'It is earth's *eye*; looking into which the beholder measures the depth of his own nature.' Tudor only saw the translucent lens coating that eye, the ice – described as 'arctic crystal' – which was known for its purity. Thoreau observed its colours:

> the Walden ice, seen near at hand, has a green tint, but at a distance is beautifully blue, and you can easily tell it from the white ice of the river, or the merely greenish ice of some ponds, a quarter of a mile off. Sometimes one of those great cakes slips from the ice-man's sled into the village street, and lies there for a week like a great emerald, an object of interest to all passers.

Like Thoreau, Tudor kept a journal. He observed the temperature and behaviour of the ice daily, recording the data in his 'ice diarie'. When customers were sceptical that the ponds could be relied upon to supply ice, he would reassure them with a favourite proverb: 'Winter never rots in the sky'. During the winter of 1827–28, he wrote gleefully: 'The frost covers the windows, the wheels creek [*sic*], the boys run, winter rules, and $50,000 worth of ice now floats for me upon Fresh Pond.' But winter did not 'rule' for long that year, and Tudor struggled to meet demand. He was not to know that the Little Ice Age was drawing to a close. By the middle of the century, there would be 'open winters' when the ponds did not freeze at all.

The ice had to be strong enough to hold both the men who worked upon it and the implements of their industry. Tudor's associate Nathaniel Wyeth had designed an ice-plough. Horses, shod with spikes as they were for winter roads, dragged a scribe over the ice; one end of the scribe sliced a section while the other scored a guideline for the next block. The neat oblongs of ice could then be prised free and edged along channels to the shore. Special tools were required to separate and manoeuvre the frozen sheets. Cold hands were sometimes clumsy. The ice-saws and grapples, the snow planes, hand ploughs and ice-hooks, the fork-splitting bars and the stricking-under bars are still being dredged from the beds of the ponds today.

Once Tudor had demonstrated how lucrative ice could be, he had to fight off competition. A map of Fresh Pond was drawn up by a Boston surveyor at the height of the trade in 1841 to show 'the Division Lines of the Proprietors Extended into the Pond and defining the right to the same'. It had become necessary to fix ownership of the surface of the pond on paper. The system was simple: all those who had rights to property along the shore got a share of the ice. 'Fred. Tudor' occupied the entire southern side of the pond, beside which the Concord Turnpike ran; his portion was valued at almost 50 acres. Much of the rest of the pond's surface was apportioned to the Wyeth family, with more modest allowances for the farmers Reed, Coolidge, Bright and Bird. The map, dissected by lines of ownership, resembles modern maps of Antarctica in which territorial claims radiate out from the South Pole.

The elaborate ritual of the ice harvest was only the beginning of the ice's journey. The blocks of ice cut by the scribe could be stored side by side leaving a minimal surface area exposed to the air. Even so, the railwaymen on the new branch line to Boston complained of their unusual cargo:

> Its demands are peremptory, and if not instantly obeyed, it weeps itself away . . . It is wet and heavy, sharp and cutting, and without grit or grain enough to keep it quiet, it is ever uneasy, and beating itself against the car and tearing off its covering . . . while today we are thus over-worked, tomorrow and next day it may give us nothing to do.

The railways transported the ice to many cities. A contemporary Baedeker for travellers to the US notes that the 'musical tinkling' of iced water was a characteristic sound of American hotels. Yet Tudor had always conceived the ice trade as an international enterprise. He knew his best markets would be in 'Tropical Climates'. The plan to ship ice across the oceans was seen by many as a joke: merchants would not charter a vessel for Tudor's first venture to Martinique in 1806, and insurance was not to be had. It took all his persistence to find a boat to transport the first cargo. Several tonnes melted on the journey, but enough reached its destination for the venture to be worth repeating. The ice from the ponds of Massachusetts was destined to travel across the Atlantic Ocean to India.

In the Concord Museum, Abigail and I admire a set of a dozen pencils, made by J. Thoreau & Co. The label, with its conventional border of printed fleurons, reads: 'Refined lead pencils | Hard, medium, and soft | Possessing the various qualities required in the Arts'. It's said that Thoreau improved the design of the pencils during the brief period that he worked for the family business, but judging by the journals on display he preferred to write with a quill pen. It is in ink that his urgent, angular copperplate races over the pages between the marbled covers of his notebooks.

Abigail calls in at the bank, and is given some free root beer lollipops by the teller. On the drive back we suck them down to the little papery sticks as we discuss the future. Abigail is planning to sell the books we're printing at a trade fair in Oxford in a few months' time. 'You have to find somewhere to live so I can come stay when I visit,' she tells me. 'I can't afford those English hotels.'

She's joking, but the idea of settling down is attractive. What began as a drive for economy has become a habitual restlessness. My quest for freedom has resulted in its own constraints. Even Thoreau left the woods eventually, his desire to 'live deliberately' tempered by his sense of obligation to his friends.

Although Thoreau was not an advocate of international travel, preferring to examine the environment close to his home, he benefitted from the global exchange of ideas. Louis Agassiz passed through Boston on a lecture tour the same winter that Thoreau observed the ice being harvested on Walden Pond, and the glaciologist's assistant, James Cabot, brought a copy of the *Bhagavad Gita* to Concord. Thoreau was excited to think of the 'stupendous' philosophy he was reading having crossed the oceans, just as the Walden ice was to do, creating an elemental connection with people in far-off places: 'our buckets as it were grate together in the same well'. The wise words of the ancient text seemed a fair exchange for the ice itself:

> Thus it appears that the sweltering inhabitants of Charleston and New Orleans, of Madras and Bombay and Calcutta, drink at my well. I lay down the book and go to my well for water, and lo! there I meet the servant of the Bramin ... The pure Walden water is mingled with the sacred water of the Ganges. With favoring winds it is wafted past the site of the fabulous islands of Atlantis and the Hesperides ... and, floating by Ternate and Tidore and the mouth of the Persian Gulf, melts in the tropic gales of the Indian seas, and is landed in ports of which Alexander only heard the names.

The Walden ice did go to Madras and Bombay and Calcutta, although there it was enjoyed by the governing elites of the British East India Company rather than by Brahmins. Frederic Tudor had noticed that ships travelling from Boston across the Atlantic to Indian ports were loaded with ballast, which could be conveniently (and cheaply) replaced with cargoes of ice. To satisfy his creditors after a catastrophic coffee speculation, he decided to take one more risk. The *Tuscany* sailed on 12 May 1833 with many tonnes of ice on board. Tudor wrote to its captain: 'As soon as you have arrived in latitude 12 degrees north you will have carried ice as far south as it has ever been carried before, and your Ship becomes a discovery ship'. By contrast to the ships setting sail in search of a Northwest Passage, this captain did not want the ice to melt.

As the *Tuscany* approached the coast of India four months later, the Board of Customs, Salt and Opium authorized the landing of the cargo duty-free to allow swift entry for the rapidly melting luxury. Such a waiver was unprecedented. Furthermore, the *India Gazette* reported, the Board directed that 'every facility may be afforded in the Customs' Department for [the ice's] conveyance, without delay or impediment, from the ship to the godown or place of store'. The crew were even permitted to unload their cargo overnight, to save it from the sun's heat. By morning the ice was already in use. The journalist Joachim Stocqueler, one of the first to board the *Tuscany*, wrote:

> How many Calcutta tables glittered that morning with lumps of ice! The butter dishes were filled; the goblets of water were converted into miniature Arctic seas with icebergs floating on the surface. All business was suspended until noon, that people might rush about to pay each other congratulatory visits and devise means for perpetuating the ice-supply. Everybody invited everybody to dinner, to taste of claret and beer cooled by the importation.

Newspapers offered advice on the best means of collecting and transporting the ice while keeping it as cool as possible ('a woollen wrapper or a basket of rice-chaff') and warned of substances, such as saltpetre or salt, which might endanger its integrity. Preserving the ice supply for as long as possible was a matter of common concern. As well as cooling claret and beer, and preserving perishable foods, ice was used to soothe the brows of invalids. It was thus claimed that the ice sustained life itself, as well as a certain colonial lifestyle. Within two years an ice-house had been built in Calcutta.

Yet some received the merchandise with scepticism. Ice is the nemesis of a foolish adjutant crane – a scavenging bird – who unwittingly swallows a chunk of it in Rudyard Kipling's story 'The Undertakers':

> Immediately [says the crane] I was afflicted with an excessive cold which, beginning in my crop, ran down to the extreme end of my toes, and deprived me even of speech, while the boatmen laughed at me. Never have I felt such cold. I danced in my grief and amazement till I could recover my breath and then I danced and cried out against the falseness of this world; and the boatmen derided me till they fell down. The chief wonder of the matter, setting aside that marvellous coldness, was that there was nothing at all in my crop when I had finished my lamentings!

Kipling intended the crane's indiscriminate gobbling as a moral on the consequences of greed. But Tudor was not lamenting: he and his partners each made $3,300 on the pioneer shipment of ice to Calcutta, and the trade with India was to redeem him from ruin. Some commentators even compared Boston's ice to the gold of California. Tudor began to export ice to Europe, China and Australia, and by the time he died in 1864 he was America's first post-Revolution millionaire.

The Revolutionary War had ended on 3 September 1783, and George Washington resigned as commander-in-chief of the US army a few days before Christmas. With time on his hands, he looked to improve his estate at Mount Vernon. He sought advice on constructing an ice-house from his fellow patriot Robert Morris, who responded on 15 June 1784 with a description of his own:

> The Door for entering this Ice house faces the north, a Trap Door is made in the middle of the Floor through which the Ice is put in and taken out. I find it best to fill with Ice which as it is put in should be broke into small pieces and pounded down with heavy Clubs or Battons such as Pavers use, if well beat it will after a while consolidate into one solid mass and require to be Cut out with a Chizell or Axe. I tried Snow one year and lost it in June. The Ice keeps until October or November and I believe if the Hole was larger so as to hold more it would keep untill Christmas.

'P.S.' he adds. 'Thatch is the best covering for an Ice House.' Washington's diary for January 1785 mentions the preparation of two wells for 'the reception of ice', one indoors and one on his estate. By the end of the month both had been filled with ice. In an entry for June, Washington laments: 'Opened the Well in my Cellar in which I laid up a store of Ice but there was not the smallest particle remaining.' The outdoor well had a larger store, and it was this ice-house that he worked to improve the following autumn. In subsequent years, his diary records ice gathering during January. The ice was taken from the frozen Potomac, only an hour's paddle downriver from the mudflats where the airport that once bore his name would be built. The river that now guides pilots previously cooled presidential drinks.

I stare at the map on the screen in the seatback. It feels like an out-of-body experience to watch the tiny white aircraft – the very one that contains me – twitch pixel by pixel up the coast of America. The flight path arcs towards the tip of Greenland, edging the Atlantic, rather than crossing the ocean directly towards Heathrow. So much for travelling transatlantic. I know the route is shorter this way, but it makes it look as if the pilot is as nervous as I am about flying over water. Before the sun disappears, I am reassured by a glimpse of the ice-covered peaks which signalled my first investigations into cold, many thousands of feet below.

A book published in Amsterdam in 1665 – *Mundus Subterraneus* – contains a map depicting an unusual island in the middle of the Atlantic Ocean. (At some point during the book's existence, the oil in the printer's ink began to seep through the paper, so that the text printed on the verso of the map can be seen, a faint moire pattern of mirror-image words.) The great Dutch mariners would never have dreamed of setting a course for Atlantis, even though it was marked on such maps, for its first mention in surviving records (by Plato around 360 BCE) details only the moment of its vanishing:

> But afterwards there occurred violent earthquakes and floods; and in a single day and night of misfortune all your warlike men in a body sank into the earth, and the island of Atlantis in like manner disappeared in the depths of the sea.

Despite its disappearance, cultural references to Atlantis persisted, from accounts by classical writers like Plato, through to its use as a representative 'fabulous island' in *Walden*, and contemporary fiction and film. As with the legendary Thule, there are many theories about its origin, its location and the reasons it sank beneath the waves. Some writers even suggest that Atlantis and Thule were the same place.

One of the most recent incarnations of Atlantis was brought into being by the American artist Robert Smithson. In 1969, five hundred years after *Mundus Subterraneus*, Smithson created a scale model of the sunken island in broken glass at a site in New Jersey, and then – as was his practice – made installation sketches, templates to show curators how to recreate the work at other locations in the future. I'd recently seen a recreation of *Map of Broken Glass (Atlantis)* on my travels and, curious about Smithson's way of working, I'd looked up the installation sketches online. The drawings are rough and immediate, one giving a bird's-eye view of jagged glass, much like the icy mountains below me. 'SEVERAL TONNES OF BROKEN CLEAR NEEDED' read Smithson's instructions in scribbled block capitals. 'TRACE OUTLINES (APPROX.) ON FLOOR LIGHTLY THAN [*sic*] FILL IT IN.' There's a side view too, to convey the desired height: 'BALANCE BIG PIECES AGAINST EACH OTHER, USE SMALLER PIECES TO SHORE THEM UP.' The big pieces are shored up by the smaller ones: Smithson understood how an artistic reputation is built. Knowing his works would erode with time, he made films and took aerial photographs to document them. Still, I get the feeling the installation sketches were an afterthought – Smithson's best-known works are not to be found in museums. *Spiral Jetty*, a large earthwork made from basalt rocks, salt crystals and mud, curls out into Utah's Great Salt Lake. He began construction on the jetty in April 1970 – the same year that Earth Day was inaugurated. It was his first work requiring the purchase of land rights, and he had difficulty finding contractors willing to be involved in such an audacious project. At the time it was made, *Spiral Jetty* was submerged in the lake. In recent years, drought has caused the water to recede far from the shore, and the jetty is visible for long periods. Where the outline of the artwork was once lapped by mineral-rich lake water, pale sand now blows across it.

Smithson was a believer in entropy, the natural movement of all things from order to disorder. Were he alive today – he died in 1973, his plane crashing after it banked too sharply as he was surveying a site for a new work in Texas – would he be surprised by how much the jetty has already changed? The shards of glass in Smithson's *Map* remind me of the fragments of ice with which Kay tried to spell out 'eternity' in the Snow Queen's castle, but rather than laying them flat to make letters, he piles them up like a treasure hoard.

An island held up by its own silica shore; mountains that must fight against falling. Only when I see Smithson's sketches do I become aware of the tension of the material in the gallery, caught between stasis and collapse. A transparent evocation of an island that is no longer visible. Strange that it should be a lake diminished by drought and a disordered pile of debris on display in a former biscuit factory, rather than the ice caps themselves, that should bring home to me the relationship between two subjects that have obsessed me, ice and books. Smithson's works reveal both the lure of cultural storehouses and their limitations. *Spiral Jetty* is more eloquent in its muta-tion under natural forces, than the controlled, static *Map*. This beautiful, turbulent heap of glass – a record of something already lost, with the potential for reproduction in unlimited locations – makes me think of the moon landings that had so recently occurred when the work was made, and humanity's dream of building colonies on other planets. However transitory our lives are, we see ourselves as poised between states: between frozen ice and fluid water, between past histories and the future homes for which we are still searching.

Islands may sink, and the seas may rise above them, but they can still provide the ground on which to anchor new islands. Average sea level rise is calculated by NASA at 3.41 millimetres per year, due to the expansion of water as it warms and the melting of the polar ice caps. If this trend continues New York, Miami, Washington and other US coastal cities will suffer the loss of iconic properties. Countries like the Netherlands, Bangladesh and the Philippines will lose significant amounts of land. The populations of some island nations are already becoming climate refugees. In recent years, the inhabitants of the Marshall Islands (a Pacific island nation which includes Bikini Atoll), finding their homes no longer habitable, have begun to resettle in Arkansas. In a statement to the United Nations in 2015 Prime Minister Gaston Browne of the Caribbean state of Antigua and Barbuda placed the blame on 'the excesses of larger and more powerful countries, who will not bend from their abuse of the world's atmosphere, even at the risk of eliminating other societies, some older than their own'.

As an alternative to such tragic and irreversible displacement, some countries are adopting new technologies and imagining future floating cities. The question is no longer how to prevent the sea overwhelming the land, but how to best enable life upon the water – initially as an extension of existing territory, but eventually as an alternative for it. The Dutch are using their maritime experience to address the question of what to do when the water defence systems that protect the Netherlands become obsolete. Engineers from the Maritime Research Institute Netherlands led by Olaf Waals have designed tessellating panels on which new cities could be built. These floating triangles of different sizes are resistant to the force of storms; they can be anchored to the sea bed or moored to the shore. At present there are only a few such panels in existence – just enough to fill the Institute's testing basin. One day this concept will be applied to make a huge, flexible island that can support a city-sized settlement of homes, farms, parks and libraries.

One of the travellers whom Robert Boyle quotes in his *New Experiments and Observations on Cold* is his friend John Evelyn. Writing from Italy during the 1640s, Evelyn told Boyle that he had seen 'snow Pits . . . sunk in the most solitary and cool'd places', often in the shade of mountains or trees. To preserve the snow which they brought down from the peaks on donkeys, the farmers 'beat it to a hard cake of an icy consistence, which is near one foot thick, upon this they make a layer of straw, and on that snow, beaten as before, and so continue a bed of straw and a bed of snow till the pit be full to the brim.' Evelyn brought this knowledge back to England with him, and the fashion for 'Conservatories of Snow' soon spread, with an ice-house being built for the king on the side of Castle Hill at Greenwich. It might have seemed like a new trend to the aristocracy who adopted it, but the ice-house was an ancient invention: the first on record was built in Mesopotamia over 4,000 years ago. A cuneiform text from Mari, beside the river Euphrates, mentions an ice-house four reeds long and two reeds deep, and lined with tamarisk boughs.

After Boyle's time, a triumvirate of ice-houses were built at the estate of Lismore Castle in Waterford, where the scientist was born in 1627. Two deep pits were dug beside the road that leads to the Blackwater River by Edmund Foley, founder of the Blackwater Fishery. The third ice-house stands on the crest of the hill in what is now Lismore's Millennium Park. I had been staying with a travel writer who was briefly at home, and was taking her dogs for a run when I discovered the ice-houses. The structures were in the process of being restored, thanks to the efforts of Lismore Tidy Towns Committee. When the dogs and I returned to the fireside, muddy and damp, Dervla told me the pits would have been used to store fish caught in the river between Youghal and Cappoquin. Some winters the Blackwater flooded and froze over the Inches, the levels opposite the castle. The stretch was used as an ice rink by children, until fishermen came and broke the ice, tore up the sheets spiked with grass blades, and hauled them a mile up the cliff to the pits. I was surprised to find a holy water source, St Carthage's Well, trickling from the rock alongside the ice-houses. As the river ice was elevated the sacred water ran downhill.

Once common by rivers, at major ports and in country estates across Europe and America, ice-houses slowly slipped out of use. The warming climate at the end of the nineteenth century diminished their efficiency, and besides, electric refrigeration was becoming available. By the 1930s many people were unaware that ice-houses had existed, and all the ice-houses were empty – or at least, they did not contain ice.

One of the first things I do when I get back to Oxford is to renew my Bodleian library card. A new library has sprung up on the corner of Broad Street during the years I've been travelling. Behind a glass façade, the ground floor provides a gallery space for visitors to explore the collection's highlights. The library stacks above also have walls of glass, so that readers on the balcony can be observed by those drinking coffee in the atrium below. *The Ice-houses of Britain* is the kind of volume library watchers might be impressed by: a labour of many years' research, it totals five hundred pages. It is bound in dark green cloth, the colour of my old school uniform. What a casual observer can't see is that it is compiled with such enthusiasm that, reading it, I feel as though I'm in the company of the Famous Five.

Campaigns to preserve ice-houses such as those in Lismore rest on scholarship like this. In 1980 Sylvia Beamon and Susan Roaf began to compile a gazetteer of all the ice-houses in Britain. It was a formidable task. They sent out hundreds of letters and surveys to local authorities, archaeological and historical groups, libraries, museums and individual estates. The hunt was a collaborative effort. The authors warned their correspondents that 'searching for ice-houses in out of the way places, struggling through nettles and brambles and dense shrubbery to reach crumbling buildings is often no pleasure'. The quest for an ice-house may be foiled by changes to county borders; the difficulty of accessing private land; even the fact that bats use ruins to hibernate, and it is illegal to disturb them.

At times, the hunters must have despaired of finding any ice-houses intact. Perry's warehouse in Bristol, where tonnes of imported ice were stored for supply to fishmongers and restaurants and hotels, burnt down in May 1895. (While this may seem paradoxical, it was a common problem as most ice-houses were lined with straw.) The bursar of Clarendon School in Bedfordshire wrote to say that their ice-house had been 'dynamited by a local farmer in 1973'; in Brockenhurst, Hampshire: 'The ice-house was filled in during the 1970s, at which time there was no roof'; the ice-house at Park Hospital, Moggerhanger was 'boarded up in the early 1970s to prevent vandalism'; and even at Waddesdon Manor: 'The ice-house could not be investigated due to its dangerous condition. The entrance is sealed . . .' The commonest responses were equally disheartening: 'It is not known if the ice-house still exists' or 'No information available.'

Ice-houses can be hard to identify because a variety of designs were employed. They could be dome- or globe-shaped pits, and the chambers circular-, rectangular- and tunnel-shaped, according to the Niven–Robertson classification system of 1953. In grand locations, they may have been disguised as small Greek or Roman temples; in suburban spaces they were just another place to keep things in and, once ice was no longer needed, soon filled with junk or were adapted for other purposes. Russell's in Watford, a former dower house which had been converted into a retirement home, reported: 'The ice-house, having outlived its original purpose, is now a boiler room.' The owners of Wydcombe Manor House, on the Isle of Wight, responded to say they had found an 'unidentified structure': a six-foot deep barrel-shaped brick pit 'the general opinion is that it is not an ice-house, but is more likely to have been a cesspit or a slurry pit'. It is not surprising that the Niven-Robertson system includes a category for 'doubtful structures' – buildings which may have been created as ice-houses, but this is unconfirmed.

As I wait to return the book, two members of staff are complaining about the cold. One librarian is due to begin a shift at the entrance to the old library, and the older one advises wrapping up well. 'The builders got a job lot of workwear in. One of the coats was XXL, too big for anyone to use. So they passed it on to us. Most people who put it on, it trails down the floor,' she says. 'You can take it with you if you like.'

'But isn't it bright fluorescent?' asks the young one.

'Well yes, but either the staff are going to glow or we need the place warmed up. There is a minimum temperature for Health and Safety, you know! Who do they think they are, making us sit below the bare minimum for a whole hour? Not a whiff of heating. You're just sat there, not moving. The doors keep opening and closing and then you get the tour groups who hold the doors open. It's not about it being a little bit under, it's degrees and degrees under. Of course *he* said we look ridiculous in the jacket. "What's the problem?" I says to him. "Do you want the readers not to know how cold we are?"'

There is no sign of the conversation ending, so I lay the volume quietly down on the desk beside them and leave. I'm perturbed to think that all the while I have been reading about cold, the temperatures the librarians work in have never once crossed my mind.

Susan Roaf, one of the gazetteers, moved on from studying ice-house construction to become an expert on low carbon building design. She is responsible for the Oxford Ecohouse, built in 1995 – the first home installed with a photovoltaic cell roof in Britain. On initiating the project, Roaf was told by the government that her designs would not work because Britain did not have enough sunshine. The Ecohouse has proved them wrong, becoming a model for sustainable design. It is easy to spot from the road, its cells laid out neatly side by side over the dark tiles, although the roof is not as striking as Oxford's other suburban landmark, known by locals as the Shark House.

I'm visiting an estate agent in search of a place to rent, when I spot the Shark House in their brochure. Simon tells me that 2 New High Street has been available for some time. Many people are curious, he says, but everyone he's shown round the modest Victorian terrace so far has decided they do not want to live with a shark. The creature appears to have nose-dived from the sky, smashing head-first through the roof, only to be pulled up short by its pectoral fins; the tail towers above the chimneypots. On the night Bill Heine bought the house in 1986, he heard fighter jets fly overhead from RAF Upper Heyford, destined for Tripoli. Not long afterwards he commissioned the 7-metre-long fibreglass sculpture from the artist John Buckley and installed it on 9 August, the anniversary of the bombing of Nagasaki, to remind passers-by that the unexpected can always happen, that the world can change in a moment. The idea that a deep-water shark might end up in a terrace at one of the furthest points from the sea in the British Isles seems less outrageous as time passes. Roaf, in contrast to Heine, is working to discover ways in which we can prepare for an uncertain future by adapting our cities for climate change; the course of her career from studying the ice-stores of the past to creating eco-houses for the future, reflects how concerns are changing too.

Eco- is such a common prefix that it is easy to forget the meaning those three letters contain. Its etymology lies in the Ancient Greek οἶκος ('house' or 'home') – a word which also underlies 'economy': the effective management of our own resources.

The storage company that had sponsored my first trip to Greenland by providing a free locker in its Tottenham warehouse had not sent me a single invoice during the seven years I'd been travelling, but I couldn't rely on their goodwill (or forgetfulness) forever. One day at the close of the year, once I had found a place to live, I took the 341 bus to Angel Road. I made my way through the draughty corridors of the warehouse to my unit, the lights flicking off behind me automatically after a disconcerting delay. I unlock the padlock. Thank goodness I'd managed not to lose the key.

Cardboard boxes are stacked up to the iron mesh at the top of the storage unit, which is shaped like a telephone kiosk. I prise one box out of the pile, then another, and peel back the tape with which I'd hurriedly sealed them. I haven't set eyes on the contents since I packed up my bedsit. Plastic bags have disintegrated like autumn leaves around the objects they once held. Why did I have so many candlesticks? My blue teapot has fallen and smashed, despite being wrapped in several jumpers. Like blocks of ice in an ice-house, the books have survived best.

I pull the first layer of boxes out into the corridor and make my way deeper into the space. A friend is coming with a van in under an hour. There's not much time – I will need to contain my curiosity until I get the boxes home.

The potential of all these boxes of books strikes me once I've got them up the stairs. I've lived without the familiar volumes so long. As I pull them back into the light, I realize how many stories I'd forgotten. I had carried a few shadowy tales around in the chambers of my memory. Now my tiny flat was transformed into a palace with infinite rooms: records of different pasts, and dreams of many possible futures.

I'd collected more books on my travels, of course. Among them was a copy of the Greenlandic–English Dictionary, the same old edition I'd consulted in Upernavik Museum. Before I shelved it I was unable to resist opening it once more. I was careful of its flaking spine, its delicate paper wrappers which had received too much wear in the last few years. I recalled my conversations with Grethe about its contents, and wondered again at both her keenness to teach me her language and her wariness of writing it down. I came to the page on which *ilisiveeruppaa* was defined: 'to put something in a safe place but be unable to find it again'. The term had once seemed to encapsulate my own doubts about the value of a paper legacy, as well as the reservations the museum had about collecting written work.

Perhaps because I was looking at the dictionary in a

comfortable armchair, rather than at a desk in a polar museum, something in the tone of the English definition now struck me as discordant. I knew the dictionary was unreliable: a previous owner had made several corrections in the margins in a shaky hand. I valued the book despite or even because of its possible inaccuracies. I decide to check the meaning of *ilisiveeruppaa* in an online dictionary, recently launched by Greenland's Language Secretariat. And then I realize the danger of learning language from a book, itself in translation and nearly a century old, for the modern definition was very different – or so I thought at first: 'To bury in a grave or a coffin'.

Either the original author was wrong, or the meaning had shifted. Or could both senses be correct? Is the grave a safe place to leave words? And is something placed in a coffin really lost? What if the burial place were not a grave but an icy pile of stones, a cairn, an ice-house – a place in which a message might rest until the right person came to find it. I thought of the objects buried under the ice around Upernavik, awaiting discovery as global temperatures warmed. It would not be long now before those stories were revealed. The disappearing ice was contained in our story, now.

I put the dictionary safely away and turned back to the boxes. Boxes of clothes, boxes of cutlery. And what was this? Reams of paper, covered in my own hand-writing. I recognized manuscripts I'd been working on before I left London. (Not a rusty paper clip in sight; I'd been well-trained.) After all this time, they looked like someone else's work – the indecipherable crossings out, the coffee rings. I closed the box again hurriedly. I would deal with them later.

NOTES

EPIGRAPH

Kevin Crossley-Holland's translation of Riddle 69 from *The Exeter Book of Riddles* (London: Enitharmon Press, 2008).

INTRODUCTION

'And if the sun had not erased the tracks upon the ice ...' in the Obituary of Simon Simonsen of Upernavik, called 'Simon Bear Hunter', 1924, from Keld Hansen, *Nuussuarmiut: Hunting Families on the Big Headland; Demography, Subsistence and Material Culture in Nuussuaq, Upernavik, Northwest Greenland* (*Meddelelser om Grønland*, Man & Society 35, Copenhagen: Museum Tusculanum Press, 2008).

'There's an Arctic myth that tells ...', see 'The coming of men, a long, long while ago' from Knud Rasmussen, *Eskimo Folk Tales*, translated and edited by W. Worster (Copenhagen: Gyldendal, 1921).

The dictionary referred to is C. Schultz-Lorentzen's *Dictionary of the West Greenland Eskimo Language* (Copenhagen: C. A. Reitzel, 1927).

'I must hasten away to warmer countries ...' in 'The Snow Queen', in Hans Christian Andersen, *Hans Andersen's Fairy Tales*, translated by 'Mrs Paull' (London: Frederick Warne & Co., 1867).

I

'*But we need the books ...*' Franz Kafka, letter to Oskar Pollak, 27 January 1904, in *Franz Kafka: Letters to Friends, Family and Editors*, translated by Richard and Clara Winston (Richmond: Oneworld Classics, 2011).

'For the Lord spake unto Job ...' and following texts, in Johannes Kepler, *The Six-Cornered Snowflake* (Oxford: Clarendon Press, 1966).

The sealskin map is in the Pitt Rivers Museum, item 1966.19.1, described as 'Painting, in black, on sealskin'; it can be viewed online http://objects.prm.ox.ac.uk/pages/ PRMUID26166.html (accessed 31 May 2018).

'However natural it may be to assist the perceptive faculty ...' quoted in *Cartographies of Time* by Daniel Rosenberg and Anthony Grafton (Princeton, NJ: Princeton University Press, 2010).

'We wish to write briefly of these first days and the beginnings . . .' quoted in *Cartographies of Time* (New York, NY: Princeton Architectural Press, 2010).

'The Noble Author being at *Oxford*, when the Book was printed at *London* . . .' and following, in Robert Boyle's *New Experiments and Observations Touching Cold* (London: 1665).

'You should have inscribed them on your mind instead of on paper . . .' and following quotations from John Evelyn and William Wotton, in Chapter 6, 'Robert Boyle's Loose Notes' in *Notebooks, English Virtuosi, and Early Modern Science* by Richard Yeo (Chicago, IL: University of Chicago Press, 2014).

'A good forger can reproduce the pattern . . .' John Finney writes about his research in *Findings on Ice*, edited by Hester Aardse and Astrid van Baalen (Zurich: PARS Foundation/ Lars Müller Publishers, 2007). Professor Finney is also author of *Water: A Very Short Introduction* (Oxford: Oxford University Press, 2015); I am indebted to him for his advice while writing this chapter.

'How are we to understand that during the fine season . . .?' in Ludwig Kämtz, *A Complete Course of Meteorology*, with notes by C. Martins and an appendix by L. Lalanne. Translated with notes and additions by C. V. Walker (London: H. Baillière, 1845).

II

'We had seen God in his splendours ...' Ernest Shackleton, *South: The Story of Shackleton's Last Expedition* (London: William Heinemann, 1919).

'We left no footprints ...' Ursula Le Guin, 'Sur', in *The Compass Rose: Short Stories* (London: Gollancz, 1983).

'They explored and explored ...' Aqqaluk Lynge's poem is collected in *The Veins of the Heart to the Pinnacle of the Mind*, translated by Ken Norris and Marianne Stenbæk (Montreal: International Polar Institute, 2008).

'across half a mile of clear blue ice, swept by the unbroken wind ...' and other material by Priestley regarding this winter, in Raymond Priestley, *Antarctic Adventure: Scott's Northern Party* (New York, NY: E. P. Dutton, 1915).

'How about giving Browning a spoonful of brandy?' Don Webster's article is in *Polar Record* – a journal managed by SPRI ('The interpretation and probable dating of conversations found in Victor Campbell's field note-book, written while in a snow-cave on Inexpressible Island, Antarctica, during the winter of 1912', *Polar Record* 51 (260): 467–74, 2015). Victor Campbell settled in Newfoundland, where his diary is now in the Memorial University Collections.

'My dearest Katie ...' and following, in Benjamin Bell, *Lieut. John Irving, RN of HMS 'Terror', in Sir John Franklin's*

last expedition to the Arctic regions; a memorial sketch with letters
(Edinburgh: David Douglas, 1881).

'Pray take care of the Pigeons . . .' in M. J. Ross, *Polar Pioneers:
John Ross and James Clark Ross* (Toronto, ON: McGill-Queen's
University Press, 1994).

'At 7 o'clock we released our first balloon . . .' in Emile
Frédéric de Bray, *A Frenchman in Search of Franklin: De Bray's
Arctic Journal 1852–1854*, translated and edited by William
Barr (Toronto, ON: University of Toronto Press, 1992).

Qivittut tale in a version told by Juliane Mouritzen in *The
Southernmost Peoples of Greenland: Dialects and Memories/Qavaat:
Oqalunneri Eqqaamassaallu*, edited by Mâliâraq Vebæk and
Birgitte Sonne (Copenhagen: *Meddelelser om Grønland*, Man
& Society 33, The Commission for Scientific Research in
Greenland, 2006). The stories were recorded during the 1970s.

'Dear Son, I wright these few lines . . .' The letter written by
John and Phoebe Diggle is held in the National Maritime
Museum, Greenwich, Object ID AGC/D/12/1–3; as is the
last record of Sir John Franklin's expedition, 'the standard
Admiralty accident form' (generally known as 'the message
in the cairn'), Object ID HSR/C/9/1.

'I noticed on his table a copy of Dean Hole's *A Book About
Roses* . . .' and following, from William Laird McKinlay,
Karluk: The Great Untold Story of Arctic Exploration (New York,
NY: St Martin's Press, 1976).

'the best part of all books ...' William Morris Hunt's *Talks about Art* quoted by Kenneth Grahame in 'Marginalia', *Pagan Papers* (London: Elkin Mathews, 1894).

'Kleinschmidt's fist ...' Otto Rosing and W. D. Preston, 'Kleinschmidt Centennial II: Samuel Petrus Kleinschmidt' in *International Journal of American Linguistics* Vol. 17, No. 2 (April 1951).

'In a manual for librarians ...' For those wishing to know more about *Disaster Preparedness*, Constance Brooks's guide, one of seven in a series of Preservation Planning Program (PPP) resource guides, was published by the Association of Research Libraries, Washington, DC, in 1993.

'Over 26,000 of the library's volumes ...' in *Lost Memory: Libraries and Archives Destroyed in the Twentieth Century*, prepared for UNESCO on behalf of IFLA by Hans van der Hoeven and on behalf of ICA by Joan van Albada (Paris: UNESCO, 1996).

'A few decades later, in 2009, the Greenlandic dialects ...' see *Atlas of the World's Languages in Danger*, UNESCO, http://www.unesco.org/languages-atlas/ (accessed 31 May 2018).

III

'Memory does this ...' Ms. 863v, in *Walter Benjamin's Archive: images, texts, signs*, translated by Esther Leslie and edited by

Ursula Marx, Gudrun Schwarz, Michael Schwarz and Erdmut Wizisla (London: Verso, 2015).

'to discover what journey *hiku* might take me on . . .' the definitions of *hiku* and the following terms, in *The Meaning of Ice: People and Sea Ice in Three Arctic Communities*, edited by Shari Fox Gearheard, Lene Kielsen Holm, Henry Huntington, Joe Mello Leavitt and Andrew R. Mahoney (Hanover: International Polar Institute Press, 2013).

'Floe giant: Over 10 km across . . .' in *Sea Ice Nomenclature* 2nd edition (Geneva: World Meteorological Organization, 2014).

'I became aware of snow and summer . . .' and 'In my short lifetime, things have really changed . . .' from *Stories of the Raven – Snowchange 2005 Conference Report*, edited by Tero Mustonen (Anchorage, AK: Snowchange, 2005), see http://www.snowchange.org/ (accessed 31 May 2018).

'A growing number of books . . .' *Kingikmi Sigum Qanuq Ilitaavut – Wales Inupiaq Sea Ice Dictionary*, compiled by Winton Weyapuk, Jr and Igor Krupnik (Washington, DC: The Arctic Studies Center, Smithsonian Institute, 2012).

'September, for hunters in Nunavut . . .' see *The Meaning of Ice* (2013) for Joelie Sanguya's definitions.

'These surreal scrapbooks are a Great Exhibition in miniature . . .' The albums of 'India-Proofs of Wood-Engravings by The Brothers Dalziel' can be viewed online at the British

Museum Collection Database, www.britishmuseum.org/
collection. The wood engravings for Albert Markham's
The Great Frozen Sea are contained in an album from 1878,
Museum No. 1913,0415.198, Nos. 325–57.

'Markham's is a dreadful story. . .' Albert Markham, *The Great
Frozen Sea: A Personal Narrative of the Voyage of the Alert during
the Arctic Expedition of 1875–6* (London: K. Paul, Trench,
Trübner, 1878).

'an *oil-stone*, a *sand-bag* or *cushion* . . .' and following, in John
Jackson and William Andrew Chatto, *A Treatise on Wood
Engraving, Historical and Practical* (London: C. Knight, 1839).

'a bone that looked like a polar bear . . .' see, for example,
the object in the Canadian Museum of History collections
described as 'Floating or Flying Bear', a Middle Dorset culture
ivory carving from the Igloolik area, https://www.history
museum.ca/cmc/exhibitions/archeo/paleoesq/pegb4eng.
shtml (accessed 31 May 2018).

'When you return to earth, send some ice . . .' Recorded in
Knud Rasmussen, *Eskimo Folk Tales*, translated and edited by
W. Worster (Copenhagen: Gyldendal, 1921).

'My playmates were native Greenlanders . . .' in Knud
Rasmussen's memoir *Across Arctic America* (New York, NY:
G. P. Putnam's Sons, 1927).

'for permanent under-secretary of state . . .' Telegram, Thule 3136 145/141 31/5/1953, quoted in Kamilla Christensen and Jeppe Sørensen, 'The Forced Relocation of the Indigenous People of Uummannaq, or How to Silence a Minority', *Humanity in Action*, https://www.humanityinaction.org/ knowledgebase/13-the-forced-relocation-of-the-indigenous-people-of-uummannaq-or-how-to-silence-a-minority (accessed 31 May 2018).

Kiviuq's tale was related by Annie Peterloosie to listeners in Pond Inlet, up the north coast of Baffin Island from Clyde River, Nunavut, in John Houston's 2007 eponymous film, produced by Kirt Ejesiak for Triad Film.

'The physical realities of the natural world' in '"Today is today and tomorrow is tomorrow": Reflections on Inuit Understanding of Time and Place' by Nicole Gombay in *Proceedings of the 15th Inuit Studies Conference, Orality* (Paris: INALCO, 2009).

IV

Carolyn Brown on Merce Cunningham, quoted in Sandra Kemp, 'But What if the Object Began to Speak? The Aesthetics of Dance', in *Thinking Art: Beyond Traditional Aesthetics*, edited by Andrew Benjamin and Peter Osborne (London: ICA, 1991).

'She gazed with her eyes open very wide ...' and following; Noel Streatfeild's novel *White Boots* was first published by Collins (London: 1951).

'after great consideration ...' Bror Meyer, *Skating with Bror Meyer* (New York, NY and Toronto, ON: Doubleday, Page and Company, 1921).

'He seemed to see, with a cartographer's eye, that string of swimming pools ...' John Cheever, 'The Swimmer', in *The Stories of John Cheever* (New York, NY: Knopf, 1978).

'The spirit of curling demands ...' *The Royal Caledonian Curling Club Handbook: Rules of the Game and the Royal Club Competitions*, issued by the RCCC in 2014.

'Mammoth Unsinkable Vessel' Geoffrey Pyke's proposal in *Max Perutz and the Secret of Life* by Georgina Ferry (London: Chatto & Windus, 2007). Pyke's quotation from the Old Testament is Habakkuk 1:5 (King James Version).

'Combined Operations requisitioned a large meat store ...' Max Perutz writes about his experience working on pykrete in 'Enemy Alien', collected in *I Wish I'd Made You Angry Earlier: Essays on Science, Scientists and Humanity* (Cold Spring Harbor, NY: Cold Spring Harbor Laboratory Press, 2003).

'All of the materials we've selected are translucent ...' 'A New Home on Mars: NASA Langley's Icy Concept for Living on the Red Planet', published 29 December 2016, https://www.

nasa.gov/feature/langley/a-new-home-on-mars-nasa-langley
-s-icy-concept-for-living-on-the-red-planet (accessed 31 May
2018).

'Chart of the Magnetic Curves of Equal Variation' in *Black's
General Atlas* (Edinburgh: A&C Black, 1844).

V

W. H. Auden, 'Journey to Iceland', first published in *Poetry*
Vol. 49, No. 4 (January 1937).

'One should simply say and do as little as possible . . .' Halldór
Laxness, *Under the Glacier*, translated by Magnus Magnusson
(New York, NY: Vintage, 2004).

The definition of '*iokel*' is from *An Icelandic-English Dictionary*
by Richard Cleasby and Gudbrand Vigfusson (Oxford:
Clarendon Press, 1874).

'The streams called Ice-waves . . .' The story of Gylfi appears
in the *Prose Edda*, in Arthur Gilchrist Brodeur's translation
(New York, NY: The American-Scandinavian Foundation,
1916).

'dynamic rivers of ice' is the definition of a glacier according
to the US Geological Survey Glossary of Glacier Terminology
(2004): https://pubs.usgs.gov/of/2004/1216/text.html (accessed 31 May 2018).

'the issue of steam from a cleft...' 'Journey to Iceland', as above. The recording was issued on CD as *W. H. Auden: The Spoken Word* (London: British Library, 2007).

Pliny the Elder on crystals and ice in 'The Natural Story of Precious Stones', Book 37, Chapter 9 of *Natural History*.

'Lucid gems are made of water ...' William Gilbert in *De Magnete*, translated by Silvanus Phillips Thompson (London: Chiswick Press, 1900).

Paul Vander-Molen and Jack Vander-Molen, *Iceland Breakthrough* (Sparkford: The Oxford Illustrated Press in association with Channel Four Television Company, 1985).

'the 6 tonnes of ice lifted from Jökulsárlón ...' Olafur Eliasson, *Your Waste of Time* (2006), http://olafureliasson.net/ archive/artwork/WEK100564/your-waste-of-time (accessed 31 May 2018).

'the expedition was overtaken by a snowstorm ...' Hakon Wadell published 'Some Studies and Observations from the Greatest Glacial Area in Iceland' in *Geografiska Annaler* Vol. 2 (1920).

'Nature's Bible ...' John Muir, *Travels in Alaska* (Boston, MA: Mariner Books, 1998).

'Here and there on the sills, ledges and crags ...' Þórbergur Þórðarson, *í Suðursveit* (uncredited English translation, Þórbergssetur, Hali).

'One should always treat stones with courtesy ...' Þórbergur Þórðarson, *The Stones Speak*, translated by Julian Meldon D'Arcy (Reykjavik: Mál og menning, 2012).

'It affected you differently whether you walked west or east. . .' and 'if a rock fell ...' *í Suðursveit* (as above).

'a slim volume illustrated with wood engravings ...' Gunnar Gunnarsson, *The Good Shepherd*, translated by Philip Roughton and illustrated by Masha Simkovitch (Reykjavik: Bjartur, 2016).

Dr Elisha Kent Kane writes of the 'pleasurable sleepiness of the story books' in *The U.S. Grinnell Expedition in Search of Sir John Franklin* (Cambridge: Cambridge University Press, 2015).

'Arnaldur Indriðason's crime novels ...' see, for example, *Reykjavik Nights*, translated by Victoria Cribb (London: Vintage, 2015): 'For years he had been reading up on tales of travellers going astray or surviving ordeals on the country's high moors and mountain roads.'

'It is cold at the choir's back ...' The original Icelandic is *Kalt er við kórbak, / kúrir þar Jón hrak. / Ýtar snúa austur og vestur, / allir nema Jón hrak, allir nema Jón hrak.* Translation quoted in 'Skriðuklaustur and the Archaeological Excavations in

East-Iceland' by Regína Hrönn Ragnarsdóttir at https:// guidetoiceland.is (accessed 31 May 2018).

'from the deep places of my sleep...' Gunnar Gunnarsson, *Ships in the Sky*, translated by Evelyn Charlotte Ramsden (London: Jarrolds Ltd, 1938).

VI

'We need not destroy the past...' John Cage, 'Lecture on Nothing' (1949), collected in *Silence: Lectures and Writings* (Middletown, CT: Wesleyan University Press, 1961).

'Then Scottish artist Katie Paterson ...' *Vatnajökull (the sound of)* (2007–8), see http://katiepaterson.org/portfolio/ vatnajokull-the-sound-of/ (accessed 31 May 2018).

'Carmen has studied ice at different stages of this cycle ...' Carmen Braden has written about her work in 'Misconceptions of a silent north' and 'Ice as instrument: using natural forms of ice for sound production' in *The Global Composition, Conference on Sound, Media and the Environment*, edited by Sabine Breitsameter and Claudia Söller-Eckert (Darmstadt: Hochschule Darmstadt, 2012). For more information, see her website: https://blackicesound.com (accessed 31 May 2018).

'soft foldings of snow ...' R. Murray Schafer, *Snowforms* (Toronto, ON: Arcana Editions, 1986).

'I call architecture frozen music.' Attributed to Johann Wolfgang von Goethe and Friedrich Schiller, *Conversations with Goethe in the Last Years of His Life* by Johann Wolfgang von Goethe, Johann Peter Eckermann, Margaret Fuller, translated by Margaret Fuller (Boston, MA: Hilliard, Gray and Co, 1839).

'This pond never breaks up so soon ...' 'Spring', in H. D. Thoreau, *Walden: Or Life in the Woods* (London: Penguin Illustrated Classics, 1938).

'unexpectedly wide and so strange ...' 'A Winter Walk', in H. D. Thoreau, *The Portable Thoreau*, edited by Jeffrey S. Cramer (New York, NY: Penguin, 2012).

'The residents of Concord have continued ...' see Richard B. Primack, *Walden Warming: Climate Change Comes to Thoreau's Woods* (Chicago, IL: University of Chicago Press, 2014).

'If a writer of prose knows enough ...' Ernest Hemingway, *Death in the Afternoon* (London: Jonathan Cape, 1968).

'I looked to the north at the two ranges of mountains ...' Ernest Hemingway, *A Farewell to Arms* (New York, NY: Scribner, 2014).

'Snow is truly a sign of mourning ...' in Giuseppe Ungaretti, *Lettere a Soffici* (Florence: Sansoni, 1981). Translation by Mark Thompson, in Chapter 17 'Whiteness', *The White War: Life and Death on the Italian Front 1915–1919* (London: Faber & Faber, 2008).

'It could be a game of Cluedo . . .' This account of the 'Alpine accident' is based on the facts given by Konrad Spindler in *The Man in the Ice: The Discovery of a 5,000-Year-Old Body*, translated by Ewald Osers (London: Weidenfeld & Nicolson, 1994).

'The men . . . sorrowed so deeply . . .' Knud Rasmussen, *The Netsilik Eskimos*, quoted in David A. Morrison and G.-H. Germain, *Inuit: Glimpses of an Arctic Past*, (Ottawa: Canadian Museum of Civilization, 1995).

'A gold mine which opened to great excitement . . .' 'The Nalunaq Gold Mine' in a special issue of *Geology and Ore* No. 11 (February 2008).

EPILOGUE

Old Icelandic Rune poem, translated by Nancy Campbell.

'a hundred men at work like busy husbandmen . . .' The editions used are H. D. Thoreau, *Walden: Or Life in the Woods* (London: Penguin Illustrated Classics, 1938) and *The Journal 1837–1861*, edited by Damion Searls (New York, NY: NYRB Classics, 2009).

'Winter never rots in the sky . . .' in Gavin Weightman, *The Frozen Water Trade* (London: HarperCollins, 2010).

'Map of Fresh Pond showing the division lines of the proprietors extended into the pond and defining their right to the same as decided by Simon Greenleaf & S. M. Felton, commissioners' by George A. Parker in the Norman B. Leventhal Map Center Collection, Boston Public Library, G3764. C2:2F7 1841 .P3x.

'Its demands are peremptory . . .' in Foster Smith, quoting the *Annual Reports of the RailRoad Corporations in the State of Mass.*, Boston, MA, 1844, in *Ice Carrying Trade at Sea: the proceedings of a symposium held at the National Maritime Museum on 8 September 1979*, edited by D. V. Proctor.

'The glaciologist Louis Agassiz . . .' For this connection, I am grateful to Laura Dassow Walls for her excellent biography, *Henry David Thoreau* (Chicago, IL: University of Chicago Press, 2017).

'How many Calcutta tables glittered . . .' in Joachim Stocqueler, *The Memoirs of a Journalist* (Bombay and London: The Times of India, 1873).

'Immediately . . . I was afflicted . . .' Rudyard Kipling, 'The Undertakers', in *The Second Jungle Book* (London: Macmillan, 1962).

'The Door for entering this Ice house . . .' in *Papers of Robert Morris: 1781–1784* Vol. 9, edited by Elizabeth M. Nuxoll and Mary A. Gallagher (Pittsburgh, PA: University of Pittsburgh Press, 1999).

'Opened the Well in my Cellar ...' in Sylvia P. Beamon and Susan Roaf, *The Ice-houses of Britain* (London: Routledge, 1990).

The map of Atlantis is 'Situs Insulae Atlantidis, a mari olim absorpte ex mente Aegyptiorum et Platonis descriptio' in Athanasius Kircher, *Mundus Subterraneus* (Amsterdam, 1665).

'But afterwards there occurred ...' Plato, *Timaeus*, translated by Benjamin Jowett, http://classics.mit.edu/Plato/timaeus. html (accessed 31 May 2018).

Robert Smithson, *Map of Broken Glass (Atlantis)*, in the collections of Dia: Beacon, https://www.diaart.org/collection/collection/smithson-robert-map-of-broken-glass-atlantis-1969-2013-027 (accessed 31 May 2018).

On sea-level rise, see J. L. Bamber and W. P. Aspinall, 'An expert judgement assessment of future sea level rise from the ice sheets', *Nature Climate Change* Vol. 3, No. 4 (April 2013) pp. 424–7, and also https://www.nature.com/articles/nclimate1778 (accessed 31 May 2018).

'the excesses of larger and more powerful countries ...' Address by Mr Gaston Alphonso Browne, prime minister and minister for finance and corporate governance of Antigua and Barbuda, in the *Official Records of the United Nations General Assembly Seventieth Session*, 23rd plenary meeting, New York, 1 October 2015, A/70/PV.23.

'snow Pits ... sunk in the most solitary and cool'd places' in Boyle's *New Experiments and Observations Touching Cold* (London: 1665).

'searching for ice-houses in out of the way places ...' and following, in Beamon and Roaf, *The Ice-houses of Britain*.

C. Schultz-Lorentzen, *Dictionary of the West Greenland Eskimo Language* (Copenhagen: C. A. Reitzel, 1927).

ACKNOWLEDGEMENTS

The travels described in this book took place over seven years. My first journey to Upernavik in Greenland in 2010 was supported in part by Grants for the Arts from Arts Council England; without this funding my explorations of cold climates would not have begun. It was an immense privilege to spend time with the people of Upernavik and this book is a testament to their generosity in sharing their abundant knowledge, as well as scarce resources. The following institutions also provided valuable space to research and write: Ilulissat Kunstmuseum, Greenland; Doverodde Book Arts Centre, Denmark; Hawthornden Castle, Scotland; Herhusið, Siglufjörður, Iceland; the Gunnar Gunnarsson Institute, Iceland; Jan Michalski Foundation, Switzerland; and Lady Margaret Hall, University of Oxford. My thanks to the staff at these institutions, who gave freely of their time and knowledge, as did others at British Antarctic Survey and Scott Polar Research Institute, Cambridge; the Lit & Phil, Newcastle-upon-Tyne and the Royal Academy, London. I am grateful to the Worshipful Company of Stationers and Newspaper Makers for a grant to travel to the United States to view Thoreau's manuscripts at the Morgan Library in New York and work at The Lone Oak Press in Massachusetts.

Special thanks to my agent Kirsty McLachlan, at DGA Ltd, for her insight and encouragement, and to editors Rowan Cope and Jo Dickinson at Simon & Schuster for their belief in the manuscript and care in guiding it to publication. Thanks also to Caroline Blake for her copy-editing, and to Jo Whitford and the wider team at Simon & Schuster. Several editors and curators gave me commissions which kept my mind on the Arctic while I was back in the UK: I am grateful to Phil Owen, of Tertulia; Francesca Goodwin, of Fabelist; Mike Sims, publications manager at The Poetry Society; Sebastian Carter, editor of *Parenthesis*; Mark Goldthorpe, of ClimateCultures; Em Strang, Nick Hunt and Charlotte Du Cann, of Dark Mountain; Sam Phillips, at *RA Magazine*; and Will Eaves, Anna Vaux and Catharine Morris, at *The Times Literary Supplement*. Thanks too, to Thea Lenarduzzi for commissioning a feature on Greenland for what turned out to be the last printed Sunday edition of the *Independent*. The section on ice cores was first published as 'The Library of Ice' on Terrain.org, having won the journal's 2012 Non-Fiction Contest; my thanks to Julian Hoffman, who awarded the prize, and to editor Simmons Buntin. Roni Gross of Z'roah Press in New York is an inspiration, in art as in life; she published my first poems about Upernavik, and I remain thankful for her continued support of my work. I wish to express my deep appreciation of Mary Jean Chan and Theophilus Kwek, friends and former co-editors at *Oxford Poetry*, who supported my decision to step down from editorial responsibilities to complete this manuscript.

I am grateful to the artists and other individuals who shared their experiences and ideas through interviews – in particular Carmen Braden, Bill Jacklin RA and Emma Stibbon RA. I also wish to thank many others, not named in the text, with whom I've discussed either books or ice or both, including Helen Barr, Kaddy Benyon, Julia Bird, Sarah Bodman, Isabel Brittain, Chris Calver, Vahni Capildeo, David Collard, Edwina Ellis, Nick Gingell, James Gledhill, Dennis Harrison, Nasim Marie Jafry, Ralph Kiggell, Bernard Kops, Robert Lock, Helen Mitchell, Eleanor Morgan, Kirsten Norrie, Judith Palmer, Clementine Perrins, Katie Potter, Russell Potter, Paul Preece, Dan Richards, Jane Rushton, Lavinia Singer, Andrew Smardon, Bethan Stevens, Stephen Stuart-Smith, Matthew Teller, Pierre Tremblay, Mark Turin, Lindy Usher, Ruth Valentine and Lefteris Yakoumakis. Thanks especially to David Borthwick, who reminded me of the etymology of 'ecology'. Last but not least a warm thank you to Nick Drake, whose collection *The Farewell Glacier* (Bloodaxe) contains a poem voiced by an ice-core sample or 'the library of ice', for graciously sharing this phrase with me. The works of numerous authors fed my imagination during my travels; many of these books are mentioned in the text. One which is not is Barry Lopez's *Arctic Dreams*, which kept me company on my journey to Upernavik and informed much of my subsequent thinking on the Arctic. With such good study guides, any mistakes which appear in *The Library of Ice* must remain my own.

On my travels I met many people who influenced the shape of this book. (To protect the privacy of individuals, some names have been changed in the text.) My thanks to everyone who helped me on the road and in the snow, especially Haukur Einarsson, Sindri Bessason and Þórey Gísladóttir at Glacier Adventure, Iceland; Lizzie Meek at Antarctic Heritage Trust; Naomi Chapman at The Polar Museum; the HERA-funded Arctic Encounters research group at the University of Leeds; Mette-Sofie D. Ambeck, and Liz and Lars Hempel-Jørgensen in Denmark; Ole and Thrine Gamst-Pedersen and Nivi Christensen in Greenland; the Scottish Arctic Club; Helena Dejak, Kristján Jóhannsson, Örlygur Kristfinnsson, Guðný Róbertsdóttir, Björn Valdimarsson and Ólöf Sæunn Valgarðsdóttir in Iceland; and Dervla Murphy in Ireland. Serge and Caroline Zvegintzov expanded my library through book loans, as did Catherine Zvegintzov with gifts. My parents Colin and Anne Campbell taught me to respect nature and encouraged me to look searchingly at writers' and artists' representations of it, and Kenneth and Eithne Campbell have fostered my curiosity about the world for years, beginning with an early subscription to *National Geographic*. Finally, my profound thanks to Anna Zvegintzov, without whose love and patient support this book could never have been completed.

ADDITIONAL COPYRIGHT ACKNOWLEDGEMENTS

Nancy Campbell is an award-winning writer, described as 'a deft, dangerous and dazzling new poet' by the Poet Laureate, Carol Ann Duffy. Her previous book on the polar environment, *Disko Bay*, was shortlisted for the Forward Prize for Best First Collection in 2016. A former magazine editor, she contributes to the *Times Literary Supplement*, *Royal Academy Magazine* and other journals. She has been a *Marie Claire* 'Wonder Woman', a Hawthornden Fellow and Visual and Performing Artist in Residence at Oxford University. She lives in Oxford.